SOME SLAVES OF VIRGINIA 1674–1894

Lost Records Localities
Digital Collection
of the
Library of Virginia

Compiled by

Sandra Barlau

HERITAGE BOOKS
2019

HERITAGE BOOKS
AN IMPRINT OF HERITAGE BOOKS, INC.

Books, CDs, and more—Worldwide

For our listing of thousands of titles see our website
at
www.HeritageBooks.com

Published 2019 by
HERITAGE BOOKS, INC.
Publishing Division
5810 Ruatan Street
Berwyn Heights, Md. 20740

Copyright © 2019 Sandra Barlau

Heritage Books by the author:

Some Slaves of Fauquier County, Virginia, Volume I: Will Books 1–10, 1759–1829

Some Slaves of Fauquier County, Virginia; Volume II: Will Books 11–20, 1829–1847

Some Slaves of Fauquier County, Virginia, Volume III: Will Books 21–31, 1847–1869

Some Slaves of Fauquier County, Virginia; Volume IV: Master Index, Will Books 1–31, 1759–1869

Some Slaves of Rappahannock County, Virginia, Will Books A to D, 1833–1865 and Old Rappahannock County, Virginia, Will Books 1 and 2, 1664–1682

Some Slaves of Virginia, 1674–1894: Lost Records Localities Digital Collection of the Library of Virginia

Cover portrait: Mary Timbers Harrison

All rights reserved. No part of this book may be reproduced or transmitted in any form or by any means, electronic or mechanical, including photocopying, recording or by any information storage and retrieval system without written permission from the author, except for the inclusion of brief quotations in a review.

International Standard Book Numbers
Paperbound: 978-0-7884-5890-3

To the Research Librarians of the Library of Virginia.
Thank you

TABLE OF CONTENTS

PREFACE......vii
INTRODUCTION......ix
ABBREVIATIONS......xi

COUNTIES

ABLEMAREL......1
APPOMATTOX......3
AUGUSTA......5
BOTETOURT......7
BRUNSWICK......9
BUCKINGHAM......11
CAROLINE......23
CHARLES CITY......31
CULPEPER......37
DINWIDDIE......39
ELIZABETH CITY......47
FAIRFAX......49
GLOUCESTER......51
HANOVER......59
HENRICO......71
JAMES CITY......75
KING AND QUEEN......99
KING GEORGE......111
KING WILLIAM......113
MATHEWS......121
MECKLENBURG......123
NANSEMOND......125
NOTTOWAY......139
PRINCE GEORGE COUNTY......147
PRINCE WILLIAM......157

RICHMOND CITY 159
ROCKINGHAM 163
SPOTSYLVANIA 169
STAFFORD 171
SURRY 189
WARWICK 191
WASHINGTON 197
WESTMORELAND 199
WILLIAMSBURG 201

INDEX 203

PREFACE

The idea for this book occurred when I asked the research librarian at the Library of Virginia if there were any other resources for wills in Prince William County.

The resource desk sent me to the Lost Records Localities Digital Collection, 1674 – 1894, on the Library of Virginia's web site: http://www.virginiamemory.com/collections/lost

"The Lost Records Localities Digital Collection consists of copies of records from counties or incorporated cities that suffered significant record loss due to a variety of reasons. The collection is divided into subcollections related to the localities which suffered record loss. The ' Source ' of each item is listed, which tells the researcher the collection in which the original ' lost ' record was found."

This site has over 1,486 records which include Wills, Deeds, Chancery Court records, and other miscellaneous papers. Only records that mention slaves are included in this book.

The site also contains biographical/historical notes for each county which I included.

INTRODUCTION

Will Books and Deed Books are good sources in the search for slaves only if the owner named the slave(s). Many times a Will lists property without specifying if it includes slaves. For example: "I will and bequeath to my (wife, son, daughter, etc.) all my estate both real and personal of every sort." or "...the property I have already given to my (wife, son, daughter, etc.)..." The documents often do not include the slave's name, sometimes only girl, runaway, boy, etc.

Each chapter contains the lost records from one county. The documents include Wills, Deeds, and other miscellaneous papers. Each slave owner is listed first, followed by the date and type of document. The list of slaves follows below. The new owner is listed if known. Surnames of the owner's children are indexed only if noted in the document.

Freed slaves are listed under Emancipated which includes Manumissions. Certificate of Freedom, Free Negro Registration, and Free Person of Color are also noted.

Not included in this summary is a slave's monetary value, if the slave was sold, hired by the estate, hired out or who hired the slave. The original text should be read to determine which occurred.

Some first names were standardized in order to make your index search easier. When you go to the original Will and Deed Books be aware that different spellings were used. Be creative in looking for first names: Sharlot (Charlotte), Ausker (Oscar), Fillis (Phillis), etc. Sometimes the written nn could be rr and many times S resembles L; n might resemble u (sou = son); e might resemble o (over = ever). Some of the entries have only a few letters separated with a blank space such as Marj__i_.

It would be a good idea to peruse the entire index. You may recognize a name under another spelling. The same name can also appear more than once on a page under different owners.

It is important to note the slave's age since the value of a slave increases or decreases with age and ability. It can also be used as a tracking tool.

Servants were included and are listed in the index. Counties without records were not included.

The Lost Records Localities Digital Collection of the Library of Virginia has two sections. One section lists documents from A-Z. The other section is by county. Some records are found in both sections.

County Court Record listings list one case after the other (i.e. not A – Z) by one date for the whole day. In that case, you will have to go by the digital page number: D/ R = digital page number right; D/ L = digital page number left. Some court records refer to the digital page and the written page. In that case, the digital page is listed first, the written page second.

ABBREVIATIONS

adm acct – Administrator's Account
exec acct – Executor Account
gdn acct – Guardian Account
inv & appr – Inventory & Appraisal
div – Division (of slaves, land, property)
comm acct – Committee Account
cert – Certificate
D/ R: digital page number, right page
D/ L: digital page number, left page

ABLEMAREL

All order books except the first and many loose papers from between 1748 and 1781 were destroyed by British general Banastre Tarleton's raid on Charlottesville in 1781 during the Revolutinary War.

Thomas PATTESON .... 25 Dec 1745, will
    boy Adam to son Thomas PATTESON; Frank, girl Moll to daughter Ann PATTESON; boy Scipio to son Charles PATTESON; girl Betty to son David; boy James to son Leonard; Bess, Cuffy, Jane, Hannah to wife, if she has a boy 1 negro, if a girl 2

.... May 1747, inv
    men Frank, Cuffy, women Hannah, Jane, boys Adam, Scirpio, girls Moll, Bess, boys James, George

William STONE .... 5 Sept 1777, will
    Delsey & her son Simon to son Caleb STONE; fellow Bob to son Elijah STONE; woman Hannah, boy Jesse to William WEELINS son of Joseph WEELINS begat on my daughter Elizabeth now dec'd; fellow Cato, woman Jane, boy Ben to son Thomas STONE; woman Moll, boy Jammy, girl Sarah, fellow Nimby to son Hezekiah STONE; girl Moll to son Marbel STONE; fellow Sam, boy Charles, girl Lucy to wife Frances Taylor STONE

APPOMATTOX

Appomattox County was created in 1845. All records except land tax books were destroyed by fire on 1 February 1892.

J.W. FLOOD .... 22 Feb 1856, will

    Louise & her child Brunello, boy Wellington to wife Eliza Bolling FLOOD; 2/5 of negroes to granddaughter Polly Walker POORE & grandson Robert Bolling POORE

Horatio GOFF .... Oct 18__, will

    girl ___ to daughter Mary; Cesar, Blake, Bob to son John G. at death of mother

David ROBERTSON .... 18 Oct 1855, will

    slaves not specifically named to wife Eliza S. ROBERTSON; Bash, Collins, Anderson, Martha & all her children, Clementine & all her children to daughter Margaret RIXEBY; Charles, Wyatt, Jane & her son, John, Patterson to son James E. ROBERTSON; Frederick, Preston, Lizza, Walker, Rachel, Arthura to daughter Elizabeth B. MARTIN; Eliza & her children Sam, Del, & Blanche, Ardinia, Lavinia to daughter Mary P. ROBERTSON

AUGUSTA

It was declared a "city Incorporate" by a royal charter in 1722, although it's actual status was that of a borough. Records were transferred to Richmond during Civil War for safekeeping but were destroyed by fire there on 3 April 1865.

Mary Blair ANDREWS .... 15 Oct 1819, will
> slaves in Albemarle to John Blair PEACHY youngest son of my father's niece Mary M. PEACHY; negroes by my husband's will to godson Alfred THOMPSON & in case of his death to his sister Mrs. Mary DIXON & Helen Ann THOMPSON or John Blair PEACHY (?); bond of Joseph WILKINSON for price of a negro boy to daughter Elizabeth ANDREWS & Catharine WILKINSON in Mississippi

.... 17 Oct 1819
> ...son Robert...after my death I divide among the servants I allowed him and Mr. WICHAM to carry to Mississippi...

.... 12 Nov 1819
> ...$20.00 to be divided among the servants at Blair Park...

Daniel CROFT .... 25 July 1826, __
> (listed under John McCUNE's will of Rockingham Co)

Kate a woman of color under my care willed to be free by John M. CUNY dec'd does not yet have papers

BOTETOURT

Botetourt County was created by an act of 1769 to take effect on 13 February 1770. Many of the loose records suffered tremendous water damage as a result of a courthouse fire on 15 December 1970. Because of the near loss of records, the General Assembly passed the Virginia Public Records Act in 1975 for the purpose of preserving local records. Volumes that record deeds, court orders, and wills exist.

Major Thomas BOWYER .... 17 Oct 1784, will

    negroes in Boetecourt County to nephew Henry BOWYER

James BOYD .... 26 May 1816, will

    man Anthony to be sold; 1/3 of remainder of my slaves to wife Mary B. BOYD; the remainder of slaves to sons Andrew, Luis BOYD, & William Watson BOYD

Lewis BURWELL .... 1 Oct 1804, will

    girl Beck given to me by my mother to sister Frances BURWELL

Derry FREEMAN .... 25 May 1804, will

    ... applied to the purchase my son Isaac a man now belonging to John BEALE & then to be set free

James A. GORDON .... 13 June 1825, will

    negroes to be hired out if wife Eliza L. GORDON does not live on the farm

William KYLE .... 26 Nov 1820, will

    Will & Rachel his wife & her child Rhoda, boy Israel, Randal, Lewis, Tom, Lily, Milly to wife Sarah KYLE & at her death divided between sons Barclay & James; boy Jim to daughter Jane WAMACK that her husband has in his possession; Jamima, Phil, Ambrose, Burwick, Charlotte to grandsons James & Robert PITZER now in the possession of their father George PITZER

Andrew LEWIS .... 28 Jan 1780, will

    2 fellows, 2 wenches to wife; wench or girl to daughter Anne; remaining negroes to be divided among sons Samuel, Thomas, Andrew, & William, & daughter Anne

John MADISON .... 19 Dec 1783, will
>   choice of slaves to wife; slaves to be divided among my children; girl Jenny to granddaughter Agatha MADISON

William MANN .... 3 Feb 1778, will
>   wench Venus to eldest daughter Ealse

James MASON .... 2 Mar 1803, will
>   Hannah & son Jim to nephew Samuel CRAWFORD.; girl Nelly to Jennet CRAWFORD wife of Samuel CRAWFORD & my sister

William McCLANAHAN .... 25 Sept 1819, will
>   negroes to wife Sarah McCLANAHAN; negroes in his possession to son Green except woman Milly

Malcolm McCLURE .... 9 Apr 1791, will
>   wench Dina to wife Elizabeth McCLURE

Thomas PRESTON .... 11 May 1807, will
>   woman Zilla, Pat age 9, Jack 11, George 4, Aleck 2, Charity 4 months to daughters Anna & Mary

George SKILLERN .... 6 Dec 1803, will
>   choice of slaves to wife Elizabeth SKILLERN; man Jim & slaves from my wife to son William Preston SKILLERN; exectors to give daughter Nancy negroes…equal to what sisters Peggy BEALE & Betsy received; woman Violet to be emancipated at pleasure of wife; slaves to be equally divided among son & 3 daughters

William TAURMAN .... 28 Jan 1842, will
>   Henry, Leonard, Carter, Nelly, Sukey, Sally to wife Martha H. TAURMAN; slaves not herein disposed: Preston, Nancy, John, Mary to be hired out

James TRIMBLE .... 9 Apr 1776 in court, will
>   …not to hurt too much the timber of my old slave (?) to son John; wench Lucy to daughter Rachel

BRUNSWICK

Created in 1720 (county government established in June 1732). Most loose records prior to 1781 are missing. Pre-1781 volumes that record deeds, court orders, and wills exist.

Henry EMBRY .... 14 July 1762, will
  negroes to wife Martha EMBRY; Mingo, Ceazor, Murrear, Amy, Luckinny, young Ceazor to wife after 2 years; Sarah, Moll to granddaughter Mary EMBRY; Pompy, Cate, little Mingo to daughter Mary MEARITT; Mingo, Ceazor, Murrear, Amy to daughter Mary MEARITT after wife's decease to be divided among my grandchildren; Luckinny, little Ceazor to granddaughter Sarah EMBRY; Dillo to granddaughter Martha ELLIOTT after wife's decease; good proportion of negroes from his father's will to grandson William EMBRY be divided to sisters Ermin, Martha, & Elizabeth EMBRY; Harry, Tarta, Nelly to son William EMBRY's children

James MASON to Richard HARTWELL .... 7 Apr 1772, slave sold
  girl Dinah to Richard HARTWELL

Henry MORRIS to Thomas SIMMONS .... 22 Apr 1765, deed
  Jenny, Judy, Beechy, Jacob, Amy, Sally, Moll, & 1 boy till he is free to Thomas SIMMONS

Henry MORRIS to Thomas & Holly STITH .... 14 Sept 1783, deed
  Judy, Frank, Sall, Mason to Thomas & Holly STITH

James PARRISH .... 12 Oct 1753, will
  Cesar, Hannah, Chloe to wife Sarah, negroes to be sold at her death; man Roger in lieu of girl Cheny before promised, girl Amy to son John PARRISH; man Mingo, boy Bob to son Joseph PARRISH; girls Cheny, Phillis, an Indian servant Farthing to daughter Mary PARRISH; boy Ned to son Charles PARRISH; girl Venus, boy Peter to son Joel PARRISH

.... 4 June 1754, codicil
  Betty & her child Cate to wife & at her death to son John PARRISH; woman Phillis which was givin to my daughter Mary to son Joel PARRISH; Margery & her child Grace to daughter Mary PARRISH in lieu of Phillis & Chany

Henry SIMMONS .... 3 Jan 1766, will
> Moses, Cupid, Sam, Jammy, David, Philip, Phebe, Patience, Isaac, Jacob, Amey to wife Susanna; negroes he now has to son Thomas SIMMONS; Will, Tom, Frank, Jack, Abram, Ted, Fortune, Lucy, Charles, Ben to son Henry SIMMONS; Robin, Ned, Daniel, Anakey & her three children, Agnes, Judith to son Benjamin SIMMONS; Sarah, Ellick, Jammy, Moses to daughter Mary TILLMAN; Charles, Dick, Milla to daughter Susanna EDWARDS; Fanny, Easter?, Solomon to daughter Mason SIMMONS

Benjamin WARREN the elder .... 8 July 1792, will
> woman Sukey, boy James, girl Amey, boy Daniel, girl Lucy to wife Temperance WARREN

BUCKINGHAM

Buckingham County was created in 1761. Records were destroyed by fire in 1869

Jesse ALLEN..27 July 178_, will

    Lucy, Sarah, Fill_o to Jesse JOPLING son of Alsey JOPLING; Will, Job to George ALLEN son of Samuel & Hannah ALLEN; Kate, __, Nan, Lu__az to Lucy ALLEN daughter of Samuel & Hannah ALLEN

William Hunt ALLEN... 28 May 1806, will

    Betsy, Fanny, Peter, Isham, little Henry, Aggy, Archer, Molly, boy Jerry, woman Conday to wife Elizabeth ALLEN; Jerry to be free at age 21; girl Aggy to Elizabeth GATES wife of Allen GATES after the death of my wife; Maggy & her child Tammy to Elizabeth GATES; girl Mourning to Samuel Hunt ALLEN son of Samuel Amherst; girl Mary to John ALLEN son of Samuel Amherst; girl Charlotte to William Hunt ALLEN son of Jesse; woman Hannah, man Tom to William ALLEN son of George; girl Candice, man Tomboy to Martha A. COTTRILL wife of Richard COTTRILL; boy George to Walter C. ALLEN son of William; boy Archer to George ALLEN son of William after the death of my wife; Rhoda to Benjamin Clapton GLOVER; Charity & her 2 children Cissely & Patty to William ALLEN son of Col. Samuel; boy Solomon to John ALLEN son of Col. Samuel; boy Ben to Sutton Farras ALLEN son of Col. Samuel; man Jim to be sold; boy Vincent to William COTTRILL son of Jacob after the death of my wife; Molly, Peter, Betty, Fanny, John, boy little Henry to William ALLEN son of George

William ALLEN...14 Feb 1824, will

    negroes to be equally divided among all my children; son-in-law Willis CHAMBERS, sons George _. ALLEN, & Baller C. ALLEN appointed as executors

Benjamin Bartley... 1 Nov 1808, cert of freedom

    age 22, 5 ft 8" and identifying marks

Elizabeth BATERSBY .... 27 Sept 1764, will
_eleaner to daughter Sele WATKINS to hold for her daughter Elizabeth Willis WATKINS; man Brunswick to be sold; woman Moll to choose to live with 1 of my 3 daughters

Bridget BEAZLEY .... 1 Apr 1792, will
girl Nelifer to son Fuqua BEAZLEY; boy Peter to son Hyram BEAZLEY; girl Neive to daughter Mary PALMER

John BEAZLEY .... 18 Nov 1781, will
negroes to wife Bridget BEAZLEY during her widowhood

Benjamin H. BELL .... 1813 – June 1821, estate acct
Alcey & her 5 children Philip, Allen, Spencer, Carter, & Rebecca, Polly & her 3 children Bolling, Mary, & Bob, man James, boy Billy son to Alcey

Benjamin H. BELL .... 14 Feb 1814, inv & appr
Alcey & 4 children William, Phillip, Allen, & Spencer, Polly, Archer & one child Bolling, man James

Henry BELL .... 4 Oct 1811, inv & appr
Ned, Moses, Maurice, Betty, Suckey, Nella, Dinah, little Nella, Molly Bigham, Tom Bigbe, Rochester, Chesses

Henry BELL .... 3 Sept 1798, deed of gift
Nat, George, Ampy, Sucky & her child Maria to Henry Cary BELL

Henry BELL .... 12 Jan 1795, deed of gift
Critt, Jack, Peter, Betty, Abbey to Henry RAWLINS

Rebecca BELL .... 1813, court order
Charles, Suckey, Betty, Nelly are exempt from taxes due to age and infirmity

Rebecca BELL .... 27 June 1834, deed
Moses, Nelly, Suckey Nancy, Polly, Bolling, Mary, Bob, Ampy, Joe, Suckey, Eliza, Maurice, William, Spencer, Carter, Becca, Phillip, Flora, Rochester, Bob, Sam, Jack, Molly, Tom, Ned, James, Abram, Martha, Maurice to her daughter Rebecca BRANCH after the death of Rebecca BELL

Rebecca BELL .... 10 June 1834, will

> all negroes to daughter Rebecca BRANCH; girl Mary to granddaughter Judith H. RAWLINGS; Philip to grandson Henry B. BRANCH; ... for the benefit of my granddaughter E.A. SCRUGGS...may not be liable for the debts of her husband's slaves; James

....27 June 1834, codicil

the increase of Mary is 6 & belong to my daughter Rebecca

Virginia BELL...20 Aug 1815, will

> a girl from my father's estate (Henry BELL) to niece Virginia BRANCH; boy Sam given to me by Martha Harrison LEED to be hired out to mother Rebecca BELL & at her death to niece Virginia BRANCH

Bolling BRANCH & Mary BELL...........14 Oct 1817, marriage settlement

> woman Nanny, given to Mary BELL by her aunt Martha HARRISON dec'd, to Maurice M. LANGORN, Benjamin BROWN, & William M. THORNTON

Benajah BROWN .... 1 July 1814, will

> slaves to wife Mary BROWN; Nancy, Betty, Lewis, Reuben, Philip, Jerry, Amy, Elijah, Liddy, Ryland, Milly, Billy, Elvia, Moses, Daniel, Henry, Titus, Monroe to sons Garland, Meletas, Benajah A., & Beverly A, BROWN, 2 daughters Martha PRICE & Catharine AYRES, grandchildren Miletas & Mary Ann JERMAN children of my dec'd daughter Sarah T. JERMAN & Addison FORD son of my dec'd daughter Mary FORD

Frederick CABELL ....25 Feb 1841, will

> man Abram & Money his wife & their 6 children to Frederick M. CABELL in trust for daughter Mildred M. HOSLEY & her children; ...all monies conveyed...should be invested in slaves for the use of Mildred M. HOSLEY & her children; Jubu & Betty his wife & their 2 children to daughter Virginia MOSBY; Reuben & Fanny his wife & their 3 children, woman Amy, Peter & Carly his wife & 1 child, woman Amby to son Lewis W. CABELL; Frederick M. CABELL as trustee for Edmund W. CABELL should lay out money for slaves; the negroes in his possession to Frederick M. CABELL

Samuel COLEMAN .... 4 Apr 1803, will

Tom, Charles, Bartley, Dick, Nan, Rose, Cloe, Patty, Judea, Anaca, Jane, Agg, Dabney to wife Elizabeth COLEMAN; man Frederick to son James COLEMAN; Tom, Charles, Dick, Nan, Rose, Cloe, Patty, Judea, Anaca, Jane, Agg, Dabney to be divided among my children George COLEMAN, Sally PENDLETON wife of Nace PENDLETON, Mary PENDLETON, Frances HARRIS wife of Robert HARRIS, Betsy COLEMAN, Ann Mourning COLEMAN, & grandchildren Benjamin PENDLETON & daughter Jane

George COX .... 28 July 1824, will

Sam, Amy, Nelly, Phebe, Amy the younger, Dafney, Phillis, Dennis, Lewis, Jesse, Isaac, Caroline, Jeremiah to wife Elizabeth COX; Robert, Louisa to Nathaniel LANCASTER in trust for son Patrick COX; Susannah, William to Palina WALTHINS; Edmond, Roseaty to son Benjamin COX; Obadiah, Martha Jane to son Matthew COX; Mary, Anna Frances to daughter Harriet K. COX; Rozelly, __lian to daughter Eliza S. COX; Betsy Ann, Jack to daughter Kejiah C. COX; Andrew, Peggy to son Josiah A. COX; Frederick, Mariah to son George H. COX

Elizabeth W. CURD .... 2 Apr 1846, deed

men Wilson, Frank, Sam, Charles, Davy, John, boys Calvin, Juba, Jim, Maria & her children Billy & Eliza to Alexander MOSELEY

Ann DAVENPORT .... 14 Dec 1825, deed

Vina, Dicy, Allen, Jinny, Madison, Adam divided among children Osburn DAVENPORT, Thomas DAVENPORT, Gabriel DUNCAN, Joseph DUCAN, & Elijah PERKINS, & children of my daughter Gracy FUQUA; the negroes to the children of Gracy FUQUA to Elijah PERKINS to manage

Thomas DAVIS .... July 1797, affidavit

on behalf of William CABELL administrator of Samuel JORDAN; ... judgment in county court...levied on some negroes...

William DAVIS .... 1 May 1816, will

Tom, Jinny, Nanney, Nelus, Prudence, Daniel, John to wife Esther DAVIS; after her decease boy David to daughter Sally MOSELY; girl Prudence to daughter Betsy FRANKLIN; boy John to grandson

Robert P. MOSELY; Stephen, Mary, Mica to son Robert DAVIS; negroes not before mentioned to grandson Robert P. MOSELY, Sally MOSELY, Robert DAVIS, Betsy FRANKLIN, & granddaughter Esther M. FRANKLIN

Joseph EADES .... 19 Aug 1827, will

slaves to stay on plantation for 10 years then divided and sold in families – not to be separated, & to choose their own masters

Martha B. EPPES .... 6 June 1861, will

6 servants to daughter Mary BOLLING; same number of negroes to Willie J. EPPES, Sarah HUBARD, Eliza W. EPPES, John, & Ann G. EPPES; Sally Haxhall, Nancy & her 4 children Eldridge, Mary, Betsy, & Sally to Nelly PAGE; I leave Ann G. EPPES the same number to be taken in Calolina from my servants there

Dougald FERGUSON .... 3 Sept 1839, will

man Alek to be sold; Charles, Lucy, Katy, Jesse, Wilson, William, Anderson, Esther to son David H. FERGUSON for benefit of wife Louisa and his children; boy Peter to granddaughter Elira Susan FERGUSON; old woman Hannah to be maintained for life

Moses FUQUA .... 29 Nov 1817 – 28 Nov1818, estate acct

John, boy Isaac

.... div slaves

Ambrose, Henry, Isaac, Spencer

Isaac to widow Amile FUQUA; Henry, Spencer to Samuel FUQUA; Ambrose to Joseph FUQUA

Moses FUQUA, heirs of vs Aaron FUQUA .... in Chancery .... 29 Nov 1817 – 15 Jan 1819, estate acct

John, boy Issac; slaves to be divided among children: Ambrose, Henry, Isaac, Spencer, Clara

Isaac to Mary the widow; Henry, Spencer to Samuel; Ambrose to Joseph

Theoderick C. GANNAWAY to William B. BOCOCK & John A. LANCASTER .... 1 June 1844, deed

men Abram, Ned, Buett, Kendal, Sam, Jones, John, George, Fredrick, Sam, Aleck, Henry, boy Peter, women Docia, Harriet, Milly, girl

Angelina, 2 unnamed children owned by Theoderick GANNAWAY to William B. BOCOCK

Laban GIPSON .... 1 Oct 1814, will

girl Charity to Elizabeth; the rest of my negroes to my wife

Archibald Turner GORDON .... 4 Jan 1850, will

Sam, Shed, George, Woodson, Sukey to be hired out if necessary otherwise to be set free

Samuel GREGORY .... 5 July 1835, will

16 negroes to Burnett & Frances HU_H

Benjamin HARRISON dec'd vs Polly HARRISON ....
.... 1812 – 1836, in court custody of Ben...hired about 1812...Polly refused to give him up...deposition of Rebecca BALL – at the division of her father's estate her sister Polly HARRISON drew a boy named Ben

John HENDRICK .... 11 July 1814, will

woman Tamar to granddaughter Harriet BILBA; girl Amis to daughter Ann HENDRICK; girl Maria to daughter Louisa; girl Patty to daughter Susanna; boy Shadrack to daughter Ann; Fanny, Lucinda, Nancy, Jack to be sold

Robert HILL to Walter S. FONTAINE & Stephen GUENAUT ....
.... 1 May 1821, deed negroes

Philip HODNETT .... 1815, will

woman Amey to sister Mary BAKER & at her death to her sons Samuel & Abraham BAKER; boy Joe to sister Esther ANDERSON & at her death to Ayres HODNETT

Charles IRVING to John C. PAGE & Randolph HARRISON ....
.... 2 May 1827, deed

George, Edwin, Armstead, Hurcules, Joe, Calib, Billy, Imy, Bob, Rachel & her 2 youngest children Nanny & Kate, Sucky, Sawny, Tarah, Susan, Buck, Hannah & child Polly, Henry, Milly & child, Celia, Edy, Lucinda, Betty, George, Phoeby, Emily & child, Lucy, P__, Sally, Francis, George, Ally to be sold

Charles IRVING to John HORSLEY .... 24 Aug 1819, deed
men Frank, Daniel, Armistead, Billy, Elick, boys Joe, Caleb to be sold

Richard JOHNSON .... 8 Sept 1823, will
negroes to wife Milly (Mildred) JOHNSON; woman _ucy loaned to Peyton JOHNSON; woman Judith loaned to John H. JOHNSON; woman Sukey loaned to daughter Sally DUNN

Edward JONES .... 22 Apr 1820, will
Gray & his wife Joanna & their 2 youngest children Paulina & Chester, Isaac, Tone, Pamela, Maria, Philis & her youngest child Hannah, Sucky & her youngest child Archer, Eliza to be emancipated; boy Johann to brother Samuel JONES for 20 years then be free; Simon, Tone to brother Thomas JONES for 20 years then be free; Carter, John to executors for brother Jonas JONES, Carter to be free after 16 years, John after 20; Rose, Peter, Moses, Hannah daughter of Sukey to brother James Jones for 20 years and then freed; Judith, Matilda to wife Polly JONES for 20 years and then freed

.... 25 Apr 1820, Codicil
boy Campbell to brother Thomas JONES to be free after 15 years; future children to be free with their mother

Josias JONES .... 27 July 1814, will
Charlotte & her child in possession of daughter Salley TALBOT to be returned to the estate; Nelly to executers in trust for daughter Elizabeth JONES; girl Fran to daughter Mary JONES; girls Louisiana, Dinah to daughter Nancy JONES; negroes in possession of daughters Salley TALBOT & Eliza JONES to executors in trust for said daughters except Charlotte & her child; boy Shephard to grandson Spotswood JONES

.... 27 July 1814, Codicil
Nelly not to go to daughter Elizabeth JONES

Samuel JONES .... 28 Dec 1837, will
slaves at Fish Pond to brother James JONES; Davy, Aaron, Hiram, Moses, John & his wife Rachel to nephew Powhatan JONES; Jack, Will, Anthony, Judy to brother Thomas JONES; Sheppard, little Ben, Susan to nephew Spotswood JONES; big Ben, Joe & his wife Mariah

with their children to my executors in trust for my brother Jonas JONES; man Nelson to be free; Will, Anthony, Joe to be free at the death of my brother to whom they are willed

William JONES .... 1823, will

Jacob & his wife Rhoda & their children, James, Jinnetta Lucy, Jacob, & Cassel, Jinney & her son Stephen, Billy & his wife Jinney & their children Robert, Jim, Randolph, Royal, Louisa, Rachel & her son Emanuel, Jeffrey & his wife Lucy, Abraham, Dorcus & her 2 sons Fountain & John, Ben, Frank, Daniel, Cate, Jesse to wife Elizabeth JONES, at her death Ben, Frank, Daniel to son Thomas S. JONES; Judy, Hal, Annis, Kiah, Billy, Kitty, Sampson, Wyatt, Spencer, Henry, Kisiah & her son Bob to son Thomas S. JONES; boy Dennis to grandson William WALKINS son of daughter Polly WALKINS; girl Chaney to granddaughter Martha JONES daughter of son William A. JONES; girl Evelina to granddaughter Sara CLARK daughter of my daughter Elizabeth CLARK; boy Billy son of Billy to grandson Edward Wiley JONES son of my son James S. JONES

Moses KIDD .... 17 July 1781, will

(Listed under Prince Edward Co. Chancery Causes but Biographical/Historical Note referred to Buckingham Co.)

woman Nane, boy David, child Frank, boy Tobe to wife Elizabeth KIDD

Zadock LACKLAND .... 5 June 1826, will

Harry, Frank, Adam, Solomon, Dick, Isaac, Franky, Phillis, Delila to wife Sarah LACKLAND; a negro named above to each daughter upon marriage: Rachel, Lillian, Elizabeth, Sarah, & Mary LACKLAND; 2 negroes of brother John LACKLAND estate to be sold

Joseph E. & Elizabeth LIGIN to Charles D. McKINNEY ....
.... 3 May 1825, deed

1 girl

Nehemiah & Elizabeth McASHAN to Philip BOLLING ....
.... 31 Aug 1844, deed

Louisa age 12

Arthur H. MOON .... 3 Apr 1853, will

Billy Fox, Henry, George, Nelson, Giles, Martin, Gilbert, Philip, Rowland, Alexander, Lucy, Kitty, Hannah & her child Sarah, Sooky, Frances, Charles, Laura, Maria, Shardack, Maria Jane, Fleming, Henricka, Aggy, Delphy, big Billy, Polly, Thomas-Anthony, Nancy, Margaret, Agnes, Ann, Anthony, Cindy, Minerva to daughter Caroline F.W. JONES

Littleberry MOON .... 14 Aug 1820, estate div

Peter, Jerry, Lucy & children Anna & Ginney to Jane MOON widow, her dower; Lot 1: Nelson to Arthur H. MOON; Lot 6: Moses to Samuel O. MOON; Lot 3: Rina to Mary H. MOON; Lot 2: Jacob to Littleberry MOON; Lot 8: Tremont? to Jane M. MOON; Lot 4: Daphine to Elisabeth MOON; Lot 7: Suckey, Elvira to James D. MOON; Lot 5: Sally, yellow Lucy to Sarah I. MOON

Richard MURRAY .... Apr 1772, will

man Harry to son John; Moch, Phillis, Frank, Jeffery to son Richard MURRAY; fellow Sampson to son Anthony MURRAY; woman Jude, fellow Andren to William TERRIL & his wife; 2 negroes to John BRYANT & his wife; woman Hannah, & boy or girl about 12 years chosen by exectors to Peter GOLDSBY & his wife; girl Jane, boy Charles to Edward WALTON & his wife; girl of about 14 years chosen by exectors to granddaughter Mary TERRIL

John NICHOLAS .... 17 Apr 1794, will

1/3 negroes among whom she may choose Bill & his mother Peg to wife, at her death to be divided between children; young fellow Giles & his sister Betty to son John; Hannah & her children, Suky, Polly to daughter Mary Rose; choice of negro girls except Lydda to daughter Elizabeth; girl Lydda to daughter Martha; remaining negroes divided between sons Robert, Joshua, & George & daughters Elizabeth & Martha

David PATTESON .... 19 Mar 1846, will

woman Dicy to son-in-law William LEWIS dec'd; woman Nancy to son-in-law _. LEWIS; boy George to grandson Charles Powhatan PATTESON; girls Tildy, Milly to granddaughters Virginia & Agnes PATTESON daughters of my son W.N. PATTESON; Pompey, Moses, Hannah, Sary, woman Emily to son James M. PATTESON;

Stephen to grandson Richard L. PATTESON; list of negroes allotted to my children: Sary, Abram, girl Harry to son I.L. PATTESON; Richard, Martha, George to daughter-in-law; Samuel, Bob, Henry to James M. PATTESON

John PATTESON etc to Trsts .... 18 May 1843, deed

man Jerry, boy Sam, women Becky, Sarah, Eliza to James M. PATTESON to hold for support of Jane PATTESON & children Hugh, Augustine, David, Lucy, William, John, & Betsy PATTESON

Hardin PERKINS .... 15 Mar 1821, will

6 equal lots to 6 youngest children: by daughter Mary L. PERKINS, sons William P., Hardin, John M., Daniel P., & daughter Eliza A. PERKINS; ...slaves already given to Sally P. MOORS, Benjamin M. PERKINS

Daniel M. SAUNDERS to Elizabeth SAUNDERS .... 17 July 1841, deed

man Sam to Elizabeth SAUNDERS

Doctor Sawney .... 9 July 1838, free negro regis

age 26, 5' 9", emancipated by George WOLL_NDGE

Betsy Scott to Clough T. AMOS .... 20 Nov 1812, deed

Betsy Scott, a free woman of color, place & bind as an apprentice her son Wilson Scott age 10 to Clough T. AMOS until he obtains the age of 21 on 15 Oct 1824

Mary SPENCER .... 1 Aug 1783, will

fellow Jack to son Moses

William SUBLETT & wife vs Zadock LACKLAND heirs .... Apr 1838, in Chancery

examination of 2 executor accts; 2 slaves sold

Thomas THOMAS .... 7th day 1802, will

the 1st child to be born which makes it to the age of 2 years to son Daniel; Juno, Peter, Juda, Keshia, Rachel, Betty to wife Rebecca; purchase of young woman or girl to daughter Lydda LANDRUM; woman Jude to daughter Lucy _ANN after decease of wife but her increase to be divided with the estate; Juno, Milly to sons Phillip & David after my wife's death but their increase to be divided with the estate; girl Betty to son Thomas but her increase to be divided with the estate; man Peter to daughter Nancy after her mother's decease; girl Rachel to daughter Rebecca after wife's decease but her increase to be divided with the estate

William WALTON to David C. JONES & Benjamin ABBITT .... 9 Sept 1836, deed

men Peter, Leville, Billy, Spencer, Sam, Page, Joshua, Jerry, John, Joe, boys Neptune, Bob, Henry, women Phillis, Pleasant, Jenny, Nancy & her daughter Lucy, Grace & her 3 children, Bib & her 3 children Winston, Charity, & another, Rachel & 5 children Mickey, Anderson, Nelson, Jesse, & Wiatt, Matilda & her 5 children Marsha, Edward, Mary, Sandy, & another, girls Caroline, Jinny, Sarah, women Rally, Silvey, also an interest in 4/9 in John, Jacob, Sally, 2 others, Judy & her 3 children James & 2 others; the other 5/9 being the Thomas WALTON's legatees to Samuel McDowell REID in trust...

William WEBB .... 12 June 1829, will

Ben, Keziah, Aron to wife Aron WEBB & Anakey's 1st child Lucy to dispose of at her death as she may think fit; man Sam to son William WEBB; man Daniel to son George WEBB; man Isham to son John WEBB; man long Jim to son Robert WEBB; man Joe to son Abraham M. WEBB; Neptune, Esther, Peter, Anica, Harry, Sarah to son Merry WEBB; Frank, Lindsey, Willis to son Martin WEBB; Miner, Mariah, Sanders, Fanny to daughter Elizabeth TRENT; George, Nan, General, Milly to daughter Nancy CONNER; Henry, Sylva, Conn to daughter Sally DINPHEY; Henry, Charles, Phoebe, Betty to daughter Willyam WALKINS; Gibson, Hannah, Micky, Stephen, Bid_g, Allen, Gabriel, Rosey, Charlotte to daughter Jane ABBITT; exectors to purchase a girl about 7 years old for granddaughter Rachel WEBB daughter of son George WEBB; long Jim, Sam, Juba, Mary to daughters Elizabeth TRENT, Nancy CONNER, Sally DINPHEY, & Willyam WALKINS at the death of my wife; Aron to be sold; Ben, Kezia to sons Merry & Martin WEBB at the death of their mother

Josiah & Jeremiah WHITNEY .... 4 Mar 1783, agreement

estate division of Jeremiah WHITNEY dec'd: Ned, Venus, Judah, Rose, Dick, Daffney, Billy, Sheppard, Venus, Crandon, Tom to

Josiah WHITNEY; Anthony, Charles, Nan, Dinah, Chloe, Silvey, Tenah, David to Susannah WHITNEY, widow; Susanna WHITNEY sold land & slaves to pay debts?

Susanna WHITNEY .... 7 Apr 1784, will

Anthony, Nan, Chloe & her child Davy to son John CHRISTIAN; Charles, Dinah, Silva to son George CHRISTIAN; Tena to daughter Elizabeth JARRETT

.... May ___

fellows Ned, Anthony, Tom, Judy & her children, Rose from Jeremiah WHITNEY to William WILSON

William WOODS .... 10 Nov 1862, will

1/3 slaves to wife to be divided among children at her death; 2/3 to children

CAROLINE

Caroline County was created in 1728. Most loose records and deed books prior to 1836 and will books prior to 1853 were stolen, mutilated, and/or destroyed by Union troops who ransacked the courthouse in May 1864. A near-complete run of order books exists.

Dabney ANDERSON..13 Feb 1735, inv & appr

> man George, woman & child

Robert ARMISTEAD..19 July 1766, will

> 2 negroes to be purchased for wife Anne; ...marriage contract...negroes to be sold after death of wife
>
> (most likely the marriage agreement of Robert ARMISTEAD & Ann SMITH, see Hanover County)

James BABER & Ambrose BULLARD to Reuben GEORGE...................
....18 Feb 1789, bond

> woman Molly to grandchildren Mary ISBELL, Daniel ISBELL, John G. GRAVIS, Benjamin GRAVIS, Francis GRAVIS, & Nancy ISBELL by will of John GEORGE which he sent to his daughter Frances the mother of the afore mentioned children...Beverly GRAVES ordered to deliver to Reuben GEORGE the aforementioned woman...

James & George BABER to Reuben GEORGE............22 Dec 1793, bond

> woman Milly willed by John GEORGE to his grandchildren Mary, Daniel, & Nancy ISBELL, & John GEORGE, Benjamin, & Frances GRAVES which at the time of his death in the possession of Beverly GRAVES who intermarried with his daughter Frances the widow of James ISBELL

James BABER & Thomas COLEMAN to Reuben GEORGE....................
....14 Feb 1788 bond

> woman Milly willed by John GEORGE to his grandchildren Mary, Daniel, & Nancy ISBELL, & John GEORGE, Benjamin, & Frances GRAVES; Reuben GEORGE to deliver the said Milly & her increase

Lawrence BATTALIE .... 7 Mar 1773, will

 1/3 negroes to wife Sarah BATTALIE; 1/3 negroes after death of my wife to son Lawrence BATTALIE; remaining negroes to said Lawrence & daughters Sarah, Catharine, & Elizabeth; Sue about 8 years old, daughter of Juno to sister Mary ROGERS; Oliver about 14 son of Oliver & Daphney, George about 14 son of Elizabeth

Timothy CHANDLER .... 29 Dec 1827, deed of gift

 Henry, John, Polly & all her children to John CHANDLER Jr. in trust for Samuel Temple CHANDLER

Timothy CHANDLER .... 21 Nov 1825, will

 slaves to be divided among my children: Samuel T., Leroy, Norborne E., Ethan, John, Hugh CHANDLER, & Frances R. JAMES; Harry, Polly, Phoeby?, Ann, John to son John CHANDLER in trust for Samuel T. CHANDLER; Janet, Baylor, Matilda, Spotswood, Eliza to son John CHANDLER in trust for son Leroy CHANDLER & on his death to his first wife; Joe, Jerry to son Norborne E. CHANDLER; old Molly, Phillis, Mary Louisa, Washington, Edmund, Susanna, Fayette to daughter Frances R. JAMES wife of Joseph J. JAMES; old Lucy, Sarah, Jesse, Walker, Martha, George, Joe, Eleanor to son John CHANDLER; Esau, Judy, Carston, Sam, Anderson, Rachel, Patty, William to son Hugh CHANDLER

John COLLIER .... 29 May 1761, will

 6 negroes to wife Sarah COLLIER; girl to daughter Elizabeth IRONMONGER; girl to daughter Frances CRENSHAW; girl to daughter Sally; girl to daughter Lucy; girl to daughter Susanna; girl to daughter Mary; girl to daughter Martha; girl to daughter Anne; remaining negroes to be divided between my children

Charles CRENSHAW .... 9 Feb 1790, will

 6 negroes to son John CRENSHAW given on his marriage; negroes to the value given to son John to son Nathanial CRENSHAW; woman Nanny, girl Mary to daughter Susanna with same proportion of slaves given to sons; woman Delphy, girl Lizer to daughter Temperance with same proportion of slaves given to sons; Agnes, girl Fanny to daughter Agnes with same proportion of slaves given to sons

Richard CRENSHAW vs Charles JACKSON ....
.... 24 July 1806, in Court

> Charles CRENSHAW shall pay unto Richard CRENSHAW 3 negroes namely 2 boys & 1 woman between the ages of 15 & 25

David DAVENPORT vs John WILKENSON .... Aug 1778, judgment

> judgment for 3 of the slaves Doll, Robert, & Judy

William DOWNER .... 5 Nov 1808, will

> Dick, Bob, Peter, Payton, Henry, James, Charlotte, Rachel to children John, Mildred, Lucy & Robert DOWNE

William FOSTER .... 17 June 1768, will

> 2 negroes belonging to the estate of James FOSTER son of William FOSTER to George FOSTER guardian of Patty FOSTER daughter of James now wife of John WULL also trustee for Lilly, Lucy, & Christian children of James

John GEORGE .... 14 May 1784, inv & appr

> Sam, Essea, George, Dick, Abel, Abram, Hannah, Esther, little Esther, Cate, Meriah, Bess, Beck, little Sam, Gilbert, Holliday, John, Shadrack, Will

Reuben GEORGE .... 14 Jan 1800, appr & div slaves

> left by will: Abram to R. GEORGE; Frank, Randol to John GEORGE; Pol, Hannah, Asher to Anner GEORGE
>
> Gilbert, Sawney, David, Brutus, Nelly, old Sarah, Dolly, Sal, Phoebe, Harry, Dick
>
> Lot 1: Gilbert, Dolly to Anner GEORGE; Lot 2: Sawney to Molley ROGERS' children; Lot 3: David to Reuben GEORGE; Lot 4: Brutus to Byrd GEORGE; Lot 5: Sall, Nelly to William GEORGE; Lot 6: Dick to John OLIVER; Lot 7: Phoebe, Harry to John GEORGE

Reuben GEORGE .... 16 May 1799, will

> man Abram to son Reuben GEORGE; man Frank, boy Randol to son John GEORGE; woman Pol, girl Hannah, boy Asher to daughter Anner GEORGE; remaining negroes to be divided among children Reuben GEORGE, Molley ROGERS, William & Byrd GEORGE, Lucy OLIVER, John, & Anner GEORGE

John HOOMES .... 1 Oct 1804, will Jacob, Dinah, Janey & her husband Tom & their children Mime, Dinah, Archibald, & Jacob, Sally & her children Lindia, Patty, & Sarah, Lye, old Jack, Cate, Nelle & children Emmanuel, Mary, & Rose, Dell & her children Charles, Thornton, & Norton, Sall & her children Lucy & Kate, old Patt, Tom, Bob, Robbin, Clary, Sukey, Eliza & her child Edmund, Frank, William, little Robbin, Hubbard, Christian George, John, Moses, Aggy & her son Isaac, Gandfry, Nelle, Moses, Phil, Molly, Tillah, Peter, Shem, old Isaac, Daniel to wife Judith HOOMES & at her death to be divided among children John, William, Richard, Armistead, & Sophia; Daniel, Esther & their children Parrot, Katy, Nancy, George, Gabriel, & Suckey, Ambrose, Moses, Bob, Aggy, Robin, Natt, Vilate (Violet?) & her children Catherine & Charlotte, Dice & her children Richard & Daniel, George & his wife Sucky & child William, Moses & his children Page, Spotswood, & Clara, Sandy, Cesar & Hannah & their children William & David to son John HOOMES; negroes in King William to grandson John Waller HOOMES; William, Joice, Nancy, Mary, Parker, Macon, Rose, Letty, Molly, Jack, Sam, Charlotte, Susannah, Sarah, Charity & child Nancy, Cynthia, Nero, Pleasant, Kitty, Peter, Robin, Tom Jones, Frank, Cato & his wife, Mack, Phillis, Ned & Phill Hedge to son William HOOMES; James, George, Aggy, Phill, Gideon, Charles, Peggy, Betsy, Mercer, Fanny, Suckey, Molly, Anna, Ede, Fountain, Rachel, Keziah, Nan, Rachel, Julia, Robin, Lucy, Rhode, Mary, Lewis, Tom & his children Maria & Lavinia, John, Jack, Dick to son Richard HOOMES; Ralph, Nan, Ned, Will & his wife Patt & their children, Spencer, Jane, Lewis, Randolph, Billy Long, Henry, Betsy, Reuben, Caty, James & his son Burwell, Joe & Suckey & their children, Cyrus, Patt, Phillis, Dick, Daniel, Milly, Unity, George, Eleanor, Rochambeau to son Armistead HOOMES; Boston, Polly, Nelson, Billy, Ursely, Ailsey, Nelly, Elliott, Henry, Isabell, Achilles, John, Frederick bought of Mrs. LAUGHLIN, Frank Hedge, Isaac, Ezekiel bought of Mr. BAYLOR, Billy & Uriah his wife & their children Harry, James, & one not named, old Daphney & John's mother, Will & Isabell his wife & children Ben, Polly, Edgar, Patrick, Jesse, & Fanny, Gilbert & Nelly his wife & children Jasper, Clay, & Armistead, Truelove, little Daphine Nelly's daughter to daughter Sophie

John GEORGE .... 29 Dec 1794, legacy
   (listed under ISBELL, Daniel to Exr of John George: Bond)
   boy Jack to Daniel ISBELL

John GEORGE .... 29 Dec 1794, legacy
   (listed under ISBELL, Nancy to Exr of John George: Bond)
   Milly & her increase to be divided...Nancy ISBELL has received man Dick...

Daniel ISBELL .... 26 Nov 1767, will
   son James ISBELL have liberty to work slaves of his own...

Nancy ISBELL to Exr of John GEORGE .... 29 Dec 1794, bond
   Milly & her increase to be divided between Nancy & Daniel ISBELL & John G., Benjamin, & Travis GRAVES; man Dick to Nancy ISBELL

Robert JOHNSON .... 20 Mar 1780, codicil
   all negroes to wife

Jeremiah JORDAN to John ALMAND .... 13 July 1763, deed
   boy Frank to John ALMAND

Edward LEVELL .... 14 Aug 1755, will
   wench Juno, Peter, Lett, Phillis, Betty, Sall to wife Elizabeth LEVELL

John MASON .... 11 July 1780, will
   young Peter, Violett, Simon, Sarah to wife Crocha MASON

Matthew MILLS .... 10 July 1753, will
   woman Jude to son Me_ain; men Housday, Sipeo to be hired out then sold when son Charly comes to lawful age

Robert MUCKLEBURROUGH .... 18 Aug 1788, will
   old Ballock, young Dick, Seller, Daniel, Grace to wife & at her death to be set free; Hannah daughter of Nan to Davie DICKERSON son of Samuel DICKERSON; Mime to Thomas GUY son of Thomas GUY; Brutus, Gift, Anny to John THILMAN Sr. to maintain his daughter Jane THILMAN; Hannah, Tom to Thomson MILLS; George, Rachel

to Susannah FENELL; Poll, young Ballock to Susannah HACKELD; rest of the negroes to be divided among John THILMAN Sr., George WILLIAMSON, Susannah HACKELD, John WILLIAMSON, Bejnamin WILLIAMSON son of Robert WILLIAMSON

Edmund PENDLETON .... 13 Dec 1824, will

aged negroes Jerry, Enos, Frank & Portia his wife, Jenny, Pat to care of son Edmund; remaining slaves to be divided into 7 lots; 1 lot to son Edmund plus Burrell as he owns his wife; 1 lot to daughter Frances TAYLOR; 1 to daughter Elizabeth TURNER; 1 lot to be divided among children of son John PENDLETON dec'd; 1 lot to son Edmund PENDLETON in trust for his sister Sarah TURNER; last lot to son-in-law Robert TAYLOR in trust for my daughter Lucy RICHARDS; negroes purchased at a sale made under a deed of trust from my son-in-law Thomas RICHARDS to Hugh N. PENDLETON will remain with said RICHARDS

.... 15 Nov 1826, codicil

slaves given to daughter Mildred PAGE dec'd to be divided among her children

Edmund PENDLETON .... 19 May 1799, will

Jem to Edmund PENDLETON Jr. son of nephew Edmund; girl Edie to John PENDLETON; slaves to wife, at her death to great nephew John PENDLETON; slaves not consumed to be divided between nephew Edmund & his 6 children; servant Hero to choose his master from them

Giles RAINES .... 8 Nov 1805, will

Barnett, Phebe & her 2 children Carlce & Walker to wife Dorothy RAINES

John REYNOLDS .... 2 Feb 1755, will

Davy, Ben, Tom, Daphney, Ralph, Nan to wife Sarah, if she marries to be divided among sisters Elizabeth GARRETT, Mary LONG, & Frances REYNOLDS

Alexander ROANE .... 9 Jan 1788, will

boy Billy to son Alexander ROANE; boy Edmund to son Thomas ROANE; girl Katy to daughter Sarah ROANE; girl Rose to daughter Dorotha SAUNDERS; girl Clary to daughter Ann ALCOCK; the remaining increase to be divided into 5 parts: 1 part to daughter Dorotha SAUNDERS, 1 part to daughter Ann ALCOCK, 1 part each to Sarah ROANE, Alexander ROANE, & Thomas ROANE

Mildred ROGERS, etc vs adm of Reuben GEORGE dec'd .... 12 Jan 1802, in Chancery

Mildred, Reuben, George, Catharine B., Achillis, Polly, Lucy, Isaac ROGERS; slaves from defendant to be delivered to plaintiffs; hire of man Sawne

Thomas STHRESHLEY .... 29 Mar 1825, will

negroes loaned to sister Fanny B. WOODWARD to be removed to friend Richard ROWZEE until her death then to nephew Thomas WOODWARD

James TERRILL .... 18 Oct 1766, will

wench Jane to daughter Betty NEWTON; wench Fortune to daughter Patty HORD; girl Rose to daughter Wiffe; boy Charles to daughter Mary HERNDON

Godney & Judy TRICE & John & Sarah ASHBURN .... 25 Feb 1736, receipt

received man George, Phillis & her increase, a legacy given by our brother Dabney ANDERSON dec'd received by James TRICE

John WATTS .... 5 Mar 1775, will

slaves to be divided among nephews & nieces the children of brother Richard WATTS & sister Elizabeth W. HARG

Zachariah WILSON .... Jan 1826, inv & appr

Celia, Rose, Randolph, Joe, Phil, Milly, Jerry, Esther, Eleanor, Christopher, Phillis, Tom, Addison, Arch, Spencer, John, Walker, Lucy, Clara, Thornton

Zachariah WILSON .... 3 Oct 1811, will

Tom, Thornton, Billy, Hannah, Sarah to daughter Catharine GEORGE; wife's negroes after her death to daughters Agnes & Catharine GEORGE except girl chosen by wife for granddaughter Louisa Catharine Wilson GEORGE

CHARLES CITY

Charles City County was recognized in 1634 as an original shire. Records have been destroyed at various times. The most damage occurred during the Civil War when the records were strewn through the woods in a rainstorm. A few pre-Civil War volumes such as deed books, will books, minute books, and order books exist.

Hannah ACRILL .... 24 Aug 1768, will

...Capt. David MINGE...for my maid Nanny who hath a husband in his farm that my executors shall sell and dispose of my said maid Nanny to him...; Ned to nephew Acrill COCKE

James ALLEN .... 10 Sept 1771, will

Jacob, Easter to granddaughter Anne KING daughter of Philip KING; little Tony to son Benjamin ALLEN; Frank, Sam to son Charles ALLEN after decease of my wife; Sampson, Agge, Dick, John, Jane to daughter Anna RICHARDSON wife of Turner RICHARDSON; Sarah, Dick, Little Cate to daughter Anna ALLEN; Dal, Isaac, __ to daughter Sarah ALLEN; Fenda, Jane, Ned, Sam, Annis now in his possession to son John RICHARDSON; girl Lidda to granddaughter Elizabeth GREEN; girl Jane to granddaughter Anne SIMS; remaining negroes to wife Anne ALLEN

William BYRD .... 6 July 1774, will

100 negroes to be sold; remaining negroes to wife Mary BYRD and to be sold at her death; 2 negroes of his choice to son John; his man, little Jack White, his choice of 2 girls to son Charles; 2 girls to daughter Jenney & the child my wife goes with; servant Jack White to be free upon death of my wife

Elizabeth CHAMBERLAYNE .... 10 Mar 1738, bond

child born after husband's death named Ann Kidby...no provision made for "post death child"...devised to her several slaves for life...Dick, Peace, Pegg...to establish & confirm the said child's right to the said slaves...

Littleberry COCKE .... 29 Oct 1768, deed of gift

Bett, Patt, Rachel, Tom, Zaga, Will to Rebecca COCKE daughter of Littleberry COCKE & Rebecca Hubbard his wife

William COLE .... 24 Oct 1750, will
    boy Dick to son Richard COLE; girl Bess to daughter Mary COLE; dower slaves of my mother to my son William COLE after her death

CHARLES CITY COURT RECORDS .... pgs 1 – 99
(The page numbers refer to the digital numbers on the menu bar. They can be changed by highlighting the number/then typing in the page you want.)

Ann HARRIS .... pg 29, 7 Mar 1693
    boy Mina to grandson William TYLOR

Ann HARRIS .... pg 30, 7 Mar 1693
    George, to grandson William, Daniel to granddaughter Martha children of son William HUNT

Thomas HARRISON .... pg 31, 3 Apr 1694
    Indian boy Frank to daughter Ann; Indian boy Jack to daughter Elizabeth

William VANGHAN .... pg 38, 24 Mar 1692
    Indian boy Will to son Nicholas VANGHAN for 15 years then to be free

Thomas GIBBS .... pg 40, 4 June 1694
    non apercell of negroes...man Czbeo, woman, boy Dick, girl Frank to Charles ANDERSON

William PEEBLES .... pg 65, 21 Nov 16__
    girl Cate to daughter Hannah after wife's decease

.... pg 81, 25 Nov 1694
    William SHERWOOD, Peter PERRY appointed Power of Attorney for Perry Thomas LANE & Richard PERRY of London; items include negroes

Thomas SHANDS .... pg 96, 3 June 1696
    man Jack, boys Tom, Matt, women Bess, Jane

CHARLES CITY COURT RECORDS .... pgs 100 – 199
(The page numbers refer to the digital numbers on the menu bar. They can be changed by highlighting the number/then typing in the page you want.)

Nicolas OVERBY .... pg 10, 30 May 1696
    girl Mott to grandson Nicolas OVERBY

John BALLE .... pg 32, 2 Feb 1690/1
    Indian wench to go free after death of wife

Phillip THOMAS .... pg 33, 20 Mar 1896/7
    woman sold to Richard GON_ER

John Gane LOTT .... pg 42, 2 Aug 1697
    old man

Thomas LANDUM .... pg 45, 10 June 1697
    man servant

James BLUNKER .... pg 46, 18 June 1697
    servant lad

Alexander DAVIDSON .... pg 59, 14 May 1697
    Indian Will & his wife & children, Indian Robin their freedom at my wife's decease

Capt. Peter PERRY .... pg 64, 1 Mar 1697/8
    old George

James HOWARD .... pg 66, 25 Dec 1697/8
    Indian girl Hannah to Elizabeth PARR daughter of Anthony PARR

Henry BATTE .... pg 100, 10 June 1695
    Roger to son Henry BATTE; woman Hannah to son William BATTE; woman Sis to daughter Mary BATTE; boy Peter to son John BATTE; girl Matt to daughter Elizabeth BATTE

CHARLES CITY COURT RECORDS .... pgs 200 – 303
(The page numbers refer to the digital numbers on the menu bar. They can be changed by highlighting the number/then typing in the page you want.)

Samuel GROTMAN .... pg 9, 15 Mar 1698/9
    old woman

Stephen FLESCHWAR .... pg 21, 10 July 1698/9
   Bess' first child to daughter Frances, her second child to daughter Elizabeth FLESCHWAR

Hen_y HARMAN .... pg 31, 24 July 1699
   2 negroes, a woman servant

Thomas SMITH .... pg 31, 3 Aug 1699
   girl

Sarah LANDUM .... pg 32, 5 Apr 1699
   servant boy

Nicholas HARRISON .... pg 33, 20 Mar 1698/9
   men John, Thomas, boy Sam, women Bess, Jean, man Jew, boys Mingo, Jack, child Tony

Stephen FLESCHWAR .... pg 44, 21 Aug 1699
   woman servant, boy servant

James HALL .... pg 49, 9 June 1699
   boy Will to wife

Matthew ANDERSON .... pg 77, 4 Mar 1699/1700
   man Tom, who previously belonged to James HEATH dec'd, to James ADAMS son of ___

George WOODLIEF .... pg 82, 9 July 1699
   cook to son John WOODLIEF; Ned to son Thomas WOODLIEF

William LUCY .... pg 95, 25 Mar 1700
   boy to brother Taylor which Hubert GAND...; wench & children may not be sold

Elias OSBORN .... pg 101, 12 July 1690
   man, woman

Ann Hollford .... pg 103, 20 ___ 1679
   ...bind my daughter Elizabeth as a mulatto apprentice unto John BAXTER...she is now 6 or 7 months old

Elizabeth EDMONDSON .... 3 May 1790, will
    Ned, Abram, Charles, Pompey, Betty, Aggy, Isaac, Becky, Moses to my ___; Henry & his wife & their children to brother Carter B. HARRISON; Patsy & 3 children Molly, Tom, & Patty to sister Sarah HARRISON; Johnny to brother Ben's son Ben; George to brother William H. HARRISON; Joe, Sarah? daughter of Polly to William Richman CAPLAND; boy ___ to husband & at his death to return to Ben's son Benjamin

William F. GRAVES to Thomas H. WILLCOX .... 7 Apr 1856, deed
    Israel, Betsy, ___ to Thomas H. WILLCOX

Francis HARDYMAN ....24 Aug 1772, in Chancery
    equal amount of slaves to wife Jane, sons Francis, Littlebarry, James, Richard, daughters Henrietta Maria CLARK, Elizabeth, & Mary HARDYMAN; ...John & Jane CROSS... Francis HARDYMAN intermarried with Jane widow of John CROSS

Benjamin HARRISON .... 17 Oct 1743, will
    slaves except Patty & her children, boy ___y son of Sarah to wife Ann HARRISON; Patty & her children, boy ___ry son of Sarah to son Benjamin HARRISON; slaves of Willis Creek to son Carter Henry HARRISON; slaves of the Estate of Sam to son Henry; slaves in the town of Peersburg & the slaves on the Chetecarah? tract to son Robert HARRISON; slaves at Amelia Courthouse to son Nathaniel; slaves of Seaman's to son Charles; 3 women, 2 men to be bought...for the 3 plantations aforementioned; man John to wife; negroes of Six? Plantation to son Benjamin; land of William Glover to be sold & slaves removed to land given to son Robert; slaves after the death of Mrs. Elizabeth WILLIS of Henry HARRISON's estate dec'd to revert to me to be divided equally to sons; Liddy, Charles, Cate daughter of Aggy to daughter Betty; girl Darcus to daughter Anne; Aaron, Hannah daughter of Timer, Martha daughter of Bess to daughter Lucy; girl Cloe to daughter Sarah; girl Sukey daughter of Bess to daughter Hannah

Robert MUNFORD .... 12 Dec 1799, will
    1/3 negroes to wife

Abigail et al .... 5 Aug 1807, cert of freedom

    age 54, 5' 6"; Lilly her daughter age 24, 5' 7 ½"; Tabetha age 12, 4' 2"; Abigail age 18, 5' 2" emancipated by will of William PARRISH

John ROGERS .... 13 Apr 1788, will

    men Johanthan, James, Venus, Sall to wife Martha ROGERS; boy Will to son Kirkland ROGERS; Sam to son John ROGERS; girl Mourning to daughter Betsey Whitt ROGERS; girl Hannah to daughter Dorcas ROGERS; girl Milly, boy Jerry to son William ROGERS

Capt Henry SOANE .... 8 Feb 1750, inv & appr

    men Johnny, Scott, Will, old Ben, Peter, Tom, boys Isaac, Jack, Glasgow, Scott, girls Amey, Betty, Lucy & child Esther, women Betty, Judy, Sue, Sarah

.... 2 Mar 1750, inv & appr

    old Will, James, Sue, Agge, Tabb, Pugg, Frederick, Hick, Jenny, Harry, Anthony

.... 1750 – 4 Dec 1754, estate acct

    Isaac, Harry, Amey, Bett sold; 2 negroes sold; maintainance of girl Bett; maintainance of boy Will, child Patt, wenches Betty, Sue, Tabb; hire of negro men & women; clothing of 11 negroes; advertising negroes to be sold; boys Scott, Glasgow, Will, women Moll, Lucy, Judy sold

Rebecca Hubbard SOANE .... 11 Dec 1752, dower

    John, Scott, Will, James, Peter, Jacob, Scott, Glasgow, Sarah, Sue, Judith

Wat H. TYLER to Robert M. CHRISTIAN .... Feb 1817, deed

    Edith & her children Garrick, Nancy, & Betsy to Robert M. CHRISTIAN to be sold at the request William E. HILL

CULPEPER

Culpeper County was created in 1749. A significant number of loose records are missing for the period prior to 1840. They were stolen, mutilated, and/or destroyed during the Civil War. Culpeper was the site of several military engagements and experienced widespread pillaging by both Union and Confederate troops. The county courthouse was used as a jail for Confederate prisoners by Union forces. Volumes that record deeds and wills from the formation of the county exist. Minute books for the periods 1749-1762, 1765-1797, 1812-1813, and 1817 are missing.

Leonard BARNES the elder .... 16 May 1805, will

man James to son Leonard BARNES; man Ralph to son Charles BARNES; Frank, Rose, George to son Henry BARNES; 3 negroes to daughter Thomsen

William BOOTON .... 1 Nov 1779, will

all negoes except Tom, Bob, Winney & the 3 I lend to my son William to wife Judith BOOTEN; boy Bob, girl Winney, fellow Tom to son William BOOTON; son Lewis BOOTON, son-in-law James BOHANON, & son Ambrose BOOTON's children to keep the negroes that I have lent to them to be returned to the estate at death of my wife; boy Dick to remain the property of James BOHANON

Henry FIELD .... 7 Nov 1785, will

Nelson, Nancy to son Henry William FIELD; Milly, Baccus, Flora to daughter Nancy DELANEY; James, Squire, Eday to daughter Molly FIELD; boy Martin to son George FIELD; sell land to purchase 2 young women & along with all slaves equally to children Joseph, John, Thomas, George, & Sarah FIELD

Paul LEATHERER .... 5 Nov 1780, will

girl Hannah to daughter Margaret LEATHERER after her mother's decease

William RICE .... 9 Feb 1780, will

Jude & her child Esther to daughter Sarah GRAVES wife of Edward GRAVES

James SIMMS .... 18 Feb 1802, will
Jacob, Poll to wife Betty SIMMS; George to son Martin SIMMS; Gideon to daughter Sally Jones SIMMS

John TOWLES .... 7 Mar 1834, will
man Davy to Rebecca RIVERCOMB, also slaves from father's estate as can be lawfully claimed, at her death to be divided among her children: Betty, Francis G. LELAND, Maryon, John M., Maria, & Virginia

Ignatius TUREMAN .... 21 Oct 1782, inv & appr
fellow Monts; wench Jude, girls Mary, Agg, June

Adam WAYLAND & etc vs John WAYLAND ....
.... 28 Aug 1792, in Chancery
widow has not received her own or her children's slaves; response was that widow has received slaves & is now in debt
.... 22 May 1782 – 22 May 1799, estate acct
appraisement of negroes, divided into 8 parts: Adam WAYLAND's interest part - James, Hannah WAYLAND's interest part - George

Joseph WOOD .... 7 Nov 1786, will
Harry, Isaac, Sally, Milley, Moses to wife Elizabeth WOOD; man Ben, Delphia to son Joseph WOOD; man Phill, boy Will to son Thomas WOOD; Lucy, Syliva to daughter Patsy ALCOCK; Daniel to disceased son John Scott WOOD; Peg to daughter Lucy WATTS; Sall to son-in-law William HILL

DINWIDDIE

Dinwiddie County was created in 1752. The bulk of court records prior to 1865 were stolen, mutilated, and/or destroyed by Union troops who ransacked the courthouse during the last months of the Civil War. Post-1830 volumes such as deed books, will books, chancery order books, and marriage registers exist.

Austin BILLUPS .... 10 Mar 1822, will

Jacob, Easter, David, Cherry, Randol, Fanny, Collonel, Ellick to wife Mary BILLUPS; Jinny to daughter Eliza M. VAUGHAN now in her possession; Mason & her child Nancy, Richard, Caroline, John, Sudley, Peyton to daughter Joicy F. BUTTERWORTH; Hollon, Belfield, Eoney, Charlotte, Peter, Harriet, Green, James to daughter Polly S. ELLIS

Robert BOLLING .... 7 Sept 1789, will

negroes to be divided between my 2 children Robert & Susanna BOLLINGS if wife remarries

Jesse BONNER .... 8 Apr 1797, will

man Jack to wife Rebecca BONNER; Judy, Tom, Tabb, Moses, Philis, Chloe, Beck, Jane, Ned, Winney, Bob, Jerry, Dinah, Nancy, Betty to be emancipated at death or marriage of wife Rebecca BONNER

Robert BOOTH .... 23 Feb 1849, will

Nelly, Mat, Adeline to wife Elizabeth

John BURROW .... 10 Mar 1770, will

Will, Betty to son John BURROW; boy Dick to be sold; boy Hardy to granddaughter Susannah BURROW; Frank, Tom, Judy, Ben to son Henry BURROW

Philip BURROW Sr. .... 13 Oct 1777, will

boy Jeremy son of Doll to daughter Martha CAIN; boy Glasgow son of Doll to son Jerrald BURROW; boy Moses to son Philip BURROW; boy Aaron son of Sue to daughter Mary; boy Lewis to son-in-law James MANQUIN; girl Cloe daughter of Doll to son-in-law William MARTIN; Bob, ___ to son Gray BURROW; Tony, Sue to wife Martha BURROW & after her death to Gray BURROW;

Indian Sue, Doll of Phillis to wife & after her death the wench Phillis to Gray BURROW, Sue, Doll to be divided between my children Jerrald, Philip, Martha, Mary, & Gray & sons-in-law James MANQUIN & William MARTIN

Bolling CLARK ....16 Feb 1809, will

Isaac, Tom to son-in-law Peter PRIDE & at his decease to granddaughter Ann ALLEN; Peter, Anthony, little Peter, Milly, Anica to granddaughter Ann ALLEN; Aaron, Lyda, Sall, Joshua, Jenny to granddaughter Mary BURNETT; Jumfred, Daniel Lewis, Rachel, Nancy to granddaughter Elizabeth NORTH; Elizabeth to grandson Bolling C. NORTH; Lucy to great-grandson Bolling C. BURNETT; Kitt should have the privilege of choosing his master

Thomas CLAY ....24 Aug 1812, will

women Amy, Luce, fellow Aaron, boy Tom to wife Luzamia

William COX ....1 Jan 1822, will

negroes to wife Mary G. COX, at her death to be divided among my children

....codicil

man Billy to son Henry willed him by his grandfather COX

John P. CRUMP ....3 Mar 1846, will

servants may be sold

William CUTLER ....7 Dec 1833, will

Isham, Edgar, Charlotte & her young unnamed male child to William H. WOODMAN in trust for daughter Maria LOVE wife of Theoderic LOVE

William EPES ....4 Mar 1762, will

little Jack to mother Amey EPES; Wood to brother Isham EPES

Francis EPPES..28 Sept 1776, will

Tom, Will that I bought of Douglas IRBY, Wood, Bett, Madon to Mary Anne Frances HARPER

William EPPES ....21 Nov 1793, will

Shadrack, Siloe, Lilly, Delsey, Jane, Mary, Lydda, Nancy, Bett, Mason, little Shadrack, Winney, Syrus, Africa, Ned, Cochener, Lucy,

Stephen, George, Joshua, Sall, Patt, Charles, Tom, Jim, Elik, Willey to wife Elizabeth EPPES & after her death to Dianelia SCOTT & after her death to her children Thomas, John, & Hannah SCOTT

....18 Mar 1806, in Chancery

SCOTT to appear here on the 17th of the next term

Alexander FRASER .... 5 Jan 1828, will

Mary & her child Juley to daughter Elizabeth GRESHAM

George Grain ....31 July 1846, cert of freedom age 31, 5' 2 ½", and identifying marks, born free

John HAMLIN .... 18 Apr 1824, will

¼ of my slaves to sons George Willoughby, Stephen Henry, John Francis, & Thomas Browne HAMLIN

John HARDAWAY.. 29 May 1824, will

1/5 value of slaves, man Bob to daughter Lucy M. MAYHEW; Billy, Isabelle, Franky, Rebecca, Ephrain, Lucinda, Manser, Richard, Cyrus to son William Edward; Hartwell, Freeman, Fanny, Temfry, Peter, Nancy, Daniel, Suckey, Jones, little Peter to son Frederick; Cresy, Tom, Rachel, Phillis, Clementine, little Billy, Roger, Sam, Travis, Ben, Nelson, David, Suckey to daughter Mary Ann; Louisa, Stephen, Albert, Henry, Dick, Betsy, Mary, Harriet, Moses, David, Sterling to daughter Eliza; James, Polly, Easter, John, Anderson, Jacob, Celia, Betty, Minon, William, George to son John

William HUDSON .... 13 Sept 1789, will

Daniel, Natt, James to be hired out if needed to pay debts; use of Natt to Nanny Wilds; James to brother Juby HUDSON; girls Abby or Fanny which is at William YATES to brother Tuttle HUDSON; boy Nelson to sister Penelope HUDSON; Daniel to brothers Juby & Tuttle; sister Penelope HUDSON to take care of Nancy Wilds

Ann JONES ....6 Oct 1806, will

women Pegg, Annica to sister Martha CLAIBORNE; woman Chener to sister Mary BRODNAX; John Brown, Patience & her 3 children ___ss, Albert, & Betsy to Augustine CLAIBORNE; boy Cosser to nephew Augustine C. JONES; boy Phill to Gracy CLAIBORNE; Tolre, Hall, Harrison, Peach to Frederick S. BRODNAX; Charlotte &

her 3 children Rose, James, & Alexander, Iris, boy John, Robert to William F. BRODNAX; man Peter to Robert BRODNAX; Sally, Caroline, Amey, Archer, Andrew to nephews Jack P. BRODNAX & Cadwallader BRODNAX; fellow Jesse to Cad CLAIBORNE; man Dick to John WITHERS

Christopher T. JONES .... 8 Apr 1819, will

2 male & 2 female servants to wife Mary JONES; 1 female slave to Elizabeth Ann NEW niece of my wife; Daniel

Mary Ann JONES .... 16 Apr 1851, will

Miranda, Robin, Betsy, Calda, Louisa, Emily, Henrietta, Martha, Lucy be emancipated

Peter JONES the younger .... 1 Dec 1770, will

Sall & her child Rachel to wife Elizabeth

Ferdinando LEIGH .... 24 May 1779, will

Lewis, girl Aggy to oldest grandson; girl Sally to grandson William Cole CLAIBORNE; girl Lucy daughter of Isbel to grandson Nathaniel CLAIBORNE; Hannah to grandson Thomas Augustin CLAIBORNE; Tom & Milly & their 5 children Prudence, Grace, Judith, Tony, & ___, Beck & her 5 children Harry, Chashin, Jany, Will, & Peggy, Betty & her 3 children Sam, Ginny, & Phill, Nanny & her child Cate, Peter, Sam, Will, Dick, Will, Fenton, Prudence, Chloe, Nancy, Lucy, Gaby, Bob, Jeffery to son William LEIGH; Harry, Joe, Warwich, Will, old Jane, young Betty, Peggy, ___, Lucy & 4 children Lucy, Thompson, Jeminy, & Will, Isbell & 4 children Dick, Esther, Frank, & ___, Nell, Lucy, Bridget & 3 children Polly, Jack, & ___ to daughter Mary CLAIBORNE & son-in-law William CLAIBORNE

Christopher MANLOVE .... 1 Oct 1802, will

Winney & her children Lizzy, Jack, Matilda, Dinah, Phillis, & Charles to daughter Jane BASS

Donald McKAY .... 1 July 1819, will

boy Adam Huks to daughter Margarey RAINEY; Eliza, Polly, Doctor, Billy to be sold; Amy, Phil to daughter Peggy SHEPPERSON; woman Fanny to choose master from one of my children; boy Manuel to son Addison McKAY, boy John to hs wife ___lia McKAY

Francis MUIR .... 11 Mar 1810, will
negroes to work land until debts are paid; Ned, York, Bristol, Shadrack, Anthony, Gary, Lenny, Titus, Tom, Aaron, Ben, Israel be kept separate property...for 4 youngest children – Gustavus Adolphus, Marianne, Douglas, & Caroline MUIR; millers, carpenters, blacksmiths to be equally divided between sons Gustavus Adolphus & Douglas MUIR when all children have been educated

Dolly P. NICHOLAS .... 27 May 1832, will
negroes to be divided between children Robert Carter NICHOLAS & Dolly P.G.B. HARRISON; Mr. LABAT to purchase? boy Billy

Ephraim PARTHAN .... 16 Mar 1779, will
___, Harry, Solomon, C_zor, Nee_, Judy to wife Ann PARTHAN; Sampson, Ben, S_rry, Jenny, Truckey to daughter Betsy PARTHAN; James, Ned, Hector, Nancy, Frank to son Nicholas PARTHAN; Peter, David, Dinah, Moll, Rachel to son Thomas PARTHAN; Jack, Anthony, Beck, Hannah, Violet to daughter Joanna PARTHAN

James PATILLO .... 1 July 1753, will
Moses to daughter Ann WILLIAMS wife of James WILLIAMS; girl Phillis to daughter Mary PATILLO; boy Peter to Cornelus FOX?; Amy to son John's mother Mary PATILLO; men Tom, Will to grandson James PATILLO minor son of my son James & Martha PATILLO; woman Phillis to grandson James PATILLO minor & his brother Solomon PATILLO

Simon REEMS / REAMES .... 12 Feb 1813, will
Agga, Bob, Lucy, Milly, Sucky & her son John to son William REEMS; Peggy, Harry, Jonas, Amy, Coleman to daughter Susannah COLE; girl Patsy to granddaughter Sally COLE; Lewis, Nancy, Charlotte, Daniel to son William REEMS & William Temple COLE in trust for daughter Polly CROWDER; when grandson Simon CROWDER arrives at age 21 to receive Lewis & Nancy

William SCOTT .... 26 Dec 1793, will
Dinah, Fanny, all my slaves to wife Ann SCOTT; boy Hall to son James SCOTT

Littleberry E. STAINBACK .... 21 Sept 1854, codicil
woman Ellen, man Tom & wife Sally, Aleck

Martha STOKES .... 12 May 1788, will
> woman Jane, boys Dumphrey, Sippio, girl Fanny to son Sterling STOKES

Robert THOMPSON .... 13 July 1851, will
> girl Agnes to daughter Mary SMITH; boy William, girl Hannah to son John; girl Rebecca & her child Jane to daughter Ann F. THOMPSON; man Henry to daughter Elizabeth C. THOMPSON; man Charles to daughter Emily THOMPSON; old Hannah to be taken care of; Harry, Aggy, Rachel, Solomon to son Robert S. THOMPSON to be used to paying debts; the remainder of the above slaves to single daughters Ann F., Elizabeth C., & Emily THOMPSON

Henry THWEATT .... 3 July 1821, will
> James, Sally to wife Jane THWEATT; Catherine, Susan to wife to be given to my children at her death; Annis, Mary, Willis to wife in trust for son James THWEATT & at his death to be divided between my children Thomas THWEATT, Mildred JONES, Lucy D. BURGE, Henry G. GREEN, & Annaliza GREEN; Nancy & her present increase to son Thomas THWEATT; Cressy, Jenny to daughter Mildred JONES & her husband Kennen JONES; Sall, boy John to daughter Lucy D. BURGE wife of Bradford BURGE; _all, Dine_, Kizey, Jacob, Peter to grandchildren Henry G. & Annaliza GREEN; man Elisha to be sold

Mary TUCKER .... 28 July 1812, will
> servants Lyda, Taber, Mina, men Peter, Charles

Peter VAUGHAN .... 6 May 1816, will
> Littis & her 2 children Rochester & Anthony to daughter Elizabeth BOISSEAU; Patience & her boy to daughter Nancy B. BOISSEAU; Anna, child Delsey to daughter Patsey Poitress VAUGHAN

Bolling M. WALKER .... 19 Dec 1811, will
> ...my share of negroes ...to Charles J. McMURDO & George FISHER in trust for sister Mary Ann BELL & her lately adopted children William, Alfred, Jane, & Mary Anne BELL

Elizabeth WALKER .... 4 May 1828, will
maid Anabella to be purchased by the legatees & to let her live with whom she pleases; all my negroes to daughter Martha BARTON; the Rev John GRAMMAR Jr. not to pay for the hires of the negroes hired by him for the present year nor Meriweather B. BRODREAX

Robert WALKER .... 29 Feb 1796, will
fellow Emanuel to son Robert WALKER; George, Sam, Africa, Eleck, Mariah, Tillor to son Richard WALKER; Peter, Able, Sally, Fanny, Hannah to daughter Barton; wench Nanny & her 4 youngest children to my wife & in liu of dower: Betty, Hannah, Anebellar, great Amey, long Amey, John, Abram, Phill, Jupiter, Bob, George, Sampson, Lucy; all the negroes she already prossesses to daughter Elizabeth WITHERS; negroes not before disposed be divided among children David, Theodore, Bolling, Mary Ann, Clara, & _ueser; those slaves left to wife in lieu of dower be divided between Robert WALKER, David, Theodore, Bolling Mumford, Mary Ann, Clarissa & _ueser WALKER

Isaac WALL .... 6 Feb 179_, will
woman Betty to son David; woman Kenny to daughter Milly; man Jim to son Daniel; small girl Easter to daughter Pattey; small girl Jenny to daughter Betsey; small boy Ben to daughter Sally; small boy Bob to daughter Polly; Lucy & her child Ned to son John; woman Jude, small child Joe to wife Sally WALL

John WATKINS .... 22 June 18_7, will
Isham, Lewis to sons Robert Edmund & John William; Charles (called Sussex) & his wife & all their children, man Dick to be sold

Alice WATTS to William WATTS .... 4 __ 1765, deed
my equal & divided part of the slaves ...from the estate of my late husband Arthur WATTS dec'd to son William WATTS

Arthur WATTS .... 9 Sept 1755, inv & appr
men Sippio, Brichche, boy Wappin, girls Jeanne, Judith, wench Bess, girls Lett, Fillis, boy Jonney, girl Tun, boy Bob

Betty WATTS & etc vs Joseph TUCKER & etc .... 20 Nov 1769, decree
estate of Arthur WATTS: Lot 3: man Jack, Breeches, Bess, Rose, Jean, Beck, ___, Lewis to William WATTS; Lot 1: Lett, Celia, Ben to

Billy KIRKLAND; Lot 4: Phillis, Bob to Sarah WATTS; Lot 5: Pru, Daniel, Winney to Edward WATTS; Lot 2: Scipio, Patt to John WATTS

Thomas WITHERS .... 2 Jan 1838, will

Moses, Hannibal, Stephen, Louis, Roger, Judy, Flora, Bob son of Beck, Kizzy, Diley, Venus, Isabella & her children, Citta & her children, Paulina to wife; man John to son Robert WALKER; man Hannibal to daughter Ann Elizabeth at death of my wife; residue of slaves to be divided among 7 children by my last marriage: Mary T., Louisa W., Elizabeth, Thomas, David WRIGHT, Edmund, William; George, Lizzy, Peggy now in possession of daughter Mary T. a part of her proportion

.... 30 Jan 1839, codicil

slaves in Alabama to continue to work there...to be divided among 7 children by my last marriage

Lucy WORSHAM .... 23 Dec 1777, will

great Will, Arter, Daniel, little Will, Ned, Frank, Chenah to son Lewelling WORSHAM; girl Sarah to granddaughter Elizabeth WORSHAM daughter of Lewelling WORSHAM; Jack, Ned, to daughter Martha WORSHAM; Milly, Beck, Peggy, Jenny to daughter Margaret WORSHAM

Phillip WORSHAM .... 18 Jan 1754, inv & appr

woman June, man Daniel, girls Nan, Doll

Phillip WORSHAM to John TAPLEY .... 9 Oct 1752, deed

Daniel, Dole, Arthur to John TAPLEY

Benjamin P. YATES .... 22 May 1815, will

land to be sold when wife marries & money used to purchase negroes or other property

ELIZABETH CITY

Elizabeth City County was recognized in 1634 as an original shire. Records were burned and/or destroyed during the Revolutionary War and the War of 1812. Additional records were burned in Richmond on 3 April 1865, where they had been moved for safekeeping during the Civil War. A few pre-Civil War volumes such as deed books, will books, and order books exist.

William ALLEN...12 July 1731, will

woman Sue to wife Elenor ALLEN & after her death to be equally divided between my children: Anthony, Elizabeth, Sarah, Thomas, & Anne ALLEN

William THOMPSON...7 Mar 1808, inv & appr

(Listed under GERRY, Anne etc. vs Henry THOMPSON, etc. Chancery)

men George, Merit, Frank, Abraham, Marcus, Robert, John, boys Cary, John, woman Betty, Molly & 2 children, girls Martha, Sophia

Robert THOMPSON..13 July 1851, will

girl Agnes to daughter Mary SMITH; boy William, girl Hannah to son John; Rebecca & her child Jane to daughter Ann F. THOMPSON; man Henry to daughter Elizabeth C. THOMPSON; man Charles to daughter Emily THOMPSON; old Hannah to be cared for by the estate; Harry, Aggy, Rachel, Soloman to son Robert L. THOMPSON & 3 single daughters

Mary TUCKER..25 July 1812, will

servants: Lyda, Taba, Vina, men Peter, Chaster

Peter VAUGHAN..6 May 1816, will

Littis & her 2 children Rochester & Anthony to daughter Elizabeth BOISSEAU; Patience & her boy to daughter Nancy B. BOISSEAU; girl Anna, child Delsey to daughter Patsey Poitress VAUGHAN

FAIRFAX

Created in 1742. Original wills and deeds as well as many other loose papers were destroyed during the Civil War; deed books for twenty-six of the fifty-six years between 1763 and 1819 are missing. Numerous pre–Civil War minute books are missing as well.

Thomas BOND .... 20 Jan 1793, will
    man Joe in the possession of Henry DEANING to be free; servant Henry Foulk

GLOUCESTER

Gloucester County was created in 1651. All records were destroyed by an 1820 fire, and most of the records created after 1820 were destroyed by fire in Richmond on 3 April 1865, where they had been moved for safekeeping during the Civil War.

Charles BLACKNELL .... 18 Dec 1761, will

negroes to wife, after her decease to all my children ....last page negroes remained in the possession of Mary BLACKNELL until her death; Peggy, Peyton are the descendants of slaves which were the property of Charles BLACKNELL and came to the possession of widow Mary BLACKNELL and on her death were divided as aforementioned

Ambrose BOHANNON ....22 Feb 1753, will

negroes

Thomas BOSWELL ....23 Feb 1797, will

Jack, Dinah to daughter Dorothy CHURCHILL; wench Polly to daughter Elizabeth ARMISTEAD; profits of Ned Branch to daughter Jane MAYOR; fellow Gabriel, wench Winney & her child Rose to grandson John ARMISTEAD; wench Beck to grandson Thomas Boswell P_HEN during his minority...his discretion to set her free or keep her as a slave

William BROOKING Sr. .... 23 Dec 1701, will

girl about 7 years old to my daughter ____; to man _ass one great cloth coat

Benjamin CHUVERIUS... 8 Jan 1782, will

old Beck, Darby, Sam, Kitt, Ruth, Else to wife Mary CHUVERIUS & after her death to daughter Kitty WASHINGTON; Kate, Henrietta, Sally to daughter Kitty WASHINGTON; negroes in the possession of William WILEY to grandchildren Irania, Holt, & Augustin CHUVERIUS; girl Sarah to granddaughter Irania CHUVERIUS; remaining negroes to be divided among sons Gibson Joseph, & Atwood CHUVERIUS

Benjamin CHUVERIUS... 7 Oct 1748, will
wench Hannah to granddaughter Grace SPILLER; Moses, Venus, Grace to son James CHUVERIUS; slaves to wife Ellonor CHUVERIUS, at her death ½ return to Joseph CHUVERIUS the other half to children Benjamin, Christian, & John CHUVERIUS

Benjamin CHUVERIUS... 8 Jan 1782, will
...Darby, Sam, Kitt, Ruth, Else & at her death to daughter Kitty WASHINGTON; Kate, Henrietta, Sally to daughter Kitty WASHINGTON; negroes in the possession of William WILEY to grandchildren Andrew, Abott, Benjamin CHUVERIUS during the life of Eleanor wife of William WILEY; girl Sarah to daughter _rania CHUVERIUS; remaining negroes to my sons Gibson, Joseph, Atwood CHUVERIUS

Mary M. CUNNINGHAM .... 16 Jan 1767, will
men Cupid, Frank, Emanuel to son Nathaniel CUNNINGHAM; Cato a male of Cloe to granddaughter Elizabeth COOPER; Phillis sold to Capt. James MAD_

John DOBSON.. 1 Oct 1833, will
1/3 negroes to wife Susan DOBSON & at her death to be divided among my children; remaining negroes to be divided among my children Rebecca, Martha Ann, Mary Frances, & Joseph DOBSON

Washington V. DUNN .... no date, will
girls Ailsey, Fanny, Sarah, boy Fallmore, & other negroes to wife Susan B. DUNN, at her death negroes to nephew George COX
.... 6 Oct 1862, codicil, in court
if funds be sufficient to buy small girl for niece Mary E. COX

Beverley HALL .... 20 Mar 1798, deposition
...Sarah HALL hired out 2 men & 1 woman...Nathan HALL sold 2 men & 1 woman, dower negroes belonging to his mother...

Henry HALL .... 20 Jan 1801, will
boy Charles to son Henry HALL; Peyton to son James HALL; girl Mottley to daughter Elizabeth MOSBY; man George to daughter Esther W. KEININGHAM after death of my wife; girl Rose to daughter Nancy GUBB; girl __oley to daughter Fanny DROINGOOLE after death of my wife

52

John HALL..20 Nov 1763, will

Isaac, David, Nan, girl Rachel to wife Sarah; woman Rose, girl Jenny to daughter Mary ALL___AN; Beck & her child Sawney to daughter Margery HOBDAY; boy Jeremy, Lucy, Gloucester to son Nathan; man Frank to son Thomas; girl Easter to granddaughter Sarah HALL; Lucy to be sold; Isaac to son John, David to son Thomas, Nan to daughter Elizabeth LOVELL after death of my wife

Thomas S. HARWOOD..26 Nov 1855, will

slaves to wife Lucy E. HARWOOD; ...in the purchase of slaves which slaves are to be sold as the residue of my estate...

Ann HIBBLE.. 6 Sept 1855, will

men Jesse, Billy to daughter Lacy F. HIBBLE

Wilkinson HUNLEY..1 Feb 1772, will

choice of 2 negroes to wife Rose HUNLEY; girl Juno to daughter Nancy

Mary JONES ....3 Mar 1835, will

Frank, Dolly & all her children except George, Lucy & her children except Judy to daughter Mary; Judy the daughter of Lucy to Becky the daughter of son Francis; George the son of Dolly to son Walter F. JONES; Anthony to be sold

.... 9 Dec 1835, codicil

having exchanged man Anthony for Billy...I dispose of Billy...have dower of Anthony

Walter KEEBLE..26 Mar 1743, will

man James, woman Abigail to son Humphry KEEBLE; Letty & her children to daughter Joye BEECHES; boys Minny & Harry, Peg's children to __; Bob Fann's boy, girl Letty to daughter Katherine ___

Thomas LEAVIT.. 3 May 1771, will

Robin, Lett, Venus, Abigail, Moses, Sawney, Michael to wife Elizabeth LEAVIT; girls Chloe, Agnes children of Hannah, wench Hannah, Frank to son Edmund LEAVIT; girl Lucy to son _o_my LEAVIT; woman Crisia to daughter Mildred BUSBIE

William A. LEAVIT .... 1 Mar 1854, will

Jackson, woman Caty to daughter Sarah A. MINER wife of Thomas MINER; man Solomon, James Carter, Lewis to son William F. LEAVIT; Tom Walker, Henry, woman Jenny, boy Peter to daughter Maria L. LEIGH; man Simon, Tomson of Caty, woman Maria to son John W. LEAVIT; man James, Wellington, Billy, Dick, Bob, Robert, James son of Beck, Nancy, Rosina, Fanny, Beck & son Abraham, Sally, woman Maria, boy Tom, little Martha, boy child to be divided among my 4 last children Catharine Lucretia, Rebecca Allen, son Wyndham Hackney, & Lucy Ellen LEAVIT; William was sold

John LEIGH .... 25 Dec 1859, will

man John Wesley, boys Stephen, little Dick, women Ann, Matilda, girls Nelly, Alice to daughter Virginia I. WIATT widow of Francis C. WIATT & her 3 children Fanny L., John M. & Frank F. WIATT; 2 boys, 2 maid servants Rebecca, Catharine to wife Jane B. LEIGH

John LEWIS .... 20 June 1827, will

Orville, Frederick & John (brothers) Jenny & her 2 children Montriville & Cupid, Becker & her 2 children Polly & Judy to wife Sara C. LEWIS; woman or girl to be purchased for sister Mary A. OLIVIER held in trust by nephew Warner OLIVIER

Warner LEWIS .... 29 Jan 1782, will

...negroes from said plantation to son Warner LEWIS; ...negroes from said plantation to son Addison LEWIS

.... 16 June 1783, Codicil

old Nell with her son Bob & youngest child Franky her daughter to daughter Rebecca LEWIS

Samuel R. MEDICOTT .... no date, will

servants to wife Mary

Mann PAGE .... 29 Aug 1778, will

2 slaves to wife; all slaves in the County of Gloucester to son John PAGE; all slaves in the County of Loudoun to son William B. PAGE; girl Peggy daughter of Letty & 2 girls chosen by wife to daughter Jane B. PAGE

Hansford ROWE .... 20 Mar 1798, deposition
> Will, Manny, Phoebe hired out by Sarah HALL; son Nathan HALL sold 2 men belonging to his mother

Francis SEAWELL .... Aug 1813, will
> Oliver, little Dick to son Overton SEAWELL; Sam, girl Cate to son Machum FULLER; John son of Billy & Clace to son Thornton SEAWELL; Bet's 2 children Henry & Polly to son Benjamin; Gregory & Bet's son Ben to son Washington; Bet & her youngest child to Robert THURSTON & John PAGE in trust for daughter Frances EDWARDS; Page's Lucy & her youngest child to Robert THURSTON & John PAGE in trust daughter Courtney CLUVERIUS?, also Billy for 2 years then to son Evertin
.... Aug 1813, codicil
sons John & Sterling shall not receive part of property; Cupid, Will, girl Harriet, Sawyer, Armistead to Robert THURSTON & John PAGE in trust for daughter Jane

John SEAWELL .... 12 Mar 1806, will
> 1/3 negroes to wife & may take Dick, his wife Lucy & her children, man Doctor, woman Sarah, Cooke, Armistead, boys Joe, Jim, girl Louisa; man Wilson, Molly & her children in lieu of Lively which I sold & was given him by Sterling THORNTON dec'd to son John P. SEAWELL; boy yellow Billy, John in lieu of Bob given him by Sterling THORNTON dec'd & sold by me to son Sterling; girl Maria, men Cats, Jimy to daughter Frances; daughters Courtney & Jane to choose a maid each not exceeding 12 years old; remaining negroes to be divided among children except sons John & Sterling & daughter Frances; boy Harry to grandson William Henry EDWARDS; boy George to grandson Sterling Thornton SEAWELL; at wife's decease negroes to be divided among children except sons John & Sterling & daughter Frances; boy Wasner to son Overton, boy Carter to son Thomas; boy Sam to son Francis THORNTON; Sam, Billy's son to son Benjamin; boy Frank to son Washington
.... 14 Mar 1806, codicil
negroes belonging to son John SEAWELL to remain with mine this year...& John should make no charge for their services

William SMART ....21 Mar 1839, will
>   ...as much out of the way of slaves;...well being of any colored people belonging to me...will of their own free choice leave forever the United States...I so freely give them their freedom

William T. SMITHER...9 Apr 1858, will
>   wife to choose negro to be sold; remainder to wife

William TABB ....2 Jan 1765, will
>   Adam, Jack, Rachel & her children Sam, Dinah, Simon, Jack, Agge, Beck, Mary, & Bob to wife, if she should marry then Sam to son Robert TABB; Jack, Esther, Hannah to daughter Mary's children; George, Bess, Susy to daughter Dorothy's children; Cate, Charles, Rose to daughter Martha's children; should my wife marry I leave Jack, Rachel & her children to be appraised to Robert TABB

Ledford VAUGHAN..16 June 1837, will
>   man Elick to wife Mary U. VAUGHAN; woman Bess to daughter Mary B. ROYSTON; Fanny, Clary to daughter Caroline S. VAUGHAN; man Jack, girl Isbell to son William T. VAUGHAN; boy Robin, woman Lucy to son Ledford VAUGHAN; women Molly, Lucendy to son James L. VAUGHAN; man George to son John H. VAUGHAN; girls Margy, Martha to daughter Lucy C. VAUGHAN

Edward WALLER...23 Aug 1845, will
>   slaves to be kept for 3 years with special care for old negroes Isaac, Esther, & Sam; at the end of 3 years if said old slaves still live they are to be supported by the estate

John WHITING..27 Oct 1790, will
>   Pati, Lucy, Easter, Abraham to wife Leticia WHITING in lieu of negroes which I have dispersed in the marriage contract & at her death to be divided among all my children as well as those by my 1st wife; wench Barbara to wife & to be divided among all children; Nelson, Dick sons of Mourning to be free at age 20; Dick, Edmond, Sarah & her 2 children Isabella & Patty, Buck the daughter of Paty to son Francis WHITING; Polly & her 3 chidren Nancy, Rachel, Jerry to daughter Agatha WHITING, also Judith the daughter of Mr. Marablis BECK

.... 28 Oct 1790, codical

Francis WHITING to be charged for the 5? negroes given him

Peter WYATT .... 20 Oct 1815, will

Harry, Cooke, Harry, Ralph, Whinney, Nancy, Kitty, Franky, Nanny, Dolly, Esther to wife Francis; Parker, Coder to brother James WYATT; at death of wife, ½ negroes to the children of sister BILLUPS excluding Peter; the other ½ to be divided into 4 parts, 1 part to Thomas BOSWELL in trust for niece Sally RANSONE; 1 part to her brother James WYATT; 1 part to Thomas BOSWELL in trust for niece Martha ROY & her children; 1 part to niece Elizabeth BRAXTON; 1 part to Thomas BOSWELL; Tom, C_hriam, Hannah & her children, Lucy bought at the sale of James ROY & now on his planatation to Thomas BOSWELL for his sister Martha ROY; girl China daughter of Martha now in the possession of Betsy BRAXTON be held by her; Aron, Adam, Milly & her 2 children, Betsy, Parker, Judy, Hany, Sam, Jack, Judy & her 2 children, Fanny also bought from James ROY to be sold

HANOVER

Hanover County was created by an act of 1720 to take effect on 1 May 1721. Most county court records, particularly deeds, wills, and marriage records, were destroyed by fire in Richmond on 3 April 1865, where they had been moved for safekeeping during the Civil War. The circuit court records were not moved to Richmond and were relatively unscathed. Consequently, there is a strong run of common law papers and chancery papers after 1831 that were generated by the circuit superior court of law and chancery and its successor, the circuit court.

ADAMS & PARKE vs Park SMITH ....7 July 1774, in court
sundry slaves; ordered Sheriff to sell the attached effects
....last page
woman Sary, boy Lewis, fellow Caesar (since dead), child Fanny, girl Molly

Henry ANDERSON .... 10 Sept 1783, will
man James to son William ANDERSON; Abraham to son Stephan ANDERSON; woman Anne to daughter Secelia ANDERSON; Ursley till she brings a child that lives to be one year old which child I give to my son Charles ANDERSON then Ursely & all her increase to daughter Jane ANDERSON; Delphy till she brings a child that lives to be one year old which child I give to my son Mitchel ANDERSON then Delphy & all her increase to daughter Sarah ANDERSON

John ANDERSON .... 19 Apr 1800, will
Austin, Clarecy, Shadrack to daughter Patsey A. ANDERSON, Shadrack to be free upon her marriage or death; Pocon, Fanny & her present increase to son John B. ANDERSON; woman Peg & her present increase that was my son Harmons to daughter Susanna A. JOHNSON; the rest of the negroes to my following children Sally PULLIAM, Betty Matilda RICHARDSON, Francisca Turnover JOHNSON, & Augusta Ann JOHNSON except Betty Matilda RICHARDSON

Robert ANDERSON .... 4 Jan 1793, inv & appr
old Barnaby, old Tom, old Phebe, young men Will, Ben, Isaac, Moses, Aaron, boy Bob

Thomas ANDERSON .... 31 Jan 1794, will
> Venus, Ned, Clary, Betty, Fanny, Peter, Keziah, London to son Thomas ANDERSON; rest of slaves to wife Fanny ANDERSON

Robert ARMISTEAD & Ann SMITH .... 23 Dec 1754, marriage agreement
> girl Sarah to Anne daughter of Gregory SMITH;...once the marriage has been solemnized 200 pounds given by...Gregory SMITH to Anne SMITH ...shall be laid out in negro slaves...girl Sarah...

John AUSTIN Jr. .... 9 June 1815, will
> Jerry, Aggy, Sam (called Quarter Sam), Lyddie & her child Charles, Mary to wife Mary; Sylvia, little Loland, Claiborne to son William Smith AUSTIN; Moses, Charles, Nancy, Alice to son Robert SPOTSWOOD; Sam, Milly to daughter Charlotte; remaining negroes to be divided at daughter Charlotte's wedding or turning 21 with daughters Susannah WINSTON, Mary C.G. SHEPPARD, Nancy OLIVER, Eliza WINN, & Charlotte AUSTIN; Matilda, Sally to be divided among my 5 daughters; girl Mary to be divided among all my children at death of my wife; the negroes in my father's possession given me by him except Claiborne to be divided among my 5 daughters

Thomas AUSTIN .... 23 Nov 1802, will
> 20 working slaves, 10 young slaves to wife Elizabeth; 1/3 part of my slaves to my 2 youngest daughters when they marry or reach age 21; 2 girls to each of the children of my deceased daughter Sarah YINSLEY; a four year old negro child to Constance AUSTIN daughter of my deceased son Chapman; friends William & Benjamin POLLARD to allot to my wife the 30 slaves lent her; when any division of slaves is made it is done that they shall go in families

Martin BAKER .... 11 June 1821, will
> Tom, Isham, Austin, Bartlett, Tom, Ben, London, Tawney, Bob, Ralph, Anderson, Rachel, Phebe, Jinny, Ailsey, Peggy, _elere, Susan, Charlotte, Cealey, Nancy, Nimey not given to my children to be divided into 9 equal parts

John BEAL .... 13 Feb 1836, will
> Warner, Agnes, Maria to son William; Hardenia & her 2 children Emeline & Nancy, Minerva to daughter Elizabeth wife of Miles H.

GARDNER; Melinda, Levinia to daughter Louisa wife of John R. WHITING; Garland, Paulina, Celiann delivered to son John

George BELL .... 2 July 1778, will

girls Mol, Dinah to son George BELL, Jenny after the death of my wife; John, Jack to Moor BELL, Janeel after the death of my wife Rebecca; Jonny, Sarah, Fanny to daughter Jemina WINSTON after the death of my wife; Angillo, Betty, Moses, Dosie to daughter Barsheba HARWOOD after the death of my wife; James & Tabitha his wife after the death of my son Nathan BELL be at liberty to live with any of my children; Betty given to my daughter Barsheba HARWOOD have the same liberty; it is my desire that all my negroes...may be set at liberty

Angello & her children and Moses (now a young man) are sold and remain in slavery (1801)

Moor BELL .... 1 Nov 1785, manumission

Jack age 35, Patty 34, Micall 25, Daniel 21, Betty 14, Tabb 11, Ned 2, William 5, Sarah 2, Frank 6 ½ months do emancipate

Nathan BELL .... 3 Apr 1783, manumission

...set free all & every of the above named slaves...(slaves listed at top of page covered up) Phillip born 15 Feb 1766, Lotty 10 Aug 1776, Alley 15 Aug 1773, Patience 5 Aug 1779 hereby set free

William A. BINFORD .... 21 Aug 1852, will

Sam, Billy, Arclin to mother Madgelena S. BINFORD

Benjamin BROWN .... 11 Feb 1781, will

Sara, Mollie, Judes to wife Susanna; Prince, Ancy to son John BROWN; Mary, Ann to daughter Milly BROWN; Lucy, Sally, Pleasant to daughter Adeline BROWN; Will, Charley to son Benjamin BROWN; Tom, Sally, Nelson to son Edward BROWN; Fill (Phil?), Aaron, Silva to daughter Huldah BROWN; Brutus, Liddy, Abram, Nancy to son Bentley BROWN; Fenton, Attiony (Anthony?), Landis, Elijah to son William BROWN

Benjamin COCKE vs John COCKE .... 1 Sept 1830, in Court

Aggy & her 2 children Henry & an infant child: John COCKE to restore the property or pay all costs & damages to Samuel COCKE administrator of Benjamin COCKE dec'd

John COLLIER .... 29 May 1761, will
(will states Hanover County, filed under Caroline County)

choice of negroes to wife Sarah COLLIER; girl to daughter Elizabeth IRONMONGER at marriage or when of age; girl to daughter Frances CRENSHAW at her mother's discretion; girl each to daughters Sally, Lucy, Susanna, Mary, & Martha at marriage or when of age; negroes left me by my father, after my mother-in-law's decease to be divided amongst all my children

Charles S. COLLEY Sr. .... 14 Feb 1811, will

boy Adain to son Charles COLLEY?; girl _itter to daughter Elizabeth ATTHISON; Grace & 4 of her children David, Matt, Kitty, & Greg to John CRENSHAW; boy Moses to daughter Milly MALLORY

John H. CONNELL .... 6 Dec 1862, deed

Daniel, Jacob to Garinter BARKER to hold for the benefit for Mary H. BARKER

William DARRACOTT .... 20 Oct 1792, will

negroes to sons Richard & John & daughters Elizabeth, Mary, & Susanna

Henry DAVIS .... 24 July 1773, will

Jo, Fan to wife Elizabeth DAVIS, on her death to daughter Rhoda DAVIS; Judah, Minor to daughter Rhoda DAVIS; Sam, Agg to be sold; rest of negroes to be divided among grandchildren by daughter Mary HARRIS & son Lewis DAVIS

.... 18 Feb 1782, pg 2, estate acct

hire of negroes; division of negroes: Nan, Seth to Lewis DAVIS; Will, Rachel, Sal to Elizabeth DAVIS; boy Joe, girl Sharlot to Rhody DAVIS

.... 15 Oct 1773, pg 3, inv

Fran, Jude, Minor, Joe, Frank, Bet, Tamer, Ned, Jacob, James, Nan, David, Siller, Tom, Sarah, Milly, Agg, Sam

.... June 1773 – Oct 1775, pg 5, estate acct

2 negroes sold

John DELMORE .... 10 Aug 1733, deed

woman Moll to Mary DELMORE

Stephen H. DILLARD................................... 3 June 1828, will
 girl Marthew to daughter Frances GAGNO; boy William to son Thomas DILLARD; negroes to wife Elizabeth & at her death be divided between Stephen, Josiah, Lucy, Eliza, Mearey, & Margate DILLARD

Thomas EUBANK Jr....................................... 18 Oct 1847, deed
 Garland PARRISH to have 1 man, _ woman; girl to nurse his children

William FLEMING....................................... 13 Sept 1742, will
 choice of 3 females to wife Elizabeth FLEMING also to choose any one young negro until age 12 when to be returned to the estate & another chosen, & etc; land & negroes to any English relations...

Nathaniel FOX... 29 June 1877, will
 woman Charlotte to wife; girl Mary the daughter of little Jenny to granddaughter Letitia PROSSER; 1/3 of remaining negroes to wife, 1 part each to my daughters Maria BOHANNON, Elizabeth W. FOX, & Mary B. COCKE

....25 Oct 1826, in Chancery
 Edwin, Charles, & Richard FOX, & mother Susan FOX against Samuel M. BOCKIUS, adm of Lewis FOX dec'd, James FOX dec'd, & Susan FOX dec'd

 negroes valuation & division: Lot 1: Joe to James FOX; Lot 2: George, _inny to Lewis FOX; Lot 3: Dicy & 2 children Dandridge & Robert to Edwin FOX; Lot 4: Randol to Charles FOX; Lot 5: Warner, Delphia to Susan FOX; Lot 6: Judy to Richard FOX

Reuben GARDNER....................................... 15 Sept 1842, will
 negroes to wife; Chester, Washington, Francis to son Thomas GARDNER; Moses, Harriet, Fanny to daughter Martha HANDLEY; slaves to be sold after death of wife

Samuel GOODMAN...................................... 7 Aug 1768, deed
 Lucy to granddaughter Elizabeth HILL; boy Ben to granddaughter Sarah HILL; girl Fanna to granddaughter Kezia HILL; boy Bob to granddaughter Juda HILL; boy Frank to granddaughter Jinny HILL; wench Dinah to granddaughter Mary Ann HILL all daughters of my daughter Mary HILL

Augustine WOOLFOLK .... will

Dick, Barret, little Sally, Gabriel, Nancy, Fan, M__ to son Joeph WOOLFOLK; Edward, David, Doll, Caty & Peggy her mother to Thomas DICKERSON now in his possession; girl Molly, man H__ to Nevell WALTON; Henry to Robert LEWIS

Bob GREEN .... 22 May 1838, Cert of Freedom age 25, 5' ½", and identifying marks

James HILL Sr. .... 12 July 1849, will

½ slaves to wife Mary HILL; fellow Harry to daughter Sally wife of David TIMBERLAKE; negroes to James HILL; ½ negroes to be divided between William HILL, Newton HILL, James HILL, Walker HILL, & daughter Susan B. READ; son William HILL has 2 negroes, Newton HILL has 3, Walker HILL has 3, Susan B. READ has 3 all of which must be accounted for

John HOPKINS .... 29 Aug 1765, will

Moses, Robin, Tamer, Joseph, Brister, Dick to wife Susannah HOPKINS & if she marries to have equal share with children David, Peter, Charles, William, Elizabeth, Mary, Sarah, & Frances HOPKINS; girl Jenny to wife then daughter Elizabeth HOPKINS; girl Dilley to daughter Mary HOPKINS; boys Ned, Patrick to daughter Frances HOPKINS

.... 1 Mar 1771, estate acct

boy Ned dec'd

.... 7 Aug 1766, inv & appr

Dick, Robin, Tamer, Brister, Moses, Joseph, Amey, Ned, Jean, Patrick, Dilley

Mary JENNINGS .... 30 July 1782, will

man Tom & his wife Jenny, boy Sawney to son Robert JENNINGS; boy Christopher to daughter Betty DUKE; man Jerry, girl Fanny to son Robert JENNINGS & Robert GOODWIN in trust for daughter Sarah YANCEY; boy Robin to granddaughter Katey Garland YANCEY; Matt, Jimmy to grandson Joel YANCEY

Robert JENNINGS .... 6 Dec 1758, will

slaves, girl Venus to son John Garland JENNINGS; girl Phoebe to be sold; 4 negroes named (but mostly unreadable) Tom _egut, old Nat,

Fanny? & Watt? to wife Mary JENNINGS to be sold at her death or marriage; girl Anaka to daughter Betty JENNINGS; boy Issac to son Robert JENNINGS; girl Betty to daughter Sara JENNINGS; girl Susan to daughter Barbara JENNINGS

Joel JONES .... 24 Mar 1829, will

old Toliman, Nelson, Solomon, George, Andrew, Jack, William, Sealy, Charlotte, Nancy, Jacob, Isaac, Chancy, Lidwell, Armstead, Martha to daughter Paulina America McLAURINE; James, Abraham, Henry, Benjamin, Joe, Claiborne, Archer, Caroline, Judith, Eliza, Fanny, Silvia, Milly, Sophia, Paulina, Zion, Miles to son Washington JONES; David, Cesar, Frank, John, Shadrick, Absalom, Garland, Emily, Lucy, Maria Oliver, Suckey, Rachel Oliver, Sam, Iverson, Harriett, Maria Jones, Mary to son Albert Timms JONES

Charles KENNEDY .... 13 Jan 1783, will

Daniel, O. Harry, Phillis, Sylva, Easter to wife & divided among children at her death; remaining negroes, not hereafter given to be divided: sons to receive ¼ part more than daughters; girl Lucy to granddaughters Croshe & Polly WASH daughters of my daughter Anne

John LEWIS .... 20 Feb 1775, will

fellows Tom, Bob, women Nan, Peg, girls Lucy, Scylla, boys Peter, Billy, Jack to daughter Elizabeth NAILOR

Nathaniel C. LIPSCOMBE .... 18 Jan 1847, will

Delphia, Agga, Elizabeth, James, Ben, Peter, David, Susan, Andreus, Ned, Edward, Ell_ to wife Mary B. LIPSCOMBE, on her death to be divided among daughers Martha P. WINGFIELD, Mary Etta McGEE, Rebecca A. GRUBBS, & Francis I. FRANKLIN; Alice, Pendleton, Mary to daughter Martha P. WINGFIELD; Taylor, Emeline to granddaughter Jane L. GREEN; Sarah, George to daughter Rebecca A. GRUBBS now in possession of her husband Peter W. GRUBBS; Agnes, Henry to daughter Francis I. FRANKLIN now in possession of her husband David B. FRANKLIN

Mahala, a free woman .... 16 Feb 1824, will

..my children that I purchased of the estate of Col. Thomas TINSLEY dec'd be free...daughter Clara be bound to former mistress Susanna TINSLEY until age 21 or death of Susanna TINSLEY

William MOSELEY .... 25 July 1825, will

Peter, Bowser, Caty, Ethalinda, Eliza, Jacob, Sally, Martha, Archer, John, Mary, Claiborne, Edwin, Bowser, Susan, Mildred to wife Sarah MOSELEY; Charlotte, Maria, Stephen, Pleasant, Albert to executors to daughter Polly COX should she become a widow; girl Sally to granddaughter Mary Ann COX at death of my wife; boy Lewis to brother Robert MOSELEY for 12 years; 1/2 remaining negroes to executors for son Philip Terpin MOSELEY's children should he have any & ½ for children of daughter Polly COX

William NUCKOLS .... 28 Dec 1819, will

a negro for each child when attains lawful age or marriage; Charlotte, Jane, a Deed of Gift, to daughter Susanna but must choose one at marriage or at lawful age; Fanny, Peter, Lidda to wife Nancy, Jane until daughter comes of age

Ann A. OLIVER .... 3 Oct 1846, will

girl Emily to daughter Margaret Isabella

Samuel OVERTON .... 18 Mar 1812, will

Armstead, London, Isaac, John, Mouring to be hired out & after 1 year to be emancipated

Thomas PRICE .... 28 June 1837, will

shop Harry, Fleming, yellow John, miller Joe, shoemaker Joe, Martin, Manuel, Waller, Caty Homes, Fleming Jr., Peter, Louisa, Randolph, Martha daughter of Shop Harry, Minor, Daphne & child Patty, Clarissa to wife Elizabeth T. PRICE; boy Braxton, man Walker to son Lucien B. PRICE; boy Leonard to son Thaddeus PRICE; 1/5 part of slaves not bequeathed to grandson Thomas P. TEMPLE; girl to daughter Camilla PRICE; girl Julianna to daughter Mary Randolph PRICE; remaining slaves to be divided among granddaughters Maria Louisa, Ella, & Eugenia TEMPLE, children of late son-in-law John T. TEMPLE

William PULLIAM .... 16 Sept 1813, will

David, Cuzzy & her 4 children Nelson, Anny, Edmund, & Eliza, Will, Woodson, Jenny, Adam, Sily to wife Mourning & at her death to be divided among the children; Sally, Fanny to son Thompson Wilson PULLIAM; Polly, Juggy to daughter Sally WADE; residue of slaves to be divided among children Robert, Thompson, Nancy

DANDRIDGE, & Sally WADE; Dolly to Archer Williams SAMBERTH now in his possession

William SIMS ....8 Aug 1814, will

Daphine, Amy, Rachel, Overton, Darcus to daughter Agnes WALTON which William WALTON dec'd her husband held in his lifetime; Nell, Anne, Kate, Huldah, Joe to daughter Sarah WALTON now in possession of her husband Joel WALTON; Nelson, Tanor, Polly, Anne, Abram to daughter Peggy SIMS widow of my son Garland; man Charles to daughter Agnes WALTON; man Martin to daughter Sarah WALTON

John SMITH..................20 July 1769, will

sale of slaves if necessary for debts; slaves to sister Mary ANDERSON; girl Lucy bought of Thomas CHAMBERLAYNE to niece Sarah HOWARD; Zack Clarke & William Spencer servants?; residue of negroes to nephews Thomas, John, Joe, William Townsend, Henry, & Samuel sons of sister Eliza SHORE
..................27 Mar 1800, letter

...improper treatment of the poor negroes...

Robert SNEAD..................1 Feb 1840, will

Abraham, Polly, Hagan, Nancy, Isaac, Annanias, Billy, Libby, Cilla, Frank, James, Benjamin, Viny, Henry, Jack to wife Sophia SNEAD, on her death to be divided among children Martha H. TAURMAN, Jesse, Moses, John, Robert, Sophia E. JONES, Erwin, Albert, Hellen HIGASON, May Ellen, Jane W. CARTER & Frances W. ELLITE

John STIFF.................. 27 May 1845 - 31 Dec 1846, estate acct

negro child supported; negro hire

John STIFF.................. 30 Apr 1846, estate div

Sally, infant John, Martha, Milly

Sally & her infant John to Catharine STIFF, dower

Charles P. STREET.................. 7 Sept 1843, will

... my negroes with the interest...; old woman Mary to brother Joseph H. STREET; old Betsy to friend John BEAL who owns her 2 sons; Matilda to brother Henry G. STREET

Ann SYDNOR..8 Nov 1816, will

   woman Delphia to daughter Mary MATTHEWS

Charles TALLEY Sr..18 Nov 1822, will

   women _ames, Minerva, boys John, Jesse to daughter Mary Richardson HUGHES; man James, girls Ann, Maryan, woman Mary to daughter Catey Ray HILLIARD wife of Benjamin HILLIARD; man Randal, woman Nancy to daughter Betsey Waide MILLS wife of John N. MILLS

Ekhanah TALLEY to Thomas POLLARD etc................ 1 Sept 1803, deed

   (Robert ANDERSON died between the years 1801 & 1703; John ANDERSON died July 31, 1787; ___ ANDERSON Jan 7, 1873; Mary ANDERSON widow of John ANDERSON & daughter of Robert ANDERSON married Elkano TALLY in 1789; E. TALLY died 1798)

   names of negroes which came by John ANDERSON: Ned & Hannah his wife – dead, George & Milly sold by B.A., Lewis at the _ house; John -- Mat; ___ Nelson sold in Richmond; Davy – died before she went; Joe, Edmund, Nelson, Maria given to her daughter Mrs. George CATTELL __, Lucy at ___; Molly & 4 children now in Mrs. TALEY's possession; Haney sold in Kentucky to ___ her in to Virginia; by Mrs. TOLEY: Chloe – dead; Charlotte, Kizzy & children (or is it Charlotte & children Kizzy…?) Mary, Sam, Harry & a younger one – Richard LAMSSON; Betsy & children Washington & Robert; Chapman sold to M.M. PAYNE; Luddy & one child Dick sold to Sally MILLER; Bob, Aaron at C'House; Milly in posesssion

Ann TERRELL ....5 Oct 1842, will

   1/3 of the money from hire of negroes from the estate of their father William PHILLIPS dec'd which I now possess as dower to sons William & Lancelot PHILLIPS & grandson William PHILLIPS

John THOMPSON ....31 July 1758, will

   Sukey, Aggey, Venus, Suck daughter of Bess, Hannah, Cupid, Moore, Tom to son Jospeh THOMPSON & his children; Rose, Lucy, Mary, Peter, Doll, Bartlet to daughter Elizabeth THOMPSON; Lucy & her 2 children Tom & Peter, Sall, Judy, Frank to the children of daughter Mary wife of James BROWN; 12 negroes to wife Kerchappuch if she marries

Henry TIMBERLAKE .... 2 Feb 1805, will
> Peter, Mary to son Chapman TIMBERLAKE; negroes to son Henry Austin, daughter Sophia, son Benjamin Arthur, & son Reuben TIMBERLAKE

Charles TINSLEY .... 5 Feb 1838, will
> estate to Mary O.D. Tinsley, a woman of color

.... 23 Feb 1842, in court
> will produced in court by Polly O.D. Tinsley, a free woman of color; William B. GREEN & Peter TINSLEY opposed the proof

.... 8 Apr 1842, in court
> will accepted as true last will & testeament

Wat H. TYLER to Robert M. CHRISTIAN .... Feb 1817, deed
> Edith & her children Garrick, Nancy, & Betsy to Robert M. CHRISTIAN, to be sold if Wat H. TYLER cannot repay bond to William E. HILL

Reuben WELCH .... 5 Dec 1729, inv & appr
> men Dick, Pompsy, Robin, woman Priss, woman & child Phillip, girl Bess, men Mingo, Jambo, Peter, woman ___, girl J__, men B__, Gary, Tom, women Sara, Combo, Abbe, girl Betty, boys _ony, ___, girl Juda, boys Peter, Will, George, boy

James WHITLOCK .... 21 Mar 1733/34, will
> woman Sue to daughter Sarah HUNT; Beck to daughter Temperance WHITLOCK; girl Cate to daughter Mary WHITLOCK; girl Rose to daughter Agnes WHITLOCK; boy Ba___ to son David WHITLOCK; boy Bob to son Matthew WHITLOCK; woman Abigail to wife Frances WHITLOCK

John WILLIAMSON .... 4 Nov 1767, will
> girl Patty to Elizabeth MITCHIE daughter of my wife Sarah; Numa, Janet, Hannah & all her children except Patty to wife Sarah & at her death to be disposed

Edward WINSTON to John G. WINSTON .... 24 July 1799, deed
> Peg & child, Patience, Rose, Mariah to John Geddis WINSTON

John WINSTON .... 19 May 1797, will
    boy Abraham to son Horatio GATES; boy Edmund to son William OVERTON; girl Julia to daughter Eliza FARRELL; girl Dilce to daughter Maria OVERTON; house Lucy to be emancipated at my mother's death

Augustine WOOLFOLK .... 27 July 1807, will
    Dick, Barnet, little Sally, Gabriel, Nancy, Fan, M___ to son Joseph WOOLFOLK; Edmond, David, Doll in his possession & girl Caty, Peggy to Thomas DICKERSON; girl Molly, man H__t__t to Newell WALTON; Harry to children of Robert LEWIS; boy Joe to Joseph WOOLFOLK; boy Dick to John L. LEWIS; Eatt__, Adam to children of Robert CLOUGHEN, W.S. CLOUGHEN & Marahan; old Molly to Mary Ann W. CLOUGHEN

.... 27 July 1807, codicil
    old Molly to Robert LEWIS

HENRICO

All county court records prior to 1655 and almost all prior to 1677 are missing. Many records were destroyed by British troops during the Revolutionary War. Post-Revolutionary War cdounty court records exist. Almost all circuit superior court of law and chancery records for Henrico County and city of Richmond were destroyed by fire during the evacuation of Richmond on 3 April 1865 in the Civil War.

Christian ALLEN Sr..17 Nov 1829, will

Patsy, Sally, George, Maria, Albert to daughter Frances E. WHITLOCKE wife of Henry WHITLOCKE; Frank, Anaky to be supported by sons Christian ALLEN & Armistead ALLEN

Campbell BLADES..3 Aug 1835, will

7 negoes to executer & trustee M.C. LACKLAND for daughter Maria AYRES

John H. CONNELL to Mary H. BARKER.....................6 Dec 1862, deed

Daniel, Jacob to Garinter BARKER in trust for Mary H. BARKER

Robert DuVAL..10 Apr 1773, will

negroes to be sold

John GUNN..31 Oct 1771, will

woman Hannah to daughter Ann VANDEWALL; boy George to granddaughter Sally VANDEWALL; Sampson, man Will to daughter Lucy GUNN; man Sam, woman Edy, girl Ann, boy Elisha to son James GUNN

John HARVIE...26 Nov 1806, will

John, Davy, Jack, Carter, Campbell, Lucy, Edy, Molly, Nelly, Tobey, Sally, boy Wilshier, girl Caroline to wife Margaret HARVIE; negroes in Hannover County to daughter Gabriella upon her marriage; Phillis' daughter Louisa, Joan's daughter Amey to daughter Juliana; negroes in his possession to son Lewis; negroes in Ablemarel County to son John; Robbin, Hardy, man Abraham to be employed

William HETH...8 Apr 1807, will

slaves to dower...any particular servant not of that family which I received by my first wife...; residue of slaves be divided to my son

Henry & my daughters Elizabeth Agnes, Margaret Thomas Jaquelin, & Mary Andrietta

William MARSHALL .... 29 July 1817, will

slaves to wife & after her death to son Thomas Griffin MARSHALL; after the death of my wife slaves received from intermarriage with their mother to son John Jaquelin & his youngest sister; residue of slaves to sons William, Thomas Griffin, & daughter Eliza

William MARSHALL vs Adm of Lewis LEATH ....
.... 22 Nov 1831, in Chancery

all the slaves now remaining in the estate of John WALTHALL to be sold: Betsy & children Randolph & Henry, Granderson, John, Sylvia purchased by Lewis LEATH; Garrison to John T. BOTTOM

MASON & COCK, etc vs Adm of Daniel BOISSEAU, etc ....
.... 29 June 1836, in Chancery

slaves sold at Bermuda Hundred Plantation, Chesterfield, Co, old China & old Sylvia to Samuel Madison FARMER
.... 27 Sept – 24 Oct 1833, expenses of sale

Ned, runaway slave; China, Sylvia; Sarah M.C. BOISSEAU allowed to purchase slaves

Joseph MARX .... 12 Sept 1835, will

slaves to wife Richa MARX...paid for slaves of Mr. Moses M. MYERS...bequeath the increase of the female slaves to Catharine, Harriet, & Julia MYERS daughters of the said Moses M. MYERS

Samuel OVERTON & wife vs Admr of Thomas P. OVEFRTON..............
.... 1 Nov 1831, in Chancery

...Samuel FORD took possession of & sold all his intestate personal property including 11 negroes...
.... 24 Nov 1796, appr & inv

man Daniel, women Abby, Clary, Betty, child Anne, boys Pleasant, Ives, girls Aggy, Phillis, man Jack, woman Gabby

John PLEASANTS Sr. .... 11 Aug 1771, will

Cooper, old Sukey, Fanny, old Robin, Will, old Nat, old Cesar, Aggy to choose their master; my man Charles White & his sons Jack & Charles...shall be free if they choose at age 30...; all slaves now born or herafter to be born...to be free at age 30; man Phil to choose his master; man Sharper & his wife Biddy to be cared for; Cuffy, Gaby, Rachel & her child, Patt's 4 children 5 of which he has in his possession to son Robert PLEASANTS, he may free them at age 30; 1/3 remaining slaves to grandson Samuel PLEASANTS, to be free at age 30; negroes conveyed to me from her husband Robert LANGLEY & labor of all negroes sold by Robert LANGLEY to John HUNT or Samuel GORDON conveyed to me by said GORDON to daughter Elizabeth LANGLEY to be free at age 30; 1/3 remaining slaves to son Jonathan PLEASANTS including his mother's negroes given to her by her father; girl Janny to granddaughter Jane PLEASANTS; Moll, Sucky, Hampton, Ned the children of Fanny to daughter Mary PLEASANTS; Pender & all her children to granddaughter Margaret PLEASANTS; Tabb & her youngest child Sypha__ to Elizabeth PLEASANTS wife of Joseph PLEASANTS; man Sam to be free; remaining 1/3 negroes to be divided between grandsons Samuel PLEASANTS & son Jonathan to son Thomas PLEASANTS; Ciss maid to daughter Dorothy wife of Gray BRIGGS

John RANDOLPH... 5 Dec 1821, will

all slaves to be freed; Essex & wife Hetty; woman Nancy, boy Johnny, Juba (alias Jupiter), Queen; confirm to brother Beverley the slaves given him; slaves given by my grandfather BLAND, ½ of them entitled to freedom at my brother Richard's death, as the other would have been at mine

....31 Jan 1826, codicil

John's father Essex, wife Betsy, Juba & his wife Celia, Nancy, Archer's wife

....6 May 1831, codicil

John called John White

Peyton RANDOLPH .... 29 Feb 1784, will

Anthony & his wife Phoebe, Delce, Betty, Kendal, Lucy Gray, Sarah, Phillis, boy Frank to wife Lucy RANDOLPH; negroes at Fighting Creek to son William RANDOLPH; negroes at Buffalo to son Richard Kidder RANDOLPH; negroes at Bush River to son Payton RANDOLPH; her choice of 4 girls under the age of 15 to daughter Betty RANDOLPH; if wife's baby is male he is to receive ¼ part of the negroes given to each of my other sons, if a girl an annuity; Tom Parret & his wife to Carter PAGE; man Warwick to be free

Robert RIVES vs William GILLIAT .... 31 Oct 1832, in Chancery
William GILLIAT administrator of Seymour SCOTT dec'd
.... 21 June 1833, in Chancery
...the slaves mentioned in this suit & there being no questions but that the slaves mentioned in the deed of trust executed by the defendant William G. PENDLETON to Herbert A. CLAIBORNE...to be sold
.... 17 Feb 1834, in Chancery
inv & appr: man James, Mary his wife, Aggy & daughter Willianna, Letty & daughters Jilina & infant Caroline, Caroline & children Eliza, Amanda, Martha, & Charles

Archibald TAYLOR .... 21 Jan 1819, will
slaves to wife Leticia H. TAYLOR

Robert WILKINS vs John ABBOTT .... 4 Dec 1839, judgment
part sale of 8 negroes

Richard WILLIAMSON .... 5 Mar 1771, will
Jammy, Bob, Buster, Beck to son Thomas WILLIAMSON, & at his death to grandchildren; Napper, Will to grandson John SPAIRS; Milly, young Bess daughter of Buck to granddaughter Elizabeth HULLARD

JAMES CITY

James City County was recognized in 1634 as an original shire. Williamsburg was founded in 1699 and declared a "city Incorporate" by a royal charter in 1722, although its actual status was that of a borough. Beginning in 1770, the courts of James City County and Williamsburg shared a common courthouse. During the Civil War, the records of both localities were transferred to Richmond for safekeeping but were destroyed by fire there on 3 April 1865.

William BARRET .... 1786, will

   the widow, since departed this life, the orator becomes entitled...a full proportion of the slaves...

Rebecca CARY .... 12 Apr 1823, will

   Jenny & her child to Wilson Jefferson CARY; money to servants Jenny, Sally, Rose

John CLAYTON .... 17 Feb 1736, will

   Davy, Frank, Phillis, Charity to daughter-in-law Mary CLAYTON widow of son Arthur CLAYTON & at her decease to John CLAYTON; Toby, Fuller, Pembroke, Tabby, Dido, Osmyn (Osman?), Dahhne, Handen to son Thomas CLAYTON

Philip COWLES .... 12 Oct 1789, free negro regis

   Thomas COWLES lets free from bondage: Joba age 9, Pers 7, Philip 4, Sally 6, Abbey R_nion 6, Hannah 4, Charlotte 1 ½

.... 9 June 1807, 2nd page

   Phil is about 22 years of age, 5ft 6" and identifying marks

Dixon & Jesse .... 13 June 1796, manumission

   Dixon to serve to 31 Dec 1798, Jesse to 1 Jan 1802 then set free by David CURLE

Leonard HENLEY .... 10 Aug 1789, sale of slaves

   Phill to Leonard HENLEY; Chesley to John COOPER; Jerry to Francis GEDDY

John W. HICKMAN .... 29 Nov 1857, will

   girl Rosey from my father's estate to Hester Ann CLAYTON; negroes in Accawmack County to sister Mary Ann CORES' children

William Ludwell LEE .... 4 Jan 1803, will
  ...all my slaves may on the first of January next to be emancipated...Joe to have blacksmith shop

William NORVELL .... 21 Sept 1802, will
  all negroes or slaves over the age of 22 at my death & after the 31st day of Dec be free; the increase of those females born after my death & before the 31st day of Dec be free; slaves between 17 & 22 at my death be free at age of 22; the increase above 17 at my death & not 22, born after my death be free at birth; slaves under age 17 be free at the age of 22

Charles PEARSON .... 20 Sept 1761, will
  man Tamos to son Henry after his mother's death; girl Sal to daughter Anne after her mother's death; boy Sam to daughter Judah after her mother's death; woman Agge to daughter Hannah after her mother's death; woman Luce to daughter Susannah after her mother's death; man James to grandson Charles PEARSON after his grandmother's death; all slaves to wife Hannah PEARSON

Fielding D. PIGGOTT .... 3 Mar 1854, will
  hires of negroes at the hospital; executrix may sell some negroes

Francis PIGGOTT .... 31 Mar 1830, will
  Henry, Peggy, Billy to wife Mary; slaves already given to him to son Nathaniel PIGGOTT; Lucy, Bob, Martha to daughter Ann B. TAYLOR wife of Edmund TAYLOR; Mima, Maria, Wilson to son Fielding D. PIGGOTT; Jack, David, Matilda to son Francis B. PIGGOTT; remaining slaves to be divided among all children

Richard RANDOLPH .... 19 Feb 1792, will
  slaves to wife Maria; man Morocco may be emancipated after the death of my wife; choice of any of Mary's sons to Gawin L. CORBIN

John SHERMER .... 11 June 1766, will
  wife Anne SHERMER has power & authority over slaves

James SHIELDS Sr. .... 11 Sept 1794, will
  as many negroes to be sold as necessary to cover debts; negroes to wife Rebecca SHIELDS to be sold at her death

Richard TALIAFERRO .... 24 Aug 1788, will
slaves to wife Rebecca to be equally divided between granddaughter Elizabeth Wythe NELSON & all my children at wife's death or marriage; men Christopher, his wife Betty & her children to son Richard

Richard TALIAFERRO .... 24 Aug 1788, will
slaves to wife Rebecca to be equally divided between granddaughter Elizabeth Wythe NELSON & all my children at wife's death or marriage; men Christopher, his wife Betty & her children to son Richard

Richard TALIAFERRO .... 1791, will
man Christopher to be free after death of my mother Rebecca TALIAFERRO, executors to purchase mother's interest in said slave then immediately emancipate him; man Sam to be free

Edmund TAYLOR Sr. .... 1 Mar 1828, will
slaves hired out; Molly & her 3 children Delia, Jemima, & Julia, girl Louisa, boy Cary to wife Sally M. TAYLOR (also written as Sarah later); woman Dicy & her child Betsy, man Israel to daughter Rebecca W. TAYLOR; men Frederick, Abram to be hired out; woman Judy & her 2 children Mary & Edloe to son Edmund TAYLOR in his possession & woman Nancy hired to Major Willis MAHONE; man Eddy, boy Pleasant, Fanny & her child George, woman Jemima, men Frederick, Abram, women Patty, Delphia to son William M. TAYLOR; Lizzy & her 2 children Dorcas & an infant, woman Hannah, girl Sally to son William M. TAYLOR in trust for daughter Mary PRILLER; women Abbey, Nancy now hired to her father Ned Dixon to daughter Susanna Catherine TAYLOR; man Tom to son Wesley H. TAYLOR; boy Otoway to son Pinkethman W. TAYLOR; lad Robert to son Richardson W. TAYLOR; woman Elvy to be free; Betty to her husband Ned Dixon, a colored man

Henry TAZEWELL .... 7 May 1797, will
Lucy & her children to daughter Sophia Anne TAZEWELL; man Cats to be free

TITHABLES 1792

John AMBLER, John HARRIS: Jacob, Milly, Joe, Daniel, Cue, Peter, Ponhatan, Harry, Moses, Mingo, James, Lewis, Harry, Dean, Betty, Caroline, Beck, Thomas, Dinah, Edy, Fanny, little Fanny, Richard, Edy, Molly, Alice, Dick, Ben, Will, York, Dick, Jerry, Henry, Moses, Nanny, Lydia, Sarah, Moll, Lydia, Nancy, Carter, Bridget, James, Armistead, free Jacob

Jones ALLEN, John ALLEN: Sam, Jacob, Jary, Lucy, Fanny, Judy

John ALLEN: Sarey, George, Dillard, John, Harry, Ampy, Moses, Doctor, Johnson, Sam, James, George, Essex, Frank, Tom, Milly, Fanny, Sarah, Hector, Bob, Charles, Larry, Janer, Pheby, Frances

William ALLEN: James, Luke, Sall, Sally, Clary

Julius ALLEN: Jack, Ned, James, Jack, Phebe

Elizabeth ALLEN, Julius ALLEN: Ambrose, Nan, Phil

Mary ALLEN: Jenny

Archer ALLEN: Sophia, Armistead, Pat

William ALLEN (H Neck): Tom, James, Joe, Robert, Stephen Worcester, Edmund, Betty, Lucy, Betty

William ALLEN, Capt. John VALENTINE: John, Daniel, Charles, Gabriel, Bob, Sal, Sue, Cibby, Alley, Fanny, Nanny, Cess, Aggy, Betty, Gaby

Alexander emancipated by Thomas WRIGHT

William AMORY: Daniel, Justin, Judy

George APPERSON, James APPERSON: Hannah

William Flounce ALLEN: Phil

Robert ANDERSON, Roy C. Richard ALLEN: Ned, George, Frank, Paisley, George, Cloe, Adam

B

John BROWNE, Richard MOORE: Will, Cyrus, George, Hawood, Dick, Godfrey, Braddock, Jack, Judy, Sukey, Dinah, Pheby, Obey, Rachel

John BROWN Jr.: William, Ben, Aggy

William BUSH: Isaac, Daniel, Harry, Cate, Peg, Esther, Sukey

Ann BERGLEY: Lewis, Phillis

Edmond BACON: Boatswain, Reuben, Anthony, Harry, Pat, Lucy

John BUSH's estate: Randolph, Roper, Charles, Lewis, Tom, Peter, Will, Atwater, Ned, Lucy, Kezia, Betty, Edy, Peg, Polly

William BIX_SOM: Davy, Cesar

John BLAIR, John FARTHING: David, Tom, Daniel, Phebe, Lyida, Winney

Henry BROWNE, Henry BROWNE Jr.: Will, Cato, Joe, Tom, Davy, Julius, Toby, Harry, James, Hannah, Betty, Milly, Pat, Lucy

Benjamin, BRIDGES, Gabe, Dixon, Milly

William BROWNE Jr.: George, Lucy, Molly

Thomas BARHAM: Phillis, Sue

William BROWNE: James, Joe, Tom, Ben, Sally, Armistead, Pheby, Kitt, Betty, Barberry, Mary, Jinny, Doll, Tom, Mya, Robin

William BANKS: Machlen, Nanny

Martha BREEDING, John BREEDING: James, Jenny, Molly, Patty

Andrew BANKS, James BOOTH: Tom, Meridith, Fanny, Milly, Lucy, Amey, Rachel, Dick

Sarah BASHIR: Cesar

Benjamin BROWNE: Phil, Tazewell, Sofia, Phebe, Sylvia, Jenny

Samuel BEALL, Basil HOLMES, James TEMPLE: Cesar, James, Jack, Sam, Joe, Molly, Judy, Jenny, Esther, Enid, Jiles

Lewis BINGLEY: Mack

Robert BARHAM, John BARHAM: Will, Jack, Cate, Lat, Lettse

John BAILEY, John HORTH/NORTH, John MONDAY: Sam, ___, Mary, Jenny, Nanny

John BROWNE, William BROWNE: Sylvia

J___ BYRD: James, Michael, Bob, James, George, Peter, Pomprey, Jack

Nathaniel BURWELL, Carter BURWELL, Edward LIGHTFOOT: Bristol, Pompry, James, Gay, Sam, Lewy, Gaby, Fredrick, Joe, Harry, Phil, Charles, Harry, Polidore, Nat, Lucy, Lewis, Simon, Jerry, Tom, Tom, Winney, Betty, Betty, Billy, Edy, Venus, Joshua, Hannah, Rachel, Nelly, Miner, Fanny, Esther, Jenny, Nanny, Mary, Tomos, Billy, Molly

C

Martha CARTER: Joe, Buck, Amy, Lucy

John COWLES: James, Ben, Cloe, Hannah, Ma_, Amey

Sarah COWLES: Jessy, Joe, Alex, Morning, David, Hagar, Judy

John CHANCEY: Edy

Edmund COWLES: Lewis, Bob, Harry, Tub, Pat, Phillis, Peg

Samuel CRANLEY: Dick, Nan, Fanny

Joseph CRAWLEY: Edmond Cate, Easter, Eave

Dr. James CARTER: Elijah, __man, Jack, Gaby, Daniel, Lewis, young Gaby, Daniel, C__o, Darl__, Moses, Peter, Jack, Coon, James, Dick, Joe, Humphrey, Grace, Pat, Hannah

John COOPER's estate: Charles, Sanny, Will, Nanny, John, Moll, Dinah, Silvia, Sabia

William CARDWELL: Phillis, Adam

Wyatt COLEMAN: Mary, Lydia, Jesse, Cumbo, Milly

Johan CHRISTIAN: Sam, Jerry, James, George, Moll, Belinda, ___, William Watt

Ann COLE, Josiah COLE: Matt, James, Peter, Jack, Lucy, Amey

Sarah CANA_Y: Sam

Margaret Crittendon MASSEY, William COLEMAN: Isaac, Sucky, Jeffery, Mary, Ned, Timson, John, Dick, ____

Thomas COWLES: Edmund, __ah, William, Charles, Milly, Pat

Bennett CURLE: Dorcas

Henry COWAN: George, Hannah

Matthew CLARK: Lewis, Charles, Dick, Jupiter, Bob, Betty, Gabey Tom, Ruben, Moll, Betty, Mary, Cate, Cate, Polly, Sal

D

William DENNIS: Cloe, Melinda

Peter DELACROUX, John WHITE: Silvia, Chisley

Wills DUNFORD: Joe, Dinah, Lucy

William DODD: James

John DAVIS: James, Dick, Tom, Ben, Dinah, Jenny, Venus, Judy

Samuel DURFEY: Dick, Sarah Cathy

John DRUMMOND: Ned, Harry, John, Sall, Betty, Nanny, mulatto Betty, Hannah, Milly, Nancy, Milly, Dinah

E

Frances EGGLESTON: Windsor, ___, Judy

Richard EGGLESTON Sr.: Primus, Charles, Henry, Tony, Daphne, Richard, ___

Ann FARTHING, William FARTHING, Richard FARTHING: Moll, Sam, Sara, Ned, David

Benjamin FAIR, Turner H. FAIR: Moses, Ramsey, Milly

John FARTHING: Moll

Camp FITZHUGH: Tossey, Will, Phillis, Phillis, Molly, Frank, Sylvia

James FREEMAN: Sukey

G

John GADBERRY: Judy

John GOODALL: Jim, Moses, Aaron, Betty, Judy, Moll, Betty, Cate

Samuel GRIFFEN: Timothy, Richard, America, Pomprey, Jenny, Anthony, Ben, Solomon, Ben, Prince, Phil, Ned, York, Tom, Betty, Polly, Molly, Ledia

Dr. John M. GALT: Davy, Nottingham, Dick, Worcester, Harry, Ben, Harry, Betty, Hannah, Sally, Violet, Charlotte, Fanny, Phillis

Samuel GEORGE: Edy

John GOODELL Sr., Turner GOODELL: Roger, Molly, Rachel, Terry

Philmer GREEN: Gary, York, Hannah, Nancy

John GRAVES: Peter, Tom, Cate, Moll, Violet, Fanny

Thomas GREEN: Jammy, __tta

William GADDY: Matt, Aaron, Denby (Joe, George went away last of April...not tithable property)

John GADDEN, Edmund GADDEN: Harry, ___tty

H

Charles HANKIN, Seth HANKIN: Joe, Harry, Peg, Alice, Sellah?, Sal

Leonard HENLEY (Pohatan): Arthur, Bat, Roger, Hannah, Nanny, Pat, Judy, Rose

William HART: Peter, Fanny

Martha HUGHES: Thomas, Betty

Joseph HIX: God__cy

Daniel HIX: Cato, Molly

William HANKIN, Archer HANKIN, Robert HANKIN: Jack, Charles, James, Phil, Peter, John, Jack, Will, George, Edmund, Jesse, Moll, Beck, Peg, Daphne, Cuz, Siller, Rachel

George HALLEN: Sukey

Elizabeth HALLEN: Hannah

John HANKIN: Sawney, George, Jenny, Beck, Milly, Judy, Josiah, Poll, Abe

Edward HARRIS's estate: Joe, Will, Peter, Geoffrey, Amey, Hannah

Joseph HORNSBY, Thomas LANSON: Jack, James, Harry, Jack, Will, Davy, Jackson, Anthony, Phillis, Pat, Dicky, Alley, Hannah

Richard HALES: Tom, Dick, Betty, Ned, Grace, Sarah, Clara

Leonard HENLEY: Drinking Spring, David, Phil, Joe, Becky, Molly, Alice, Lucy, Sall

William HARWOOD: Sawney, Milly, Will, Ben, Duffin

Richardson HAZELWOOD: Sarah, Elizabeth, Henley, Sarah, Tellah

J

Catharine JOHNSON: Joe, Mark, Jenny, Tenor, Sue, Dinah

James JONES, John AMMONETH; Bristol, Ned Abram, Flemming, Cloe, Hannah, Lyddia

William JAMES: Robin, George, Milly, Aston, Lucy, Dinah, Hannah, Dosha

Daniel JONES: Bess, James, Esther, Sella

Edward JONES: Clara

John JAMES: Isham, Julius, Tom, Sarah, Kato, Sal dec'd in Mar

Barbara A. JONES: Mary, Nanny

Silas belonging to William PORVELL orphan of Willam PORVELL of Warwick Co dec'd living with Hannah Jackson his wife on Capt. John WALTER's land

K

Ann KNEWSTEP: Will, Venus

John KERBY: Will, Tony, Daniel, Ben, Lewis, Sarah, Bess, Lucy, Nanny, Aggy, Edy

L

Timothy LESTER: Frank, Fanny

William I. LEWIS: Daniel, Jane, Judy

William LIGHTFOOT: Isham, James, Siller, Silvia, Beck, Fanny

Jestina LINSEY, Sandy LINSEY: Tom, Beck, Fanny

Jesse LINSEY: James

John LEWIS's estate, John WILLIAMS: Primus, Fanny, Jenny, old Edmund

William LEE, William L. LEE, Lewis BOOKER: Joe, Michael, Ned, Jacob, Jack, Guy, Mary, Betty, Cesar, Edy, Grace, Ge__, Beck, John, Cupid, Aaron, Isaac, Daniel, Sterling, Davy, Isaac, George, Tom, Sarah, C_ss, Lydia, Peg, Letty, Nancy, little Lyddy, & a man at Green Springs

34 including 3 whites

Robin, James, Frank, Humphrey, Harry, B. Jude, Y. __rte, Edy, Amey, Milly, Kezia, at Scotland Quarter

Richard LESTER: Jack, Squire, _rah, Betty

M

Ann MENETREE: Betty, Sek

Gabriel MAUPIN, Turner WELLS: Sam, James, Joe, Hannah, Peg

Major MAHONE: Matt

William MAHONE: Alice

Rev. Bishop MADDISON: Gilbert, James, Radnor, Charles, Flora, Edy, Sall, Winney

Elizabeth MARTIN: Moll

Joshua MORRIS: Tony, Silvia

John MACTYRE: George

Joham MENETREE: Will, James, Martin, Fanny, Amey, Edy, Dick

Sarah MULTON: Fanny

John MACHANDREE: Pompey, Daniel, Roger, Milly, Hannah

P

Frances PEGGOTT: Thomas, Sylvia

John PONER: Seley, Nanny, Milly, Roger

Eleanor PITT: Gabey, George, Isaac, Nancy, Daphney

Edward PARVER, Edward PARVER Jr.: Daniel, Moses, Machlin, Minor, Bristol, Ned, Jack, Moll, Aggy, Sukey, Doll, Rachel, Bett, Amey, Sall, Doll

Mary PERKINS, Baker PERKINS: Sam, Gabey, Adam, Lucius, Fanny, Sall, Milly

John PARADISE, William LONG: James, George, Jack, Phil, Cyrus, Ben, Nero, Lett, Lace, Esther, Betty, Nancy, Sylvia

R

William RICHARDSON: (Nightsfeld) Rippon, Beth, Beck, Betty

Luc_ia E. RANLEY: George, Tom, Ben, Fanny

Edward RICHARDSON, Ned CLOPTON: Daniel, Lewis, Dick, Lucy, Phillis, Dosha, Rippon

Harold RAN_ISON: Sib

James RATCLIFFE: Daniel, Sal, King, William, Redwood, Silvia

Stan__ RICHARDSON, Allen RICHARDSON: Harry, Peter, Hannah, Charley, Dasha, Amey, Ally, Kitty

Mary RICHARDSON: Fanny, Patt, Aggy, Jenny, Doll, Dinah, Rachel

William RICHARDSON: Simon, Julius, Charles, Frank, Beck, Feby (Phoebe?), Milly

Dudley RICHARDSON, Dudley RICHARDSON Jr.: Bosen, Daniel, David, Carter, Hannah, Sylvy, Thoedosia

Edmund RANDOLPH: Philip, Woody, Stephen, Benson, Dick, ____, Nat, Doctor, John, Mars, Betty, James, Gaby, Billy, James, Bob, Roger, Sam, Sam, Sam, Watt, Robin, Jacob, William, Sue, Sandy, Aggy, Lidya, Betty, Aggy, Fanny, Jenny, Nancy, Jenny, Judy, Stephen, Betsy, Molly, Sukey

Frances ROUNTREE: Jane

S

James SHIELDS, John SHIELDS, Page SHEILDS: Jack, Jamy, David, George, Sam, Squire, Dick, Warwick, Billy, Betty, Betty, Fanny, Pheby, Judy, Molly, Molly, Nan, Silvey, Sarey, Amey, Cutty, Cate, Sukey?

James SHIELDMAN: Lucy, Peter

Robert SANFORD: Ben, Rachel, Nan

Lewellin SPENCER John ASHLOCK: Aldren, Spencer, Jack, James, Lucy

Eugene SULLIVAN: Patt

William SHOTTY: Seleg, Dinah, Phil, Homer, Tenor

John SAUNDERS, William HENLEY: Betty, Daphnie, Letty, Sarah, ___, Will, Stafford, James

Rebecca SLATER: Dinah, Nancy

Hamilton USHER Sr., George's children, Jacob, Will, James, Cato, Fanny, Phillis, Beck, Lucy, Manny, Rose, & Betty

Kezia SPRATTOY: George, Joe, James, Martha, Lucy, Phillis

John G. SCULLY: John, Otey, Jack

James SOUTHALL, John APPERSON: Dublin, George, Will, Will, John, Grace, Milly, Flora, Jenny

Sarah SPENCER: Tarr, Esther

Mary SPRAGGINS: Sillah

Stephen a free negroe emancipated by Frances BATES

T

Isham TAYLOR: Phil, Nutty

Edmund TAYLOR: Sam, Tom, Belinda, Jenny

Henley TAYLOR: Peter, Nanny, Lucy

Robert TAYLOR: Beck

Mary TYNE: Nanny

Elizabeth TAYLOR: Ben, Jerry, Siller, Phillis, Sylvia

Jeremiah TAYLOR: Scipio, Jenny, Doll

Charles TALIAFERRO: Gaby, Charles, Sarey, Jack, Sarah, Ambrose

Col. Richard TALIAFERRO estate: Thomas, Bradley, Sam, Kit, Sam, Tom, Roger, Nat, Letty, Nanny, Nelly, Peter, Daphne, Edy, Betty, Dinah, Hampshire, Richard, Tony, Garrett, Jack, Dabben

Champion TRAVIS: Garthwright, Sam, James, Ned, Gandy, Giles, Sam, Arthur, Champion, John, Cromwell, Agge, Michael, Frederick, Will, Betty, Juba, old Fanny, Diana, Silvia, Anaky, Jenny, Fanny, Violet, Violet, Milly, Hannah, Nanny

William TAYLOR: Littleton, Tazwell, Silvanus, Prince, Cesar, George, Peter, James, Danbar, Robin, John, Peter, Topsam, Lydia, Rachel, Fanny, Betty

Henry TAZWELL: Slaughter, Joe, Sampson, G_cy, Pomprey, Hampton, Janny, Cupid, Tony, Frank, George, Sophia, Luke, Ned, George, Johnny, Cato, Silvia, Cloe, Peggy, Nanny, Esther, Sall, Tab, Sarah, Lucy, Mariah, Milly, Titus

Pinkethman TAYLOR: Sambo, Sal, Rachel

James TENNY: Cloe

V

John VALENTINE Jr.: Belinda, Sillah

W

John WALKER, Capt. Robert WALKER: David, Bess, Ben, Peter, Gilbert, Will, Herbert, Jammy, Tom, Harry, Judy, Lucy, Cate, Suckey, Silvia, Amer

James N. WALKER: Frank, Lydia, Doll

William WALKER, Capt. ABRAM: Dick, Charles, Daniel, Peter, Sarah, Dinah, Sarah, Alice

David WALKER: Andrew, Mourning

John WEATHERS: Sarah, Trak, Will, Ned, Doll

William WILKINSON Sr.: Ned, Harry, Beshley, Aberdeen, Abram, Venus, Amey, Sall, Phillis

Matthew WADE: Charles, Peg

John D. WILKINSON: Jupiter, Lucy

John D. WILKINSON: Cupid, Sam, Tom, Peter, Letty, Nancy

William WILKINSON Jr., Vincent D. NUEMAR: Dick, Antony, Bristo, Will, Joe, Jack, Aaron, John, Pat, Joan, Sarah, Nanny, Patt, Daniel

John WALKER: Judy

James WILLIS: Sarah

Robert H. WALLIS: James, Bradberry, Michael, Tom, Joe, Caleb, Bob, Sarah, Betsy, Isbell

Judith WADE, William WADE, Ch__y WADE, David WADE: Charles, Betty, Cate, Sal, Cate, Dizey, Aggy, B_in_y

Elizabeth WILLIAMSON: John

TITHABLES 1793

John AMBLER: Jacob, Will, Joe, Daniel, Cupid, Peter, Harry, Moses, Mingo, James, Lewis, Davy, Aberdeen, Betty, Caroline, Beck, Thomas, Dinah, Edy, Fanny, Fanny, Rachel, Molly, Sarah, Else, Dick, Ben, Will, York, Dick, Jerry, Harry, Moses, Nanny, Lydia, Sarah, Moll, Lydia, Nanny, Cusy, Bridget

John ALLEN: (Surry Co) John, Ampy, Moses, Doctor, Johnson, Sam, James, Hector, Bob, George, ___, Frank, Harry, Charles, Tom, Fanny, Junior, Frances, Milly, Fanny, Sarah, Phebe

William ALLEN, Capt. James ALLEN: John, Bob, Sue, Siby, Alley, Fanny, Nanny, Betty, Sis, Aggy

William ALLEN: James, Luke, Sall, Davy, Lucy, Siller

William ALLEN Jr.: Tom, Robert, James, Joe, Worster, Edmund, Stephen, Lucy, Billy, Winney

William F. ALLEN: Phil, Cate, Nanny

Jones ALLEN, John & William ALLEN: Jacob, Sam, Jerry, Lucy, Jenny, Judy, Fanny

Archer ALLEN: James, Scypio, Armistead, Patt

Robert ANDERSON: Ned, George, James, Rawley, George, Adam, Cloe

Julius ALLEN: Hamlin, Thomas, Jack, John, David, Phebe

Elizabeth ALLEN, Julius ALLEN: Ambrose, Phil, Nan, Lucy

George APPERSON, James APPERSON: Hannah

Alexander emancipated by Thomas WRIGHT

B

Samuel BEALL's estate: Jimmy, Cesar, Sam, Jenny, Sally, Molly, Marinda

William BUSH: Isaac, Daniel, Harry, Pegg, Esther, Sukey

Robert BARHAM, John BARHAM: Will, Jack, Cate, Sally, Lette__

Thomas BARHAM: Phillis, Lucy

John BLAIR: Lewis, Michael, James, David, Daniel, Tom, Phebe, Jenny

Nathaniel BURWELL, Edward LIGHTFORD, Francis DRAKE: Jerry, Tom, Tom, Bristor, Nanny, Guy, Sam, Venus, James, Edy, Betty, Porc__, Rachel, Hannah, Jimmy, Charles, Phil, Hester, Fanny, Harry, Nanny, Tenor, Lewis, Simon, Federick, Fanny, Pompey, Frank, Jenny, Billy belonging to the estate of M. BURWELL Jr.

John BROWNE's estate: Will, Braddock, George, Syrus, John, Godfrey, Dick, Hawood, Rachel, Obey, Beth, Dinah, Sukey, Sall, Judy

John BROWN Jr.: Will, Ben, Aggy

John BROWNE, William BROWNE: Phyllis

William BROWNE: Isaac, Roper, Joe, Tom, Moll, Mary, Sabra, Chester, Tom, Will, Ben, Robin, Will, M___, Armistead, James, Doll, Jinny, Betty, Pheby, Hit, Barberry, Dinah, John, Hornsby, Phillis

William BROWNE Jr.: Lucy, Molly, Tiller

Henry BROWN, Henry BROWN Jr.: Will, Joe, Julius, David, Tom, Toby, Cato, Harry, James, John, Betty, Hannah, Pat, Milly, Lucy

Lewis BINGLEY: Mack

Andrew BANKS, Joseph BANKS: Meridith, Tom, Dick, Fanny, Lucy, Milly

Benjamin BROWNE: Tazwell, Sepio, Phil, Jane, Sylvy

Martha BREEDING: James, Jenny, Molly

Benjamin, BRIDGES, Gabe, Dixon, Milly

William BARROM: David, Nelson Cesar

John C. BYRD: James, Billy, Mike, George, Bob, Jimmy, Jack, Pompey, Peter

Joseph BOND: Sarah

Edmond BACON, Edmond BACON Jr.: Boson, Reuben, Ned, Anthony, Pat, Lucy, Delsy

Jon BAILEY Jr.: Munday, Molly, Judy, Jinny, Nanny

James BINGLEY: Amey

Martin BINS: Silvy, Lucy

Ann BINGLEY: Lewis, Phillis, Davy

Mary BRACH: Harry

Sarah BARKER, William __: Lucy

C

James CARTER, Elijah FROMAN, John ROGERS: Gaby, Jack, Jack, Crusoe, Tom, Squire, Humphrey, Grace, Gaby, Daniel, James, Joham, Charles, Daniel, Dick, Ian, Hannah, Lucy

Sarah COWLES: Alexander, Joe, Hagar, Mack, Judy

Rebecca CAMP, William K___E: Frank, Joe

Charles CARTER: Jesse, Pointer

Bennett CURLE: Dorcas, Tiller

William COLUNAN: Isaac, Dick, Seth, Howett, Ned, Sam, John, Phil, Gaby, Sam, Ben, Suky, Mary

George CARDWELL: Venus, Bet

William CARDWELL, Thomas CARDWELL: Charity

Samuel CHARLES: Edy

Joham CHRISTIAN: Sam, Edmund, Lander

Henry COWAN, John COWAN: George, Hannah, Ben, Disey

Joseph CRAWLEY: Edmond, Cate, Easter, Eve

William CHARLES: Pumetia, Patt

Lewis CHARLES: Dick, Tom, Billy, Juboy, Bob, Moll, Kate, Sall, Kitty, Polly, Mary, Betty

Elizabeth CHANCEY: Kate, Doll

Martha COOPER: Amey

Ann COWLES, Josia COWLES: James, John, Lucy, Silvy

John COWLES: James, Ben, Blue, Tom, Hannah, Mackey, Amey

Henry COWLES: David

Edmond COWLES, Edmond COWLES Jr.: Harry, Phillis, Patt, Pegg

Thomas COWLES: Edmond, Dinah

D

Goodrich DURFEY: Sam, Silvy

John DUNBAR: James, Bradbury, David, Lancastor, Aaron, Addy, _omund, F_ak, Peter, Beck, Jack, Robin

Peter DELACROUX: Chisley, Silvey

Wills DUNFORD: Dinah, Lucy, Silvey

John DAVIS: Tom, James, Dick, Ben, Jenny, Judy, Venus

William DODD: Jack

Samuel DURFEY, Samuel DURFEY Jr.: Jim, Dick, Sarah, Cutty

William DENNIS: Cloe, Melinda

John DRUMMOND: Gill

ditto for WARBURTON's estate: Milly, Betty, Sall, Betty

E

Frances EGGLESTON: Windsor, Tom, Judy, Sukey

Richard EGGLESTON: Simon, ___, Charles, Winney, Lyddia, Daphne

F

Elijah FROMAN: Daniel, Jenny, Patt

Benjamin FEAR: Sarah, Peter

James FREEMAN: Sukey

Camp FITZHUGH: Tony, Charles, Phillis, Molly, Sylvy, Frank

John FENTON: Joe, Jack, Bib, Siller

John FARTHING: Milly

Edward FARTHING: Godfrey

Ann FARTHING, William FARTHING, Richard FARTHING: Sam, Edmund, Moll, Sary

G

James GLAREBROOK: Winney

John M. GALT: David, Harry, Dick, Harry, Nottingham, Worcester, Ben, Betty, Violet, Phillis, Charlotte, Fanny

John GADBERRY, Samuel MANNING: Patt, Judy

Samuel GEORGE: Edy

William GADDY: Joe, Austin, Jerry, Amey, Clary

Richard GEDDY: Jemmy, Amey

Thomas GUNN: Primus, Peter

John GRAVES: Peter, Tom, Cate, Moll, Fanny, Violet

John GADDEN, Edmund GADDEN: Harry

Alexander GREEN: Mack, Fanny

Philmer GREEN: Guy, York, Mary, Hannah

William GOODALL: Fanny

John GOODALL Jr.: Moses, Judy, Moll, Betty

John GOODALL: Roger, Rachel, Molly

Samuel GRIFFIN: Tim, Richard, Jenny, Tom, America, Pomprey, Anthony, Ben, Solomon, James, Prince, Ben, York, Betty, Molly, Lyddia, Polly

H

Leonard HENLEY: Dick, David, Phil, Joe, Beck of Molly, Else, Sall, Temp, Patrick

Stephen HAZLEWOOD: Ben

William HART: Fanny

John HAZLEWOOD: Phil

Humphrey HARWOOD: Sawney, Milly, young Milly, Ben, Duffin, Peter

Martha HUGHES: Tamor, Betty

Richard HALES: Sam, Dick, Will, Ned, Grace, Sary, Clary

Elizabeth HATTON: Hannah

Elizabeth HENLEY: Siller

William HENLEY, Leonard HENLEY: (Pouhatan) Arthur, Batt, Roger, Hannah, Nanny, Judy, Rose, Patt

John HANKIN: Sawney, George, Jenny, Milly, Beck, Judy, Sarah, Obey, Senah, Polly

William HANKIN, Archer HANKIN, William HANKIN Jr., Robert HANKIN: Phil, Jack, _aues, James, Peter, John, Edmund, Jack, George, Joe, Will, Sue, Moll, Beck, Pegg, Cuz, Daphne, Rachel, Siller

Charles HAUKINS, Nathaniel HAUKINS: Harry, Joe, Tom, Pegg, Alice, Teller

Bristo HEMING: Abraham, Frank, Hannah, Cloe, Lyddia

Joseph HORNSBY, Archer SAUNDERS: Harry, old Jack, James, Jack, Joham, Dave, Will, Anthony, Phillis, Hannah, Dicey, Alley, Pat

Thomas HARWOOD, William SPRAGGINS: Mary

J

Daniel JONES: Ben, Easter, James, Siller, James

Catharine JOHNSON: Joe, Mark, Sue, Tinah, Jenny, Dinah

William JAMES: George, Robin, Reuben, Milly, Aston, Lucy, Dinah, Hannah, Doshe, Will

John JAMES: Isham, Julius, James, Sarah, Kato

Jeffrey freed by Edward HARRIS

Silas belonging to William POWELL

Barbara A. JONES: Nan

K

John KERBY: Tony, Will, Ben, Lewey, Daniel, Sarey, Bess, Nanny, Lucy, Edy, Aggy

Ann KNEWSTEP: Will, Venus

L

Thomas LAWSON: Jack, Kate, Lyon, Julius, Phillip, Timothy, Lester, Frank, Fanny

William I. LEWIS, Edward LEWIS: Daniel, Jenny, Judy

William LIGHTFOOT, Jacquelin LIGHTFOOT: Isham, James, Harry, Edmond, Beck, Fanny, Silvey, Seller

Jesse LINSEY: James, Sall

Jestina LINSEY: Tom, Fanny, Sanday, Lindsay

John LEWIS's estate, John WILLIAMS: Primus, Edmund, Harrison, Seany, Fanny, Jenny, Sall

William LEE, William L. LEE: Joe, Mick, Jacob, Jack, Guy, John, Aaron, Cupid, Isaac, Ned, Davy, Isaac, George, Johney, Mary, Grace, ___, Betty, Lyddia, Peggy, Sarah, Edy, Letty, Nancy, Lydia, Amey, Nancy, James, Robin, Frank, Humphrey, Harry, Milly, Edy, Jude, Judy, Kezia, Silas, Damus, Edmund, Joe, Tinken, Suckey, Temp, Rachel, Phillis, Charlotte, Betty, Kit, Lewis, Sall, Milly, Phillis, Sabina, Charles, James

M

John MACHANDREE: Pomprey, Roger

Major MAHONE: Matt

John MACTYRE: George

Joham MENETREE: Will, Johnny, Amey, Edy

Ann MENETREE: Suck, Pat

Elizabeth MARTIN: Moll

Joshua MORRIS: Tony, Silvey

Gabriel MAUPIN: James, Sam, Joe, Peg, Moll, Hannah

James MADDISON: Charles, Gilbert, Cato, Peyton, Winney, Sall, Edy, Nanny

N

William NOVELL, Nicholas LIGHTFOOT, William BUFFIN; Isaac, Jack, Jimmy, George, Tom, Jack, Gilbert, Easter, Pegg, Pat, Fanny, Jenny, Nan, Mackey, Moll, Barberry, Cressy, Moll, Nancy, Hannah, Abbey, Isabel

P

John PARADISE, William LONG: Syrus, Nero, Ben, George, Jack, Phillis, Lett, Sue, Esther, Nancy, Betty, Sylvey, John

John PIERCE, John PIERCE Jr.: Joe, George, Rippon, Billy, Edmond, Ned, Pegg, Kitty, Beck, Betty, Pat, Milly, Silvey

John PEGGOTT: David, Judy, Siller

Mary PERKINS: Sam, Gabey, Addin, Lucius, Fanny, Sall, Milly, Baker, Perkins

Eleanor PITT: Gabey, Isaac, George, Amey, Daphney

Benjamin PREWITT: Thomas, Pate, Ben, Betty, Kate, Cloe, Betty

Francis PEGGOTT: Jack, Nanny

Edward POWER, Edward POWER Jr.: Daniel, Machlin, Moses, Minor, Ned, Jack, Joe, Taff, Bristol, Moll, Aggy, Sukey, Doll, Rachel, Sall, Bett, Amey, Doll

R

Randolph ROSSER: Pegg

William REDWOOD: Silvey

James RATCLIFFE: Daniel, Sal, King, George, Rice

Edmund RANDOLPH: Dick, Dimbo, Pouringer, Gaby, John, Doctor, Nat, Mars, Billy, Jamy, Bob, Roger, James, Jacob, William, Stephen, Jim, Betty, Watt, Ned, Robin, Sam, Sam, Charles, Lydia, Fanny, Aggy, Aggy, Nancy, Judy, Jinny, Jinny, Betsy, Sukey, Sue, Lu__ordy, Molly, Stepney

Hewlett RAWLISON: Lib

William RICHARDSON: Rippon, Beck, Betty, Beck

William RICHARDSON: Julius, Simon, Charles, Frank, Beck, Pheby

Edward RICHARDSON: Dick, Daniel, Lewis, Rippon, Lucy, Phillis, Dosha, Janny

Stan__ RICHARDSON: Harry, Peter, Hannah, Ally, Kitty, Dosha

Mary RICHARDSON: Aggy, Fanny, Pat, Doll, Dinah, Dudly

Dudley RICHARDSON, Dudley RICHARDSON Jr.: Boatswain, Daniel, David, Carter, Hannah, Thoedosia, Sylvia, Obey

S

James SOUTHALL: Dublin, Grace, Will, Will, John, Marcus, George, Flora, Millia, Jinny

John P. SHIELDS: Joe, Ned, Charles, Martin, Billy, George

Solomon belonging to B. TAYLOR

Eugene SULLIVAN: Pat

Mary SPRIGGINS: Priscilla

James SHELBURNE: Peter, Lucy

Lewellin SPENCER, John ASHLOCK: man Spencer, Joe, James, Lucy

Sarah SPENCER: Hester

John G. SCULLY: John, Otey Jack

Rebecca SLATER, William SLATER: Dinah, Nanny

Hamilton U.S. GEORGE: Jacob, Will, Janny, Edmond, Phillis, Phillis, Beck, Lucy, Nanny, Rose

Robert SANFORD: Ben, Rachel, Nan, Robin

William SPRATTEY, William HOPKINS: Joe, James, Stephen, Lucy, Nanny

John SAUNDERS: Lucy, Clary, Phillis, Billy, David, Betty, Sarah, Jack, Letty, Effy

James SHIELDS, Page SHEILDS: James, David, George, Jack, Squire, Dick, Warwick, Betty, Betty, Moll, Moll, Nan, Dinah, Judy, Fanny, Pheby, Sarey, Amey, Cutty, Silvey, Charlotte

T

Henry TAZWELL, Littleton TAZWELL, Richard GRAVES: Joe, Sampson, George, George, Sucke, Sucke, Guy, Pomprey, Frank, Sam, Scipio, Jancy, Hampton, Cato, Johnny, George, Venus, Tab, Sarah, Lucy, Maria, Easter, Cloe, Sall, Peg, Clara, Rachel?, Milly, Ned, Charlotte, Marg

Littleton TAZWELL: Silvanus, Prince, George, James, Dunbar, Peter, Joe, Lyddia, Milly

Champion TRAVIS, Sam TRAVIS, Joel GATHRIGHT: James, Jiles, Arthur, Sam, John, Champion, Ned, Frederick, Peter, Michael, Syrus, Cromwell, Sam, Will, Tom, Gandy, Fanny, Betty, Silvy, Jane, Diana, Anecy, Anecy, Fanny, Violet, Violet, Milly, Hannah, Nan

Richardson TAYOR: Fanny, Sary, Batt

Richard TALIAFERRO estate, Benjamin TALIAFERRO, William EARNEST: Sam, Hampshire, Kit, Roger, Sam, Nat, Tom, Booker, Tony, Paul, Daniel, Letty, Nelly, Nan, Edy, Betty, Kate, Daphne, Rachel, Dinah, Lucy, Judy, Lyddia, Nelly

Charles TALIAFERRO: Gaby, Jack, Sam, Will, Sary, Hannah

Robert TAYLOR: Harry, Beck

Jeremiah TAYLOR: Scipio, Doll

Edmund TAYLOR: Sam, Jenny, Belinda

Pinkethman TAYLOR: Adam, Phil, Tom, Sambo, Sal, Rachel

Elizabeth TAYLOR: Ben, Siller, Phillis, Sylvey

Isham TAYLOR: Bartlet, Phil, Nut

Henley TAYLOR: Peter, Joe, Nanny, Lucy, George

V

John VALENTINE: Lender Rachel

W

David WALKER: Andrew, Mourning

John WARBURTON: Tom, Sam, Cupid, Peter, Sam, George, Nancy, Lutty

John WEATHERS: Frank, Will, Ned, Sary, Doll

Dudley WILLIAMS: Margaret

David WADE: Milly

Matthew WADE: Isaac, Pegg

Judith WADE, William WADE: Lewey, Charles, Nate, Betty, Cate, Aggy, Sabina, Ben

John D. WILKINSON: Cupid, Lucy

William WILKINSON Sr.: Harry, Ned, Aberdeen, Joe, Abraham, Amey, Venus, Sall

William WILKINSON: Dick, Bristo, Antony, Will, Daniel, Jack, Aaron, King, Joe, Daniel, Pat, Joan, Pat, Sarah, Kate, Priss, Nanny, Viney

William WALKER: Abraham, Dick, Bob, Will, Mingo, Charles, Alice, Pat, Sary, Dinah, Sary, Doll

James N. WALKER: Frank, Sam, Lyddia, Doll, Judy

Richard WHITAKER: Moses, Paul

John WALKER: James, Siller, Milly, Judy

John WALKER Sr., Robert WALKER: Hubert, Judy, Nan, Lucy, Silvey, Rose, Delsey, Amey, Suck

William WILKINSON .... 30 Sept 1800, will

King, Priscilla & her 2 children Charles & Jack, Viney & her son Thomas, boy Sam who I had in exchange of William P. HARRIS, woman Fanny, Betty daughter of Lucy to daughter Elizabeth WILKINSON with 1st wife Sally TALIAFERRO daughter of Col. Richard TALIAFERRO dec'd; remaining negroes to wife Elizabeth C. WILKINSON

KING AND QUEEN

King and Queen County was created in 1691. Records were lost in courthouse fires in 1828 and 1833. Records were again destroyed by a courthouse fire set by Union troops on 10 March 1864 during the Civil War.

James Harvey Atkins .... 8 May 1833, Cert of Freedom
  21 years old, 5 ft, 2", and identifying marks

Richard BAGBY .... 31 Mar 1854, will
  slaves are to be divided in kind or the whole or any part of them sold for division

Townley BANKS .... 30 Dec 1817, will
  woman Cloe to sister Lucy BURKE

John BLAND Jr. .... 1 July 1846, will
  girl Martha to daughter Nancy TODD; slaves in possession of my son Roderick BLAND & daughter Fanny TAYLOR to be divided equally among my children

Isaac BOOKER .... 28July 1841, will
  woman Rachel to sister Ann COURTNEY; Obe, Penellepet, Lewis, Harrison, Tom, William, young Penellepet to sister Ann COURTNEY

George BRAXTON .... 13 Sept 1749, will
  all negroes to remain on my plantation till my son George attains the age of 21 then to be divided between my sons George & Carter; man London to wait on them

Lewis BROOCKE .... 13 Feb 1832, will
  woman Sally, girl Phillis to wife Elizabeth BROOCKE; Henry to Lewis E. BROOCKE; girl Nanny to daughter Frances A.E. BROOCKE; boy Jack to son Cornelius C. BROOCKE

Ann BRUSHWOOD .... 7 June 1851, will
  woman servant Mary to son Robert D. DIDLAKE; at the death of my son Robert all the servants have the privilege choosing their own masters

John CAMM...17 Mar 1766, will

1/3 slaves to daughter Ann BOOKER; 1/3 to daughter Mary GARLICK; 1/3 to daughter Elizabeth WHITE

George K. CARLTON..15 Oct 1846, will

1/3 slaves to wife; balance of slaves to be divided among children at his death

William CARLTON..4 June 1812, will

man Ben to be sold; girl Easter to daughter Elizabeth CARLTON

Etheline CHRISTIAN vs Fanny C.C. CHRISTIAN.................................
....12 Dec 1853, in Chancery

James CHRISTIAN dec'd left will naming wife Catharine CHRISTIAN...John, Henry, Billy, Thomas, Patsy, Williams, Aleena, Jane, Betsy, Ailey, Betty, Lucy, Elnora to be equally divided among children Lavinia, Mary, Ethelena, & Fanny at her death...

James CHRISTIAN..30 Dec 184_, will

after the death of my wife Catherine...I give to my children Levina, Mary, Etheline, & Fanny to be equally divided among them...
....Chancery continued

John age 4, Billy 16, Tom _4, Betty 40, Alrina 27 & 2 children Lucy & Nora, Jane 15, Betsy 13, Alice 12, Patty 10, William 5

Lot 1: Jane, Tom to Etheline PHILLIPS; Lot 2: Alice, John, Betty to F. NELSON trustee for Lavinia PAGE; Lot 3: Betsy, Alrina & 2 children Lucy & Nora to John F. WOOTIN in right of his wife Mary; Lot 4: Patsy, Billy, William to Fanny C.C. CHRISTIAN; Henry now in possession of John CHRISTIAN

Johnathan CLARK..9 Apr 1734, will

1/3 negroes to wife Elizabeth CLARK; rest of negroes to be divided among my 4 children John, Ann, Benjamin, & Elizabeth CLARK

James CLAYTON..7 Feb 1818, will

girl Anna to daughter to daughter Maud Henden EUBANK; woman Maud, boy John to daughter Polly Ruffin SPENCER; man Je__y to son William Hemden CLAYTON; girl Milly, man Billy to daughter Harriet Byron COLLINS; boys George, little Billy to son Thomas

Smith CLAYTON; man Humphrey, woman Leah, girl Mary to daughter Rebecca Parke Farley CLAYTON

Jeyeux COLLINS .... 14 Feb 1840, will

Judith, Lavinia, John to wife Maria Ann; woman Maria to son Jeyeux COLLINS; negroes divided among my 3 children William, Juliett, & Susan COLLINS; girl Betty to daughter Susan _. COLLINS

Alice COBIN .... 26 Apr 1791, will

Sally & her child to my sister Braxton; Samantha to cousin Alicy ROBINSON

John CROCKFORD .... 30 __ 1757, will

old woman Beck, man Sawney, girl girl Beck to daughter Mary FAULKNER; girl Frank to daughter Elizabeth Meriah JEFFRIES; boy George to daughter S__ecy CARTER

Charles DOBBINS .... 8 Sept 1789, will

man Harry to William COVINGTON & Sarah his wife; girl Fanny to Catharine ABBET

Charles R. EVENS .... 7 May 1856, will

Mary, Delcie to wife Mary E. EVENS

Robert FARINHOLL .... 19 Dec 1832, will

girl Kitty, boy Billy to son Beverley; Jenny & 4 children Charles, Simon, Mary, & James to daughter Ann ALBRIGHT; Hannah & 4 children Esther, Absalom , John & Chancy to daughter Sarah HUGHES; man Jim, Clara & 2 children Lucy & Kitty, women Lucy, Harriet, boy George, old man Jesse to daughter Betsy; Fanny to daughter Martha

Moore G. FAUNTLEROY .... 25 Jan 1859, will

man Nathan to mother; woman Fanny to wife

Christopher FLEET vs Jacob VALENTINE .... 16 Mar 1831, in court

Jacob VALENTINE's negroes sold

Richard GAINES, Frances TAYLOR, & Henry MICKELBOURROUGH ....10 Dec 1777, deed

    slaves to Henry MICKELBOURROUGH in trust for Frances TAYLOR until her marriage to Richard GAINES; slaves: Phoebe & her children Rachel & Jerry

James GARDNER .... 8 Mar 1784, will

    Kit, Wapping, Phebee, Bette to son John GARDNER; Humphrey, Adam to son Anthony GARDNER

William GARDNER .... 5 July 1854, will

    girl Rebecca to daughter Mary Frances

Robert L. GARRETT .... 1832, will

    Judy, _ffc_, John, Barco__, George to brother Edward GARRETT; Patty & her child, Emily to brother Edward GARRETT in trust for nephew John H. PARRISH; the residue of slaves to child or children of late brother Richard GARRETT

William George VIDAL ....29 Aug 1821, inv & appr

    (listed as William GEORGE)

    Bill, Nace, Tom, Tom, Abraham, Joe, Major, Lewis, Billy, Amos, Warner, Cesar, John, Sam, Marmion, Jackson, Napoleon, Patty, Lucy, Hannah, Polly, Aggy, Lucky, Jane

Samuel GRESHAM .... 7 Feb 1842, will

    negroes to wife Susannah GRESHAM

William HOSKINS .... 13 Dec 1802, inv & appr

    men Lewis, Toby, George, Robin, James, Randolph, Ben, boys Vernal, Sam, Nelson, women Patty, Lydia, girls Martha, Jane

X Ann W. HOWERTON ....10 Oct 1846, will

    girl Maria to daughter Eleanor A. SMITH; woman Mary to son Walter G. COVINGTON

Robert HOWERTON .... 8 May 1854, will

    Handy, Walker, June, Ruffin, Anderson, Mariah, Eliza, ___ to wife Sara HOWERTON & her children Etta, William, Robert, & Evelina; Bob, Martha, Betty, Henry, Lavinia, Matilda, Andrew, Solomon,

James to daughters Mary C. BRUMLEY, Anna ARCHER, Jane TRICE, & Ellen V. HOWERTON; boy Moore to sons-in-law G.W. TRICE & Joseph BRUMLEY; Sam, Charlotte to L. ARCHER; Archer, Susan to daughter Ellen V. HOWERTON; Alice to choose her master or mistress; girl Harriet to Eliza St. JOHN

Francis KERR to George KERR .... 11 May 1830, deed

men Bob, Burnett to son George KERR

Francis KERR to William KERR .... 11 May 1830, deed

man Iverson to son William KERR

Francis KERR .... 23 Dec 1830, will

men Bob, Burnett to son George KERR; man Iverson to son William KERR; woman Charlotte to granddaughter Mary Susan EDWARDS

William LYNE .... 19 Dec 1806, will

negroe children received to be accounted for: Lewis, Tillar, Peter to son William; Matt, Milly, girl Betty to son Henry; Lender to daughter Betty; Vina to daughter Mary Ann; Hannah to daughter Lucy CARTER; Judah, Harriet, Cloe to daughter Catharine TEMPLE; Esther, Cuffy to daughter Ann Foster HUTCHESON; Sam, Hannah to son Edmund

Robert MANN .... 5 Dec 1825, will

Daniel, Mira to wife Susan D. MANN

Thomas MANN .... 4 Oct 1856, will

1 or 2 negroes to children as they come of age or marry; man Davy to be sold if necessary

Edwin MOTLEY .... 5 Oct 1808, will

Kitt, Agga & her child Anderson, Sawny, Dawson, James, Charity, Judith, Ann & her child Wilson, Reuben, Moll, Nancy to wife Elisabeth; negroes in his possession in Caroline to son Thomas; negroes in her possession to daughter Ann ANDREWS; man Ned to son Henry; a negro each to grandchildren Thomas, Edwin, & Lucy KETCHION when they reach a lawful age; negroes in her possession to daughter Betsy BROADUS; negroes in her possession to daughter Rosey RYLAND; choice of 1 negro to son John; choice of 1 negro to son William; choice of 1 negro to son Richard; choice of 1 negro to sons Sanford, Andrew, Robert, & Silas when they arrive at a lawful age; girl Milly & 2 choice of negroes to daughter Fanna; girl Jenny & 2 choice of negroes to daughter Polly; man Tom to be sold

Absalum MUIRE to William OLIVER, etc ....
....29 Dec 1840, marriage settlement

young fellow Bob, Lucy & child Martha possessed by Rutha Ann OLIVER & young fellow Shawn loaned to Martha OLIVER the mother of said Rutha Ann OLIVER...given to her by Catherine __ dec'd...

John NICHOLS .... 17 Sept 1764, will

girl Frank to daughter Mary NICHOLS; boys Harry, Reuben to son John NICHOLS; girl Alice to daughter Anna NICHOLS; girl Winney to daughter Hannah NICHOLS

Philip B. PENDELTON .... 7 Dec 1839, will

Lewis & his wife little Aggy & her children to wife as well as 6 to be chosen out of the remainder of my slaves except my man John Smith; Maria, now in the possession of Dr. William B. PODD, young woman Cordilia, boy Dick to grandson Marcus P. PODD; servants John Smith, Jack, Anderson; remaining slaves to be given to my grandson

Peter Thornton POLLARD .... 1 June 1839, will

girl Winney daughter of Kitty to wife Elizabeth P. POLLARD; woman Winney daughter of Nancy which Nancy died in the possession of Samuel G. FAUNT to choose her master

Thomas ROANE .... 27 Jan 1799, will

40 slaves to wife including man Billy; James, Jerry, Bland, Winney, Lydia, Suckey, to daughter Sarah CAMPBELL wife of Hugh CAMPBELL, old Bit, old Jenny, Dixon having died; Amy & her 2 children to daughter Margaret GARNETT; boy & girl their own age to sons of Margaret GARNETT Archibald & Thomas HARDWOOD; Peter, Sam, Charles, Anthony, Violet, Judy, Sarah, young Sarah, Sally, Pickles to son-in-law Sterling RUFFIN; Isaac, Gilbert, Bob, Amy, Jinny, Judy, young Shill, Pegg to son-in-law Richard BARNES; George, Dick, Billy, Jerry, Cate, Janet, Easther, Mary, Robin to son Thomas ROANE; George, Nelson, Tom, _ George, Charles, Nanny, Tillah, Lydia, Sarah to son Samuel ROANE;

Charles, Godfrey, Hancock, Aggy, Hannah, Patience, Venus & 2 others to sons Thomas & Samuel ROANE in trust for daughter Patsy Hipkins RETCHIE wife of Archibald RETCHIE; a young man to sons Thomas & Samuel ROANE

John N. RYLAND .... 16 Feb 1865, affidavit

owner of Tom 26 in June 1863, John 31 in May 1864, Lawrence 19 in June 1864; it is believed Tom fled the possession & went into the U.S. Army in June 1863; in May 1864 the army carried away John, & in June 1864 carried away Lawrence, all slaves have been lost

George SCHOOLS .... 12 Aug 1835, will

Polly SCHOOLS wife of Elijah SCHOOLS nor her 3 sons George, Major, & Elijah SCHOOLS are to have no part of my negroes at my death; Bob to daughter-in-law Nancy SCHOOLS wife of Thomas SCHOOLS; balance of negroes to sons Jeremiah, John, & Waller SCHOOLS & Nancy OWENS & Polly PATTERSON

Waller SCHOOLS .... 13 May 1843, will

woman Martha to wife Rebecca SCHOOLS

Thomas SEARS .... 14 Feb 1850, will

1 negro to each child at marriage or coming of age

Samuel SHEPHERD .... 9 Nov 1751, will

boy Jime to son Robert SHEPHERD; negroes to wife Mildred SHEPHERD

William SHEPPARD & Mary DIX .... 11 July 1832, deposition

William SHEPPARD's deposition: at the death of my wife slaves to be divided; Mary DIX deposition: believes that the will as copied in said deposition of William SHEPPARD is a true copy from the will of Lewis CARLTAN

Dorothea Ann SMITH .... 8 Mar 1841, deed

Dorothea Ann SMITH wife of Robert B. SMITH in a conveyance to John D. McGILL & James M. JEFFRIES trustees; Judy, little Judy, Betsy, Maria, Sarah & 3 children William, Louisa, & Thaddius, Walker, Letty to Dr. William SMITH trustee of Dorothea Ann SMITH for her use

James SMITHER .... 7 Mar 1839, will

    Henry, Delphia, Maria to wife Eliza SMITHER; balance of slaves to be sold

John SPENCER .... 4 Sept 1858, will

    girl Polly to son William W. SPENCER; man Sam to daughter Nancy; man Andrew, part of Thomas MANN's estate, to daughter Sarah widow of Thomas MANN; man Henry to Sarah Elizabeth & James Spencer ANDERSON, children of deceased daughter Elizabeth ANDERSON; Salena & all her children to daughter Nancy

William STUART to William SAUNDERS .... 18 Sept 1816, deed

    Sam, Aggy & her 2 children Leland & Sanford, Esther to William SAUNDERS

R.J. SUTTON to R.H. DICKINSON .... 8 Mar ___, letter

    ...lay out in negroes before the 1st of April...

Francis TAYLOR .... 15 Jan 1766, will

    woman Winney to son John TAYLOR; boy Randolph to son Samuel TAYLOR; Joe, Lett & her child James to daughter Ann DUMPHIN; Phill, Feel to daughter Frances TAYLOR; Cambridge, Nan, Moll to daughter Mary MICHELB__Y

William TAYLOR .... 14 June 1845, will

    girls Delpha, Martha, Nanny to daughters Frances NOEL, Ellen EUBANK, & Lucy MARSHALL; negroes to be divided; Fanny, Norman to have choice of living with either of my children & is not to be sold

Cornelius VAUGHAN .... 6 Nov 1735, will

    men Antony, Tom, Sam to wife Elizabeth VAUGHAN, Hannah, Bess, Judy, Charles, Sary to wife to be divided among 4 youngest children: Bridget, Cournelius, Elizabeth & Margaret & the child yet to be born; Anthony, Tom, Sam to be divided among James, John, & Ambrose VAUGHAN, Mary CHAPMAN, Ann MARTIN, Sarah HUDGEN, Catharine SILVAN, & Christian SCOTT

Richard WALDEN Sr. .... 22 Apr 1845, will

    Spencer, C_ssa & her daughter Isabella to wife Maria WALDEN; Mary & her children Sophromia & Mahala to son William

WALDEN; slaves loaned to children Richard WALDEN Jr., Edward WALDEN, Elizabeth HART, Sarah KERR, & Lucy Ann ALBRIGHT be returned to the estate for general division

Spencer WARE's orphans vs Exr of John GARDNER............................
....16 Aug 1804, in Chancery

Robert Spence WARE, Spencer WARE, & Lydia WARE, orphans of Spencer WARE; ...3 negroes...part of the estate of John GARDNER...1 negro delivered on 18 Dec 1784 to Ann FIELD daughter of Stephen FIELD...
....16 Mar 1787

Mary DIDLAKE & Staige DAVIS, the first is the widow of John GARDNER dec'd, the other by marriage of the only daughter & child of said John GARDNER dec'd have the possession of sundry slaves Thomas ROW as exec of John GARDNER dec'd delivered to the said Mary DIDLAKE...said slaves to be disposed of...refused to suffer the said slaves...
....15 Aug 1798

...Mary DIDLAKE became possessed of 3 slaves – Billy, Sam, & Beck...delivered about 13 years ago...Billy died about 5 or 6 years ago, Beck died about 4 years, consequently Sam is now about 45 years old, boy Peter a child of Beck's is about 10 years old are the only remaining negros in her possession.
....13 July 1801

...woman delivered to Ann FIELDS...said Ann FIELDS hath since married John WOOD who by virtue thereof is possessed of said woman slave who now has 3 or 4 children...to be sold to pay...
....13 Oct 1801

...delivered up the one female negro named Charlotte...said negro 4 children James, Peter, Joe & the other at her breast not named...
....17 Aug 1804

...negroes left by John GARDNER dec'd which Mary DIDLAKE the widow of the said John afterward had in her possession: Will called Billy, Beck, Amey are since dead, that Billy died sometime about the year 1792, Beck died about the year 1795, & Amey died about the year 1797 & that Mary DIDLAKE has no negroes by the above names in her possession...

.... 11 Oct 1800, deposition

Olive, Hagar, Will called Billy, Beck, Amey are since dec'd...Olive, Hagar, Amey, Hampton, Ned, Beck, Cate were negroes that Henry MACON father of Mary DIDLAKE...sent after her marriage with John GARDNER dec'd, that Olive, Hagar, Amey are some of those stated above to be dead... several negroes were sent down by said MACON to said GARDNER...

....28 Mar 1801, deposition

...in the possession of his brother the following negroes: Hampton, Ned, Olive, Buck, Stephen, Amey, Hagar, Cate, a girl, a woman & child...were sent to him by Henry MACON...in the year 1786...all the negroes by name: Hampton, Ned, Olive, Stephen, Buck, Amy, Hagar, Cate, a girl, a woman, a child, Robin lent to his daughter Mary GARDNER during her life & at her death to be divided among all her children...Robin was placed in his brother William's lot...the deed of gift from his father to his sister Mary was not recorded therefore all the negroes were the property of William MACON & self...all of which has died...(except the woman & child)...

....28 Mar 1801, deposition

...1784 about the month of Nov there was a fellow called Smith Bob that was sold by ROW & he believes that DEJARNETT purchased him...GARDNER received 11 negroes...Amy, Hagar, Cate, Ned, Hampton, Buck, Olive...Amey, Hagar, Olive are since dead. ...fellow Will called Billy, woman Beck...William DILLARD has hired the negro...should keep the negro himself...Isaac DIGGES...purchased at the sale of said GARDNER's estate 2 negroes...

.... 2 Oct 1792, deposition

man James belonging to Spencer WARE orphan was struck out to William DILLARD in 1782 & since that year lived with John GARDNER the guardian to Spencer WARE...Robert A. WARE had no chargable negroes in 1783 but 1 woman & child...

.... 2 Oct 1792, deposition

...negoes belonging to the orphans of Spencer WARE...man James...

.... 13 May 1794, deposition

negroes alloted in will to Mary GARDNER...Sam, Billy, Beck.

.... 12 Feb 1799, deposition

appraisal: Sam, Will, Olive, Hampton, Ned, Beck & children Peter 12, Frank 12 twins, Milly 7, Hagar & child Violet, Buck, Amey, Cate & child Kitty...

.... 27 Sept 1784 – 13 Apr 1789, estate acct

woman Betty to Dr. GARDNER; man Kit to Lewis SEGOUGUE; boy Peter; negro to James

.... 26 Dec 1789 – 7 July 1791, estate acct

sundry negroes sold; Dinah to Samuel H. H_RY; Phebe to William EDMONSON

.... 14 Mar 1792 – 15 July 1794, estate acct

for crying negroes; Anthony, small boy Billy, an infant, boy Abraham, Lewey, girl Betty sold

.... 28 May 1791, in Chancery

sale of sundry negroes in Nov 1784, Bob sold healthy but was not

.... 15 May 1792, in Chancery

Bob's sale under dispute

Francis WILSON vs Heirs of Fanny C.C. CHRISTIAN, etc ....
.... 13 Apr 1854, in Chancery

Fanny CHRISTIAN is possessed of 3 negroes which were in the division of her father's estate

Fanny B. WOODWARD .... 2 Nov 1857, will

Sarah to daughter Caroline SMITH

John WYATT .... 26 Nov 1773, will

boy Lewis to daughter Frankie BURNS; boy Phill to son John; Harry to son Joseph; boy Gabriel to son Thomas Turner WYATT; girl Jeanie to son Willam; girl Mary to son Henry; girl Delilah to son George; remaining negroes to wife Sarah & at her death to be divided among the sons

KING GEORGE

Created by an act of 1720 to take effect on 19 May in 1721. Most loose records prior to 1830 are missing. Volumes that record deeds, court orders, and wills exist.

William BOON .... Feb 1792, will
> man John to son George Green BOON; Guley, Ben, Hannah to daughter Molly HARRISON wife of Richardson HARRISON

Elizabeth CARTER .... 12 Apr 1836, codicil
> Aggy & her 4 children Lucy, Fanny, William, & John to be emancipated but not at the time of my death: Aggy to live with her father & mother at son Otway's farm in Fauquier where she is now residing with them...to care for them until their death; Lucy & Fanny to be hired out until they are 21...granddaughter Elizabeth Landon BRADFORD for the use of her 2 sons Osmond & Landon; William & John to be bound out until they are 21...their father Billy Fergerson, who lives in Richmond City with a Mr. PILCHER...; Bartlett & his sister Matilda – Bartlett to be hired out by son St L.L.CARTER...for the care of daughter Harmar CARTER wife of Robert C. CARTER for her daughter Emma at whose decease the said Bartlett is to be free; Matilda & her son James to live with her mother to take care of her & with her death they are to be free

Samuel SKINKER .... 24 Jan 1752, will
> slaves bought of James HAY to son Samuel; negroes to son John SKINKER; negroes to son Thomas SKINKER; negroes to son William; negroes to son George; 1/3 negroes to wife Dinah & at her decease divided between sons Samuel, Thomas, John, George, & William

John TAYLOE .... 21 July 1824, will
> wife Ann TAYLOE to choose 12 house servants, to have slaves from farm called Pitsworth, to be sold after her death; 20 working hands & 5 children to grandson John TAYLOE Jr. at estate in Charles Co. MD in lieu of children Alfred, Emanuel, Martha, Becky, George at Mount Airy formerly given to him; said children & other slaves at Mount Airy to son William; son William is to surrender the slaves at "Windsor", "South Hill" & "Society Hill" to his brother Benjamin Ogle TAYLOE; slaves at Brunswick & Clover Dale estates in

Botetourt Co to all my sons; settlement of slaves made to daughter Henrietta Hill KEY; Archy to be free
....Dec 1827, codicil
sons switching estates & their slaves

KING WILLIAM

King William County was created by an act of 1701 to take effect on 11 April 1702. Most records were destroyed by a courthouse fire on 17 January 1885. Only a few order books and deed books exist.

Dorothy ANDERSON .... 15 Feb 1729, deed

 widow of William ANDERSON; Shion, Betty to son William ANDERSON

William ANDERSON .... 25 June 1719, inv & appr

 man Harry, woman Betty, man Ben, boy Shion, girls Hannah, Sarah, Bess smaller, Irish servants Patrick Welsh, Timothy Bryant

David ARNETT .... 22 Jan 1738, will

 wench Lucy to daughter Mary ARNETT after my wife's decease, Martha ARNETT; Phillis, Ledia to son James ARNETT after my wife's decease; girl Fanny to son Robert ARNETT after my wife's decease

William AYLETT .... 8 Nov 1730, will

 Jack, Sue, Peg, Manuel, Cangelow now in her posession to daughter Lydia BOYD wife of John BOYD & at my decease Ben, Jimbo, Backus, Mary, Cate; the said slaves to my son Benjamin AYLETT; several slaves to daughter Ann wife of Benjamin WALKER; Jenny, Yousy, L__, Brass, Milly, Tippis, Abraham, Baker, Angelo, Moll & child Warrick, Dolly, Malcom, Venus, Delph to daughter Elizabeth AYLETT; Nelson, Pheby, Esther, Fuller, Charles, Daniel, Tom, Violet, Luce, Jenney, Peter to daughter Jane AYLETT; Molbourgh, John, Sambo, Ciss, Beck & her son Jappo, Matthew son of Ciss, Sam, Billy, Fidler, Venus, Gayney, Caesar & his wife Cate, Manuel, Abby to son John AYLETT; Jupiter, Cyrus, Rachel, Nell, Roger, Pacience, Davy, Jacob, Gloucester, York, Sall & her child Lucy, Frank, Simon to son Benjamin AYLETT; George, Grace, Ashley & her child Grace, Bristol, Robin, Phillis, Catchanah, Will, Mary, Matthew the child of Phillis, Sarah, Watt, Cupit, Gla_co, Grace, Bowler, Silis, to son Philip AYLETT

.... 6 Jan 1732, codicil

 Peg, Arthur of Peg to son Philip AYLETT

Augustine A. BLAKE .... 9 Mar 1857, deed
(listed under BLACK)

Billy, McKenzie, Annanias, Aggy & 3 children, Joice & 2 children; Gabrelly & 3 children to John H. BARCH the same left in trust by the late Richard COCKRAN dc'd to Nancy HAY

Carter BRAXTON .... 11 Aug 1783, deed

Simon, James, Malbrough, Billy, London, James, Boatswain, Abram, Joe, Stephen, James, Will, Andrew, Harrison, Randolph, Davy, Harry, Bob, Frank, Matt, Daniel, George, Isaac, Tom, Ralph, Dick, Tom, Cyrus, Billy, Davy, Joseph, Sue, Delph, Alice, Dedo, Harriett, Mercia, Phillis, Lucy, Lett, Rachel, Jinty, Sukey to Augustine CLAIBORNE

Corbin BRAXTON .... 25 Feb 1848, will

to my son William BRAXTON...the negroes...lend him during another's life, at her death...all negroes to be divided between my 5 children William A., Tomlin, Fanny C., Betty, & Lucy BRAXTON after my wife's death

Nathaniel BURWELL .... 30 Mar 1802, will

man Jerry & his wife & children to wife Martha BURWELL

John CLEMENTS .... 13 Oct 1766, will

Fillis (Phillis), Rachel to son William Martin CLEMENTS; boy Moses to daughter Lucresa CLEMENTS; boy Sam to daughter Mary CLEMENTS; girl Temp to daughter Lavine CLEMENTS; boy Isaac to daughter Elizabeth CLEMENTS

Richard COCKRAN .... 6 June 1837, will

boy Isaac to grandsons Richard & William EUBANK; Fanny, Joice, Billy, John, Winney, Aggy, Nelly, Gabriella, all other slaves I may leave to be held in trust by George LIZER for daughters Catharine TUCK & Nancy HAYES

Reuben DUGAR .... 5 Dec 1833, will

Burwell, Joe, Billy, George, Caty, Lucy, Viney, Ralph, Frederick, Amanda, Sam to wife; balance of slaves except 2 negroes to daughters Susan & Kitty to son James; first choice of women, girl Sally to daughter Kitty

Richard EUBANK.. 20 Dec 1871, will
> Spencer Tayler (col'd) given money bond when he turns 21

Benjamin FIGG... 20 Mar 1839, will
> Jim, Malinda to Mary W. FIGG; Eliza to daughter Martha P. WORDY; Catharine to son Robert _. FIGG; Ginny, Adeline to daughter Sarah Frances FIGG
> .... 15 May 1839, codicil
> boy George, girl Susan to be sold

Mary C. GARLICK.. 19 Mar 1856, will
> Richard, Billy, Robert, Susan & her children Sophia, Sarah, Reuben, Winney, Tommy, & Wattes, Dorinda & her children James, Nat, Robert, & Eliza, Lucinda, Joe, Henry, Octavia, George, to daughter Mildred C. GARLICK; girl Maria to Mary TEMPLE wife of James TEMPLE, daughter from 1st marriage; 1/3 of servants not herein specifically divided to daughter Mildred C. GARLICK; Maria, Lucy, Shirley, Reuben, James, Henry, Emma, Susan, Nelly & her children Robert, Sophia, & Armstead, Martha & her children Amy & an infant, Sally & her children Juliet, Ellen, & her children William & Nat, Andrew, Martin to daughter Sarah SELDON; Anora, Jerry, James to nephew William P. BRAXTON in trust for daughter Sarah SELDON; Robert was sold improperly by Mr. SELDON, Sarah's husband; Delphia & her children Milly, Joe, Becky, Owney, & Reuben, Ben, Robert to son Braxton; 1/3 part of the servants at my death to nephew William P. BRAXTON; man Custer to nephew William P. BRAXTON; Maria, Nat's wife, to choose her mistress from my 2 daughters; my undivided servants: Ourney & her children, Martha, Anne, Ben, Frank, Johnny, Beverly, Louisa, Sally & her children, Charlotte, Vince, Andrew, Bartlett, Tena, Addison, Richard Jr.

Major Joseph GWATHMEY.. 1 Oct 1823, will
> at death of wife Mary GWATHMEY executors to purchase a girl about 15 years of age in trust for daughter Mary GARLICK; a male & a female each to son John GWATHMEY & daughters Susanna & Martha GWATHMEY at the death of my wife
> .... 6 Aug 1824, inv & appr
> Simon, Lorain, Sam, Peter, Harry, Julius, Amos, Oliver, Kit,

Frederick, Ben, Billy, George, Osmond, old Hannah, Hannah, Lucy, Jenny, Annis, child Simon, William, Fanny, Caty, Jacob, Jack, Alice & 2 children, Phoebe, Humphrey

....15 June 1824, Exhibit 2 received of Mary GWATHMEY: Jack, Pheobe, Alice & her 2 children William & Cretty

....29 Dec 1826, Exhibit 3 slave Mary to John GWATHMEY executor & trustee from Harry B. GAINES & Agnes his wife nee GWATHMEY

Edward & Martha HAY to John L. SWEET & John H. BURCH...............
....20 June 1851, deed slaves to John L. SWEET & John H. BURCH

James H. HAY to John H. BURCH ....5 Dec 1856, deed
Billy, McKanzie, Amania, Aggy & her 3 children, Gabriella & her 3 children, Joice & her 2 children to John H. BURCH

John H. BURCH to Richard HAWES............................7 Mar 1859, deed
slaves, acquired by deed from James H. HAY as trustee for Nancy HAY & her children, to Richard HAWES

Joseph HILLYARD...13 Nov 1830, will
slaves to wife Mary Eliza

John LIPSCOMB .... 5 Dec 1776, will
Dingo, Judy, Glory, Moll to wife Ann; fellow George to son Pember; fellow James to son John; wench Rachel to daughter Elizabeth; wench Mourning to daughter Ann; fellow Peter to son Henry; girl Lucy to daughter Sally; boy Wilbert to son Madison; girl Sylvia to daughter Martha; boy Lewis to son Reuben; boy Carter to son Anderson; girl Phoebe to daughter Patty; Boatswain, Sampson, Frank kept on land to maintain my 3 youngest children, to be sold when youngest turns 18

Madison LIPSCOMB .... 11 Mar 1815, will
Lucy, Jainett, Sally, Lucy to wife Mary; man Peter, boy Kendal to son Conway O. LIPSCOMB; woman Phillis, girl Mary to daughter Polly POLLARD; Jinney & children Francis & Jefferson to daughter Nancy P. LIPSCOMB; boy Warner, girl Betsy to son John H.

LIPSCOMB; Warner to be bound to William B. LIPSCOMB until he is 20; boy Russell, girl Harriet to be sold; Harriet to son Conway O. LIPSCOMB if money not needed for debt

Lucy Ann Littlepage .... 24 Aug 1824, cert of freedom

age 18, 5 ft, 6 ½", no marks or scars, emancipated by will of Edmund LITTLEPAGE

Thomas B. MARTIN .... 22 Feb 1853, will

Lucinda to Julia Harriet Thomasa MARTIN; boy Edward to son Thomas Brumby MARTIN; girl Isabella to son John Buckler MARTIN; servants to be hire out privately

Elizabeth McGEORGE etc vs Exr of William McGEORGE .... 27 Jan 18__, in Chancery

to divide the slaves, except Caroline, Cyrus, Franky, & Rachel of William McGEORGE dec'd into 4 equal parts, one lot to Elizabeth & William & John F. McGEORGE as trustees for Catharine WOODDY; 1 to John F. & Wily R., & another to William McGEORGE

.... allotment & div

men ___, __per, Abraham, boys Harry, Hanover, Carter, woman Judy, Polly, Jenny, Nanny, Levina

Harry to Elizabeth, William, & John F. McGEORGE trustees for Catharine WOODY; Abraham, Lavinia to John F. McGEORGE; Nelson, Carter, Nanny to Wily R. McGEORGE; Sharper, Jenny to William McGEORGE

William McGEORGE .... __ Nov 1822, will

Caroline, Cyrus, Franky to wife Elizabeth McGEORGE; girl Rachel to sons William & John Franklin McGEORGE in trust for granddaughter Mary Ann McGEORGE

Augustine MOORE .... 26 Jan 1742, will

Catina, old Jemmy, Dinah to wife Elizabeth MOORE; Hannah, great Daniel's wife & their children to daughter Elizabeth MACON; Judy, Robin's wife, great Patty & their children to daughter Lucy ROBINSON; 1/3 part of slaves to wife – Neptune & his wife Violet, Sambo, York, Sawyers & at her death to sons Bernand & Thomas; 1/3 of slaves & those in his possession to son Augustine; 10 working slaves to daughter-in-law Ann MOORE if left a widow; 1/3 slaves to son Bernard; 1/3 to son Thomas

PORTER .... , will

__tan, Jude to wife; 2 __cy to son Israel PORTER; Adam, Hanner to daughter Ann PORTER; __n, Jenny to daughter Mary PORTER

Levi RICE to B.F. DABNEY ....29 July 1844, deed

all slaves of the late Richard COCKRAN died possessed to B.F. DABNEY; my title derived in right of my wife Patsy, the daughter of Nancy HAY the daughter of Richard ACKRAN which said slaves are 11 in number, Fanny & her 2 children Henry & __ Kenzie, Billy, John, Cornelius, Joice, Aggy, Jane, Gabriella, Annanias

William S. RYLAND .... 26 Dec 1861, will

slaves to be sold only if necessary; Spenser, Matt, Louisa to son Robert S. RYLAND; Joe, Henny to daughter Ann S. RYLAND; Cate, Mary Ellen to daughter Sally B. RYLAND; Ned, Betty to daughter Susan F. RYLAND; Obadiah, Margaret to daughter Pricila E. RYLAND; Ben, Coly to daughter Dora RYLAND; Seal, Matilda to daughter Willentina RYLAND; Jerry, Laura to daughter Josephine RYLAND; Baylor, Martha Brown to daughter Maria P. RYLAND; Lewis to wife Susan; slaves lent to wife to be divided at her death among all children including daughters Catharine & Mary & son Robert

John SANDAGE ....28 Feb 1750, will

girl Lucy to wife Jane SANDAGE

Betty SEATON .... 15 June 1782, will

woman Cug to son Augustine SEATON, to be free at his death; girl Betty child of Aney to granddaughter Jenny SEATON daughter of son Augustine SEATON; man Cook to grandson George SEATON son of my son Augustine; woman Aney to grandson George Watson SEATON son of my son George SEATON; man Berkeley to executor to be sold for purchase of a wench to be divided among childen of son Augustine & his wife Mary

James SEAY..15 Feb 1752, will

6 Jan 1746 married wife, widow of Nathan BREEDLOVE; man Harry to wife & at her marriage or death to so Gideon SEAY; boy

And__ to son John SEAY; wench Janny to son Jesse SEAY; girl Gilly to daughter Phebe BIDGNAY; boy Peter to daughter Tirviah BREEDLOVE; girl Grace to daughter Anna SEAY

John SIZER .... 11 Feb 1860, will

Jenny, Jack to wife Hannah SIZER; 4 slaves (too faint to read) plus Sara Jane to son Augustus SIZER; 3 slaves (too faint to read) plus Elizabeth, little Charles, George to daughter Ann Willis FAUNTLEROY; William, Letty & her son John, Harriet, Betty's daughter Adeline to Henry W. DANGERFIELD in trust for daughter Lucy Ellen

.... 9 Aug 1860, codicil

boy little Charles to son Augustus

James TRICE .... 22 Feb 1769, inv & appr

fellows Sam, Abram, Daniel, wench Sukey, boy Isaac, wench Hosa, child Ballard, boys Will, Ralph, Jack, Harry, David, wench Sarah

Thomas WARE .... 20 June 1822, will

Isaac, Ellison, Joe, John, Plummer, Adam, Richard, George, Washington, Moses, Tom, Molly, Polly, Lucy, Betty to wife Sarah WARE & at her death a deed of gift to Charles S. EDWARDS; Esther & her children Joe (who is with Thomas FOSTER), Maria, Betty Jane or Jinny, Alarny, Delphy to granddaughter Emeline CHRISTIAN & if dies before age 20 to daughter Ann NEALE

MATHEWS

Mathews County was created by an act of 1790 to take effect on 1 May 1791. Most records were burned in Richmond on 3 April 1865, where they had been moved for safekeeping during the Civil War.

Alfred BILLUPS ....29 July 1845, deed
    Plenty & her 3 children Lucy, Charlotte, & Eliza to Edmond JONES, trustee to hold for Joice BILLUPS the wife & Octavia BILLUPS the daughter of Alfred BILLUPS

Edmond BORUM ....8 Feb 1798, will
    ¼ part of ½ of my negroes to my son John BORUM; ¼ part to grandsons William THORNTON & Benjamin BORUM; ¼ part of ½ of my negroes to my daughter Susanna GAYLE; ¼ part of ½ of my negroes to my daughter Mary MACHEN; the other ¼ part to be divided among all their children; the ½ of my negroes lent to my wife Mary BORUM shall after her death be equally divided among all my children and 2 grandchildren

John BORUM Sr. ....11 Jan 1842, bill of sale
    Sarah & her infant child without name to Sterling BORUM

William H. & Betsy CALLIS .... gdn acct
    division of negroes

Thomas EDWARDS ....29 May 1857, will
    negroes to wife Mary T. EDWARDS widow of Walter G. HUDGINS dec'd; son Charles H. EDWARDS to account for negroes advanced to him – he sold girl Courtney & boy Andrew; daughter Sarah F. AMISTEAD wife of Francis AMISTEAD to account for negroes advanced to her

William S. THURSTON ....8 Feb 1861, will
    all the slaves which I am entitled under the will of my father (except girl Violet daughter of Sally) men Tom, Jim, John to brother Edward T. THURSTON, if John refuses to move to Gloucester he may be sold; girl Violet daughter of Sally to sister Sarah M. ROSE, wife of John N. ROSE; Sally & her children to brother Edward T. THURSTON

MECKLENBURG

Created in 1764. Numerous loose records prior to 1783 are missing. Volumes that record deeds, court orders, and wills exist.

Joshua MOSS & others vs Exr of Joshua MOSS dec'd .... 18 Jan 1813, in Chancery

9 slaves given up by Elizabeth MOSS widow of Joshua MOSS dec'd for purpose of dividing among her children, first allotting 3 slaves of her choice

.... 14 Jan 1842, slaves sold

George & his wife Charlotte to Alexander PA__CAR; woman Rhoda, boy London to William B. ___WOOD; man Joseph, boy Byas to James WILLIAMSON; woman Elenor to James JONES; woman Lucy to Robert ___; Jinney to John O BRION

.... 5 Feb 1813, acct of sales

girl Betty to John SPEED; Cate, Frank, Jane the youngest child, Sam, Lucy to John OLIVER; boy Gilbert to Brown ___

Thomas REEKS .... 27 Apr 1846, will

Isaac, James, Jack, Cary, Finton & 4 children Lovlip, Harriet, Kitty, & Pantha, Maria & her child Rachel to wife Patsey C. REEKS, John, Barker, Osborne, Keziah, Mima to daughter Polly H. NORTHINGTON; Mima & her 2 children Phoebe & Keziah to daughter Elizabeth C. ROBERTS; man Reuben to son Thomas C. REEKS; Matilda & her child Lucy, Robert, Philip, Aaron, Hope, small girl Martha to daughter Margaret Anne; woman Eliza to daughter Elvira E. TARRY; executors to purchase 5 girls, one of which I give to my daughter Margaret Ann, the other 4 one each to my other 4 daughters Polly H. NORTHINGTON, Elizabeth C. ROBERTS, Francis HARRIS, & Elivra E. TARRY; woman Narsetta to daughter Francis and afterwards sold by Mrs. HARRIS

NANSEMOND

Nansemond County was created as Upper Norfolk County by 1640 and renamed Nansemond in 1646. Records were destroyed in three separate fires: the earliest consumed the house of the court clerk in April 1734 (where the records were kept at that time), the second was set by British troops in 1779, and the last occurred on 7 February 1866.

Aaron .... 14 Sept 1801, cert of freedom
    age 30, 6 ft, 9", emancipated by Thomas TROTTER

Edward ALLEN .... 18 May 1814, will
    allotment of negroes to be equally divided among sons Henry Jno ALLEN, Archibald ALLEN, Cornelius Edward ALLEN, & Thomas William Gilbert ALLEN; man James to son Henry Jno ALLEN

Diana Ash .... 8 Dec 1856, cert of freedom
    28 years old, 5 ft, 7" and identifying marks

Hetty Ash .... 12 Feb 1855, cert of freedom
    23 years, 5 ft, 3 ½" and identifying marks

William H. BAKER .... June 1798 – 9 Apr 1801, estate acct
    Bob, Cloe & children, Penn

William H. BAKER to John DORLON .... 4 Feb 1798, deed
    Will, Penn, Wallace, Miles, Ester, Bridget, Betty, Julia, Cloe & her child, J___ & her 3 children, Julia, Chuchaluck, Ned to John DORLON

Benjamin BAKER .... 6 Apr 1735, will
    boy Ned to son Richard BAKER; boy Jack to son Benjamin Blake BAKER; boy David to son William Henry BAKER; girl Nan to daughter Mary BAKER; girl Lucinda to daughter Julianna BAKER; girl Hannah to daughter Elizabeth BAKER; girl Belinda to daughter Emela BAKER; wench Cherry to Thomas BLUNT which he has in his possession

.... 10 July '05, bill of complaint
    David devised to William BAKER was sold with a number of others that had come to him from his father's estate

Richard BENNETT .... 1674, will

> to all servants & negroes each of them 1,000 pounds of tobacco, only the 2 hirelings excepted: Richard Higgins & John Turner; the rest of my personal & real estate to grandchild Richard BENNETT

Robert CARR .... 1 May 1773, will

> boy Harry to son Joshua CARR after his mother's death; fellows Sam, Venus, Pompey, wench Kate, Rose to wife Mary CARR; girl Jenny to daughter Elizabeth; boy Jim to daughter Martha CARR; boy Abram to daughter Lidia CARR; a negro of his choice to sons Robert, Mathew, & Titus CARR; remaining negroes to be divided among all my children

Samuel COWLING .... 16 Aug 1857, will

> girl Sal sold; wife Ann L. COWLING to select a girl; negroes not to be sold

Benjamin CROSS .... 29 May 1849, will

> negroes to be hired out

Hardy CROSS .... 20 June 1856, will

> Charles, Daughtry, Allen, Albert, Cate & children (Jackson, Isaiah & Caroline with all her smaller children), Angeline to wife Martha N. CROSS; woman Caroline except her oldest, Edith, to niece Sarah RAWLS; woman Edith now in the possession of Justin RAWLS to niece Martha SMITH; girl Mary to niece Margaret CROSS; boy Kadas to niece Martha Susan EA_LEY; boy Willis to nephew William H. CROSS; woman Peg to nephew Patrick H. DAUGHTNEY & the dower right of the negro slaves held by Mrs. Elizabeth HAYNES; boy Jackson to nephew Edwin SMITH; girl Mary, Veria to Mary Effa SMITH daughter of Edwin SMITH; girl Adalaney to Margaret Maria SMITH daughter of Edwin SMITH; 25 – 30 slaves already given to daughter Mary Louisa

....20 June 1856, codicil

> man Anderson, now blind, & wife & children held by my wife as dower, Anderson to Dr. George W. PEETE for eye surgery; negroes in wife's possession at our marriage not be be included in my estate

Dennis .... 13 Feb 1797, free negro cert

> age 31, 5 ft 8 ¾" freed by Willis PITT

Jacob DICKINSON .... 11 Sept 1798 estate acct
   hire of: Isaac, Harry, Charles, Nero, Billy, Nanny, Sam; Nanny, Sam, Grace & child sold

Mary DICKINSON .... 16 Mar 1796, in Chancery
   sons Henry & William DICKINSON seized all lands & slaves & refuse to assign dower; property to be divided - Lot 1: Isaac, Nero, Violett, Willis, Peter, Deck to Henry DICKINSON; Lot 2: Charles, Harry, Nanny, Violett, James to Jacob DICKINSON; Lot 3: Sam, Bob, Grace, Dick, Frank, Dinah to William DICKINSON

John FRENCH .... 26 Sept 1839, will
   negroes acquired by intermarriage with my present wife back to her

Ralph GIBBS vs Nathaniel GRAY .... 18 May 1799, District Court
   Sam, China, Nan, Judah, Tony, November, Ned, Isaac; Ralph GIBBS to recover against the cost

James GOODMAN .... 4 June 1845, will
   Cader, Burton & wife Amey, Noar Sr., Willis, Nancy, Sam, Penny to wife Pricilla GOODMAN, after her death Cader, Burton, Sam, Nancy, old Penny, Amery to brother Barnes GOODMAN's son James GOODMAN; girl Betty to sister Cheary DAUGHTNEY; man Sam in their possession to John LANGSTON wife Nancy LANGSTON; boy Cader, girls Marthey, Sealy to niece Susan DAUGHTNEY ; man Sam to James B. GOODMAN; Noar Sr., Willis Sr., to Benjamin RIDDICK; boy Noar to sister Cheary DAUGHTREY son Barnes DAUGHTREY; Armistead, Jorden, Prentise, Willis bought of James PARKER dec'd, Mandey & 2 children Bob & her youngest child a boy, Sally & 2 children Harry & a girl to Barnes GOODMAN; boy Gilbert to Barnes DAUGHTREY

John HARTWELL .... 1 Jan 1806, will
   man Orange to be free

Brumage HEFFINGTON to William H. WHITEHEAD ....
   .... 4 Mar 1843, deed
   (listed under HEFFINGTON, Bromager to Trst of Wm B WHITEHEAD of the 3rd part)
   man Cyrus to William H. WHITEHEAD

Thomas HOLLOWAY .... 10 Apr 1798, will

    negroes to wife, at her death divided among her children & if there are no children to be freed

Exum JENKINS .... 20 Nov 1857, will

    Sam, Nat, Jaky, Dina, Lewis, Harry, Mendy to wife Elizabeth JENKINS; Cary Jr., Rufus, Jack, Tom, Netty, Billy, Sallie, Lucy, Oliver to daughter Leora B. JENKINS; Chloe, Nelson, Joseph, Dallas, Taylor, Osco, Charlotte, Fannie, Mira, Franklin, Mourning, Anthony, Ben to daughter Lucretia J. LANGSTINE wife of Isaac LANGSTINE; man Abram to daughter Sophia Ann HASLETT wife of Jethro HASLETT; Anderson, Ned, Barbara, Agga, Jim, Stephen, Dick, Adeline, big Carry, Edmund to son John B. JENKINS; if man Drew is disobedient he can be sold

Solomon JOHNSON .... 29 Nov 1852, will

    negroes to be hired out for heirs of daughter Nancy

Ann JORDAN .... 29 Mar 1829, will

    Christopher, Nany, Maria, Jim, Jack to be free

Jacob KEELING Sr. .... 8 Jan 1844, will

    Nancy, Matilda & her 2 boy children, Ann, Sam the son of Sam Sr. whom I purchased of Richard RIDDICK to wife Charlotte KEELING; James Jr., Nat, Joe Sr., Joe Jr., James Sr., Jerry, Amy & her 2 daughters to son John W. KEELING; Nancy, Matilda & her 2 boy children, Ann, Sam loaned to my wife during her life, Anthony, Max, John to grandchildren Sarah, Arthur, Lucretia, & William WILSON Jr.

John R. & Martha KILBY to James M. Mile .... 29 Dec 1866, deed

    land to James M. Miles (a colored man)

John R. KILBY Trst. to William B. WHITEHEAD ....
.... 24 Aug 1843, deed

    Amelia & her children Sukey, Lizzy, Washington, Sam, & Harriet from David HENDERSON in Deed of Trust of 6 Aug 1842 to John R. KILBY; man Luke to William B. WHITEHEAD

John LAWRENCE .... 7 May 1795, will
> Bob, Mingo, Doll, Hannah, Beck, Rachel to wife Phoebe LAWRENCE; man Jim to son Lemuel LAWRENCE, at his death to grandson Jonas LAWRENCE; man Pocker to granddaughters Mary MOORE & Elizabeth COTTON daughters of James DICKINSON dec'd; man Pierce to 5 grandchildren sons & daughters of daughter Martha DICKINSON & John DICKINSON; girl Dinah to granddaughter Patsy CARR daughter of John CARR dec'd; woman Rose & her children to daughter Abigail LEE

Elizabeth LAWRENCE .... 27 Sept 1739, will
> woman Nan, girl Nanny to eldest son Michael LAWRENCE & Susanna his wife; negroes to daughter Sarah; girl Sarah to daughter Pleasant BENTON wife of John BENTON; girls Moll, Beck to daughter Isabella; girl ____ to granddaughter Martha wife of John MACHEY

Joseph J. LAWRENCE .... 14 Mar 1864, will
> all slaves except those given by Deed of Gift to wife Mary

Michael LAWRENCE to John LAWRENCE ....26 July 1754, deed
> M__, Tony, possibily others

John LEAR .... 12 Nov 1695, will
> boy Charles, girl Nancy to Charles COVINGTON; Jack, Vido to John GEORGE

Solomon McClure his Exr to John R.KILBY .... 18 Jan 1854, deed
> Solomon McClure is a free negro

Andrew MEADE .... 8 Aug 1744, will
> negro stock to grandson David CURLE

John W. MILES to Owen R. FLYNN trustee for Andrew McALISTER....
.... 8 Oct 1841, deed
> Monroe to Owen R. FLYNN to sell?

Moses of Boon .... 14 Aug 1848, cert of freedom
> age 30, 5 ft, 5", and identifying marks was free born

Rachel of Ash .... 11 June 1832, free negro cert
  age 42, 5 ft 1", free born

Jacob RANDOLPH .... Jan 1798 – 12 Apr 1800, estate acct
  Ben

Jacob RANDOLPH .... 4 Mar 1797, will
  children of color Joe Taylor, Peter Nobby, Agge

Randolph .... 20 Apr 1799, free negro cert
  age 21 years & 4 months, 5 ft 7", emancipated by Archibald WHITE on 14 Sept 1795

Uriah RAWLS Jr. to William B. WHITEHEAD .... 9 July 1841, deed
  Trecy & child Jacob, woman Claressa, boy Henry, girl Cate, boy Nathan to Edwin SMITH, sheriff, to be sold; Trecy & child Jacob, woman Clarissa, boy Henry, girl Cate, boy Nathan, men Cyrus Jr., Sam to John R. KILBY; Uriah RAWLS Jr. to remain in possession of all the negro slaves until a sale is actually made

Josiah RIDDICK .... 16 Sept 1838, will
  Ann age 15 the daughter of Phillis, Fabries 12, Willis 9, Millicent 10, & James 8, children of Maria to be free, females at age 18, males at age 21; Moses, Beit, Albert, Fester, Zelpha, Maria, Lydia, Lucy, William, Matilda, Jennie to nephew Josiah RIDDICK Jr. also the slaves liberated in this will

Robin .... 26 Sept 1782, manumission
  age 23, freed by John PORTER

Samuel .... 19 Sept 1782, manumission
  age 7; Ann PORTER, owner, to act as guardian until he reaches age 21

Jesse R. SAVAGE to John R. KILBY .... 14 Oct 1859, deed
  sheriff to sell George, slave of of Gilbert W. GRAY; purchased by John R. KILBY

Arthur SMITH .... 25 Aug 1838, will
  girl Lucy to daughter Martha Jane Louisa SMITH

Arthur SMITH .... 26 Nov 1849, inv & appr
   Lucy & 2 children, 1 two years old, the other a child

John WARDROP .... 9 Oct 1765, will
   all negoes to wife Ann WARDROP until daughters & sons come of age or marry & at her death to be divided among children sons John, Alexander, & daughters Elizabeth, Margaret, Ann, & Lillias

Matthew I. WHITE .... 20 Aug 1840, will
   man Jack, obtained by marriage with her, to wife Eliza K.

Daniel WILLIAMS .... 21 May 1767, will
   Cate, Isabell, More, Venus to wife Mourning WILLIAMS to be sold at her decease

Robert WILLIS .... 1798, deed of gift
   fellow Lewis to son David WILLIS

John S. WILLS to Thomas J. KILBY Trus .... 3 Aug 1838, deed
   man Newsom to Thomas J. KILBY trustee of Samuel H. HOLLAND to be sold

Ann WODDROP .... 7 Sept 1785, will
   Tom, Bailey, Essex. Jack, Fortune, Junn, Boller, woman Congo to son Alexander WODDROP

Charles WRENN to Sally K. GODWIN ....
   .... 30 Jan 1834, marriage settlement
   Daniel, Jeffrey, Sam, Luke, Rachel, Caroline, Nelly, Pallas, Cherry, Rose property of Sally K. GODWIN

John YEATES .... 18 Sept 1731, will
   Bess, negroes

NEW KENT

New Kent County was created in 1654. Records were destroyed when John Posey set fire to the courthouse on 15 July 1787. Many records were lost when the courthouse was partially destroyed by fire during Civil War hostilities in 1862. Additional records were burned in Richmond on 3 April 1865, where they had been moved for safekeeping during the Civil War.

John ALFORD .... 1 May 1726, will

    Tom, Jack, Jeminy, Sue, Bess, Lucy, Sam, Charles, Jenny to daughters Elizabeth, Unity, & Charity ALFORD

William ARMISTEAD .... 20 May 1791, codicil

    Bob, Peter, Sam, Gilbert, Betty, Edey, Sarah, Nell to be free now, children Sally, Ned, Esther, Gilly, Edey, Nancy to be free as they arrive to the age of 21; Stepney at the end of 3 years, Fanny, Gary at the end of 2 years, John at the age of 21

.... 17 Apr 1827

    Sarah, the woman mentioned in the forgoing, was mother to Nancy (also mentioned among the children therein named) and Nancy grew up, came to Richmond, & became the mother of John, alias John Warden, now at work at Miss COSBY's

Frances BARHAM .... 3 May 1851, will

    girl Lena to daughter Martha WOODWARD

Charles BINNS .... 2 Sept 1851, will

    Lott, Wieson, Tom, Cary, Stephen, Beverly, Betsy & her 2 children Robert & William to nephew Otway P. BINNS; Martha, Ann, Lucy, Albert, Charles, Delia, Nancy to niece Martha E. BINNS daughter of Charles H. BINNS & Martha E. his wife; J_done, Henry, Davy, Doctor, Dick, Sam, Louisa, Amy, Harriet, Lockey & her 2 children Fleming & Maria Louisa to be divided among Charles H. BINNS' children at his death; old Elly, old Aggy to be supported by nephew Charles H. BINNS

.... 13 Aug 1851, codicil

    man Beverly given to nephew Otway P. BINNS be revoked & given to friend John Henry CHRISTIAN?

Elizabeth CHAMBERLAYNE to William ACRILL ... 10 Mar 1738, bond
I, Elizabeth CHAMBERLAYNE, am bound unto William ACRILL...no provision for child Ann KIDLEY born after husband's death...several slaves to wife for life; slaves of plantation in Goochland County purchased of one Stephen HUGHES & all slaves devised by husband M__ CHAMBERLAYNE's will, also Dick, Peace, Pegg purchased since husband's decease the said Ann KIDLEY to have said land & slaves after the decease of said Elizabeth

William CLARKE .... 30 Dec 1842, will
girl Barbary to son James CLARKE

William CLAYTON vs. Ann Kidley POSEY ....
....14 Nov 1789, in Chancery
Ann Kidley POSEY widow of John Price POSEY dec'd, Mary of Martha POSEY's children of the said John P. POSEY & infants under the age of 21

Jeffrey, Hagar & her child Moses, Absalom, Molly Brown & her child, David, Forest, Priss, Annaka, Sam, Possom, Michael, Davy, Sarah & her 2 children, Jenny & her child James sold at auction

William CLAYTON vs. Armistead RUSSELL .... 12 Nov 1792, judgment
defendant took & sold negroes

Mildred CRUMP .... 15 May 1837, will
negroes to be sold after death of my sister Mary CRUMP

Moses DAVIS .... 1687/88, will
woman ___ to wife

John ELLYSON .... 7 Jan 1783, manumission
Peter, Lucy, Taner, Cate, Frank, Milia, Robert, Daniel, Roper, Elizabeth, Amy, Jemima, Sarah, Mary, Jane, William to be free

William GRAY to widow of William CHAMBERLAYNE ....
....3 Aug 1744, marriage record
negroes

Samuel JORDAN .... 2 Oct 1718, will
 wife Elizabeth to keep negroes until last child comes of age then to be divided among them

Sarah Lewis .... 7 Jan 1783, free negro regis
 31 years of age, 5 ft 1", emancipated by John ELLYSON

Gideon MACON .... 25 Sept 1767, will
 girl Mildred, Jack, girl Nancy to son Edmund MACON; wench Bess, boy Billy Boller, girl Cate to wife Rebecca MACON & at her death divided between daughers Elizabeth MACON & Rebecca Walker MACON

Sarah MACON .... 1 Sept 1847, will
 servant Tom to son Thomas L. DABNEY; servant Mary Jane & all her children to daughter Mary S. NELSON
 .... 1 June 1849, codicil
 I have disposed of certain slaves conveyed to me by my late husband William H. MACON

Samuel MEREDITH .... 22 Jan 1838, will
 negroes to be divided between children Albert F., Martha A.E., & Mary F. MEREDITH & my wife's daughter Elizabeth TRO_VER

Charles PEARSON .... 16 May 1855, will
 slaves to wife except those otherwise disposed of by this will; girl Fanny to daughter Sarah; girl Agnes to daughter Mary BACON
 .... 1 Oct, 1857, codicil
 girl Parthena to daughter Robinette CRUMP wife of George P. CRUMP
 .... 5 Apr 1860, codicil
 Agnes to go to the general distribution of my estate

John Price POSEY .... 25 July 1789, appr
 man Day Gun, boys Absalom, Billy Collins
 .... 14 Nov 1789 – _4 Jan 1790, estate acct
 Davy, Absalom, small boy Billy sold to Mrs. POSEY

.... 10 Mar & 12 Nov 1792, judgment
> judgment against Armistead RUSSELL for selling part of the mortgaged negroes

.... 6 Jul 1791 - 12 Nov 1793
> man Moses claimed by C.M. TALBOT

Armistead RUSSELL vs Exrs of Austin HEWLETT ....
.... 14 Mar 1794, judgment
> woman Molly Brown seesed (seized?) by sheriff; sold although William CLAYTON under a mortgage which he charges to have been made to him of the said slave hath forbid the sale

John SHERMER .... 11 June 1766, will
> wife Ann SHERMER to have full power & authority over slaves

James STAMPER .... 4 Feb 1853, will
> Nancy & her 2 children Eliza & Isaac, boy Murray to daughter Octavia E. who calls herself Bettie

Francis TIMBERLAKE .... 6 Apr 1794, will
> man Riger to be free on his paying 5 pounds per year to the support of Patty & her children; man Isham to be free during the term of his servitude on his paying 5 pounds per year to be applied to the support of Patty & her children & old Davy; Patty & her children Amey, Aaron, Alley, Clary, & Martha to be free; Venus & her child Avery to be free; man Sam's bond to nephew Armistead HILLIARD; girl Mary to Sally HILLIARD daughter of Richard HILLIARD until she reaches age 25 & then freed

Mary TYREE .... 29 Mar 1836, will
> little child Louisa to daughter Mary & her husband Edmund HOWLE; woman Sylvia to William B. MORECOCK & Thomas E. DAVIS in trust for my 2 daughters Nancy WRIGHT & Matilda BINNS

John VAIDEN .... 20 Dec 1783, div of slaves
> man Micael, wench Hannah, girl Elvey, boy Richard, child Betty
>
> Micael, Betty to to Jerimiah VAIDEN; Elvey, Richard to Isaac VAIDEN; wench Hannah to Henry VAIDEN

Bartlett WILLIAMS .... 10 Jan 1791, manumission
Aggy, Clara & her children Wilson, Jane, Nancy, Lavin, Gabe, Sam, Jerry, & Jim to be free

NOTTOWAY

Nottoway County was created by an act of 1788 to take effect on 1 May 1789. Many records were destroyed or heavily mutilated in 1865 by Union troops during the Civil War. A few volumes that record deeds, court orders, and wills exist

Alexander BRUCE Sr. .... 7 Sept 1795, will

Jim, Doll, John to wife Ann BRUCE; Peter, Isham to son Woodson BRUCE; Jesse to son James BRUCE; girl Silva to daughter Lucy BRUCE; girl Molly to daughter Janey BRUCE; boy Charles to son Lamma BRUCE; boy Dick to son Armsted BRUCE; girl Aggy to daughter Ridley ELLINGTON; remaining negroes to be divided among my children Prudence HUDSON, Rachal CLAY, Polly CUSHENBURY, Lamma, Alexander, Armisted, Woodson, James, & Janey BRUCE

Allain CRENSHAW .... 1 Mar 1842, will

negroes to wife Mary CRENSHAW & at her death to be divided into 7 equal parts; negroes to choose own masters

William CROSS .... 1 June 1801, will

Jack, Jenny, Jim, Easter & her child Sucky, __arn, Dick, Milly the youngest child of Sarah, Cinow, Rose, Asabell, Hall, to wife Rebecca; remaining negroes & those which I may be entitled at the death of my mother to be hired out; William Ellis COCKE to have first choice of all my negoes

Charles A. CRUMP .... 6 Apr 1861, will

negroes might be sold

Elizabeth DAVIS .... 12 June 1813, will

negroes except little Dick, Sterling, Nancy & her youngest child to son Thomas DAVIS; woman Clitty to granddaughter Elizabeth DAVIS daughter of my daughter Elizabeth by John DAVIS; Nancy & her youngest child to be sold; negroes to be sold after death of son Thomas DAVIS; boy Allen, man Freeman now in his possession to son Matthew DAVIS; little Dick to William Watkins ELMORE son of Elizabeth ELMORE; boy Sterling to daughter Rebecca ELMORE

Jacob DAVIS.. 23 May 1794, will
> girl Silvia to son Jacob DAVIS; boy Tony to son Mathew DAVIS; boy Peter to son Stephen DAVIS; girl Suckey to daughter Rebecca ELMORE; girl Betty to daughter Nancy HIGHTOWER; woman Isabella to son Thomas DAVIS; girl Patt to daughter Elizabeth DAVIS; Bob, Sylla, Rachel, Nancy, Bristor, Boatswain, Kate, Freeman, Will, Dick to wife Elizabeth DAVIS

Reuben H. DEJAMATTE & wife vs Joseph TODD & wife......................
.... 1 July 1847, in Chancery
> Rachel DEJAMATTE had slaves as her dower widow of Bowler DEJAMATTEs...distribution of estate...his children Reuben H. DEJAMATTE, John DEJAMATTE, Martha W. DEJAMATTE who has married William C. RUDD, & Judith W. DEJAMATTE who has married Joseph TODD...division of slaves should take place...

Thomas DICKINSON .... 5 May 1860, will
> negroes on Bellgrove Plantation to brothers William & John; the balance of negroes to be divided among Mary A., William P., Asa D. DICKINSON & the children of my niece Elizabeth G. KNIGHT dec'd; old woman Dilsey; negroes to remain as families in division; all children & grandchildren of old woman Dilsey to William P. & Asa D. DICKINSON

Mary DUPUY .... 20 Mar 1793, will
> woman Nancy to nephew Milton FORD; boy Charles to nephew Samuel FORD; girl Ancy, Rachel & her child Milton to nephew Waller FORD; girl Patty to niece Mary OVERTON; girl Milly to niece Lucy MORDIGS; boy Elijah to niece Ann FORD; Betty & her child Mary & her child Morning, Lucy, man Peter, Lucy her 2 children Jenny & Keziah to nephew Thomas GEERS; boy Sam to nephew Robert GEERS; boy Davy to Anne OLIVER daughter of John OLIVER dec'd; girl Tabitha to nephew Zachary FORD

Francis DYSON .... 6 Jan 1866, will
> Jesse, Louisa, Randol to daughter H.I. DYSON to be sold or divided

Francis EPES .... 8 July 1833, will
> 6 negroes to sons Francis & Thomas W.; negroes to son Peter; 1/3 part of slaves to wife Sarah G. EPES; 3 slaves loaned to daughter Sarah MIDDLETON...a part of her share; boy Simon to son Francis

Francis FITZGERALD...7 July 1859, will
    old Lewis, Prudence, Mary, Rachel & her son Cornelius, Phil, Harry, Thomas, Mariah & her children Ben & Booker, Sally & her child Richard, Ann & her child not named to son George; Booker, Diana, Nathan, Allen, Mary, Jane, Nancy, Frank, Charles, Fanny, old Nelly to son Charles W.; Nanny, Edward, Robert, William, Sambo, Joseph, Cloe, Martha, Frances, Frank, Grace & her son Jim to son James H.; Aggy & her children Sidney, Branch, Prudence, Nathan, Mary to son Charles W.

William FOWLKES...18 Aug 1834, will
    big Dick, Asa, Solomon, Eliza, Paul, Elizajane, Aden, Branch, Delia, Sylvy, little Bush to wife Sally FOWLKES; Booker, Dicy, Mary, Parker, Miner to son Hiram FOWLKES; man Tom to son Rafe FOWLKES; man Mondica to son Edward B. FOWLKES; man Ben, woman Cindy to son William C. FOWLKES; Julian, Vilett, Nelson, Fanny, Keziah, Peter & others which they hold to sons Opie & Ranson FOWLKES; Ned, Hardy, Hogin, Phillis, Abby, little Joe to son Kennen FOWLKES; Josey, Martha, Louisa, Rachel, Syfox to daughter Pamelia FOWLKES; said children to return the negroes they received into the estate for equal distribution; slaves to be sold at the discretion of executers: Ned, Peter, little Dick, Abraham, David, Tunin, little Essex, Jack, Archer, Jesse, Rolling, Henry, Peter, Meles, Molly, Jerry, Sam, Manuel, Peg, Nelly, Ann, Molly, Martha, Ann, Jane, Hanner, Manda, Nancy, Sam, Daniel, Harriet, Patience, Edmund, Sophia, Matilda, William, Parker, Labia, Sindi, Letty, Lucy, Jeanings, Susan, Winny, Joe; the money divided among children Rafe, Edward B., William C., Opie, Ranson, Kenner, & Pamelia FOWLKES; Ana to son William C. FOWLKES; Rafe FOWLKES' part to be divided among his 5 children: William A., Samuel H., Nancy B. FOWLKES & Martha E. K__TON; Edward B. FOWLKES to be trustee for Nancy B. FOWLKES portion

Reuben GILLIAM...20 Dec 1823, deed
    man Ned, Hannah & her child Rachel to Richard Y. BLAND

Reuben GILLIAM...9 July 1822, deed
    Hannah, Ned, Simon to John MADDUX in trust

Burwell GUNN .... 2 Jan 1855, will

negroes that I have already given to my children James W. GUNN, William B. GUNN, Jamima J. ROGERS, Mary B. MA__, & Henrietta K. WELLS; Lucy & her child, Richard, Brian to daughter Sarah F. SHACKLEFORD; Peter, Martha Ann to son Elisha G. GUNN; Joe, Emily to son Roth C. GUNN; Julianna, ___ to daughter Ann E. GUNN; Minerva, Henry Wilson to son Thomas J. GUNN; at wife's death Jane to granddaughter Laura A.H. SHACKLEFORD

Daniel H. HARDAWAY .... 1 Oct 1853, will

1/3 slaves in my possession to wife Sarah Ann, not those in possession of my mother at my death; remainder to be divided among children

Phillip HAWKES .... 25 Nov 1845, will

Aggy & her children, man Crawley, boy John Archer, boy Edward Branch to George A. HAWKES until Aggy's children arrive at the age of 21 then be set free; if he misbehaves man Crawley to hire out for 5 years and then be free; man Daniel to George A. HAWKES until Aggy's youngest child arrives at the age of 21 then be set free; Delphia & Harriet (2 of Aggy's children)

Reuben HAWKES .... 17 Oct 1844, will

Daniel to select his master; Fanny & her children Armistead, James, Louisa, Branch, & Henry to Alexander H. HAWKES & to have their liberty when youngest reached age 21

Jane JACKSON .... 27 Mar 1856, will

girl Fanny to granddaughter Susan Jane THOMPSON daughter of Ty__ B. JACKSON; boy John to grandson John L. JACKSON son of Thomas JACKSON; girl Olive to granddaughter Lucy Jane JACKSON daughter of Thomas JACKSON; girl Emily to granddaughter Virginia Mir__ JACKSON daughter of Thomas JACKSON; boy Albert to grandson Thomas L. JACKSON; boy H__ to grandson Richard Worth JACKSON; girl Maria to grandson Edwin B. JACKSON; boy Henry to grandson William H. JACKSON; Julia & the balance of her children not disposed of to son Thomas JACKSON

Robert P. JENNINGS .... 3 Dec 1862, will
> Nancy & her children Richard, Eliza, Mary & George to be free & also Elnora & George Boler children of Eliza; Jordan, Caty & her child Caty to nephew Henry Archer JENNINGS; boy Calvin to Rotert H. JENNINGS son of Henry Archer JENNINGS; Hannah, William, Henry to nephew William M. JENNINGS; Taylor, Sarah, Peter to nephew James R. JENNINGS; Sam, Sally & child to niece Patty ROBERT__; Wyath to nephew Richard OLIVER, Charles to Micajah OLIVER; Isaac to Joseph _. OLIVER; Dolly to Molly OLIVER; Linda to Martha OLIVER; Delia & her 2 children Ella & Roger to George W. OLIVER's 3 youngest children George W., Iman, & Ann OLIVER; Dinah to Betty; Armistead to Bruce; Miranda to Elvira all children of brother Micajah; Peter, Addin to brother Joseph JENNINGS

Albert A. & Susan C.I. JETER to John WILSON .... 25 Jan 1844, deed
> negroes

Catherine JONES to Joseph Addison JONES .... 3 Nov 1858, deed
> Harry & his wife Chancy & their 2 sons Solomon & Aser, her daughters Martha Ann, & Julia Johnson & her child Royal Souter Betsy & her child Alice to Joseph Addison JONES in trust for me & remain in my possession

Elizabeth JONES .... 10 Nov 1853, deed
> to Travis H. EPES & Thomas H. CAMPBELL of 2nd part & Catherine JONES, Eleanor JONES, & Sarah F. JONES of 3rd part ...slaves...

James JONES .... 9 Oct 1845, will
> slaves to wife; James Oliver son of Agnes to his wife Maria Cooper a free woman of color after death of my wife but he will remain with his wife in Richmond; Agnes' 2 daughters Patty Martin & Mary

Joseph Addison JONES to Thomas H. CAMPBELL ....
.... 19 Dec 1855, deed
> slaves except James Oliver & Patty Martin & her children to Thomas H. CAMPBELL

Judith W. JONES vs Elizabeth Chamberlain JONES ....
.... 3 Jan 1828, in court

    Tom, Dinah, Brannum, George, Sally, Allen, Pleasant, Solomon, Aggy, Isabel, Jenny, Susan, Miles, Nancy, Eliza Jones, Catherine, Mary, Polly, Nathan allotted to the legatees of said Peter JONES, dec'd; Patram, Rowland, Asa to John H. KNIGHT

Sterling LAMBERT .... 2 Sept 1827, will

    Burwell, Solomon to be sold

Richard S. MARSHALL .... 16 May 1860, will

    8 negroes to children; daughter Martha's negro with her children I give to her (woman Taylor)

Anderson B. MILLER .... 28 Jan 1858, will

    girl Molly to daughter Emma

John MILLS .... 8 Oct 1822, will

    Bolling, Dick, Mima, Rachel, Jenny, Huny to daughter Patsy TANDY's children; Aggy, Daniel, Stephen, _usery dec'd, Ned, Stan to daughter Sally WATKINS; Peter, Burwell, Fanny, Lucy, Charles to daughter Nancy

John ROBERTSON .... 10 Aug 1855, will

    Isaac, Becky, Rhoda, Matilda, Lewis alias Martin to wife Melvina J. ROBERTSON

Peter ROBINSON .... 19 Nov 1814, will

    ½ the slaves I got by my wife to Nancy GHOLSON & her 2 children William YATES & Cary Ann; the other half of the slaves to Sally Taylor CARY sister of Nancy GHOLSON, George B. CARY, & Charlotte L. CARY

Elizabeth SYDNOR .... 21 July 1814, will

    woman Jenny to daughter Jane LAMKIN

Eliza J. WILLIAMS .... 5 Mar 1853, will

    Creary, Clay to son Joel B. WILLIAMS; Am_ & her children to daughter Sarah B. STREET; Joanna, Su_ea to son Richard H. WILLIAMS; girls Susan, Lucy to daughter Camelia R. WILLIAMS;

girls Nancy, Eliza to daughter Martha V. WILLIAMS; Enos, Liddy to son Thomas W. WILLIAMS; Tazwell, Rhody to daughter Anna L. WILLIAMS; Moses, Minah to son James L. WILLIAMS; Jamy, Winney to son Frank S. WILLIAMS; 2 negroes apiece to sons David D. & William O. WILLIAMS; Mary, Julia, Helen to daughter Mary A. WILLIAMS; remaining negroes kept for the benefit of my single daughter & 5 youngest children, James & Frank

Thomas R. WILLIAMS .... 14 July 1798, will

James, Tom & his wife Patty, Izbel, Grace, Patty & her 6 children Abram, M___ier, Sinder, Pompy, Amelia, & Phebe, Nancy & her 7 children Simon, Amos, Harry, Amica, Sally, Nanny, & Molly, Ben, Joe, Luis, to wife Catherine WILLIAMS, at her death 1/12 part to son William WILLIAMS, also boy Anthony to him; the remainder at her death to be divided among 11 children; girl Peggy now in the possession of William IRBY to daughter Elizabeth IRBY & to be returned to the estate at daughter's death; girl Dolly to daughter Catharine EPES; girl Phillis to daughter Rachel EPES; boy David to son David G. WILLIAMS; girl Clarissa to daughter Sarah G. WILLIAMS; boy Vivian to son James T. WILLIAMS; boy Limehouse to son Joseph G. WILLIAMS; boy Truman to son Samuel G. WILLIAMS; girl Susannah to daughter Martha G. WILLIAMS; girl Betty to daughter Lettice G. WILLIAMS; girl Cloe to daughter Ann A. WILLIAMS; Jesse, Burrel, Betty, Pheby to executors in trust for son Thomas WILLIAMS; boy Mingoe son of Judah to grandson Thomas R. EPES; boy Tom son of Patty to grandson John EPES; remaining negroes to be divided among children; Sinder, Pompy, Amica, Sally, Nanny interlined before signed, sealed, & acknowledged

Charles WILSON .... 5 June 1818, will

Sam, Will, Ned, Joe, Letty, Milly & her children to wife Rachel WILSON; blacksmith ___ to sons John WILSON & William B. WILSON; blacksmith Isham to son-in-law Thomas JORDON; Fanny, Lucy, __y & her children, Fillis & her children, Gilbert, Amey as 4th lot & to remain in possession of executors for daughter Elizabeth JORDAN wife of Thomas JORDAN

Jane WINN .... 21 June 1851, will

Lewis, Phill to daughter Mary P. GUY wife of Warren W. GUY

Peter WINN .... 9 May 1839, will
   man Phill, interest in man Lewis to mother Jane WINN

James S. WRIGHT .... 10 Apr 1856, will
   son William Thomas Jr. to take charge of slaves

PRINCE GEORGE COUNTY

Created by an act of 1788 to take effect on 1 May 1789. Many records were destroyed or heavily mutilated in 1865 by Union troops during the Civil War. A few volumes that record deeds, court orders, and wills exist.

Mary AVERY .... 28 Nov 1853, will

    servants to brother George; Jane, the wife of my husband's man Daniel, to my husband John AVERY

John BAIRD .... 13 Dec 1825, will

    man Tom & his wife Dinah, men Fred, Edward, girl Judy, woman Evie, my boy Jack to son Colin; girl Becky to son Herbert's oldest daughter

Robert BATTE .... 8 Feb 1805, will

    Aggy & part of her children except Sally to daughter Mary EPES; Lilly & all her children to daughter Martha CALLEY; Betty, Sally, Charles to Milly's children; Peter, Fanny & child to Fanny; Moses, Arter, Frank to Archy

Peter BRICHETT Sr. .... 9 Jan 1852, will

    Robert to son William G. BRICHETT; Nat to son Peter BRICHETT Jr.; girl Maria to granddaughter Mary S. WEBB; remaining slaves to wife Martha BRICHETT

James BLAIR .... 14 May 1770, will

    Billy Mankey, John Cesar, Jenny, Betty to wife Ann BLAIR; Billy, Frank, Catchena to son Archibald BLAIR; Ben, Sall, Joshua to son John BLAIR; Jack, Amy, Nan to daughter Marion BLAIR; Jenny, Judy, Dick to daughter Henrietta Maria BLAIR; Sucky, Molly, old Jeanny to daughter Ann BLAIR

Theodonick BLAND/BLUND .... June 1858, will

    all negroes to wife Mary B. BLAND/BLUND

Robert BONNER to Charles DUNCAN .... 18 Feb 1765, bill of sale

    fellow Dennis, wench Nan, girl Mall, boy Arthur to Charles DUNCAN

Randolph Brandon .... 21 Sept 1829, letter of emancipation

    Randolph Brandon emancipated by Richard RANDOLPH

Bridget et al vs John TUCKER .... Sept term 1812, Superior Court

    Bridget, Sall, Frank, Pat, James, Bob, Roger, Dick, Billy, Jim, George, Dinah, Viney, Maria, Celia, Catherine, Caroline, Jenny, Jacob, Kizzy, Frances, Rachel, Lizzy

    Special verdict: the Plantiffs are lineally descended in the maternal line from a native American Indian, named Bess, who was of the Appalachian tribe of Indians...and kept as a slave by Robert HICKS...found free & not slaves

William BROWN .... 5 Dec 1775, will

    Deds, Daniel, Letty, Dafney, Delphy, Will, Yunker, Matt, Harry, Surry, Davey, Robin to wife Sarah BROWN; Nancy, Simon, long Betty, Sukey, Jane, Will, short Betty, Hanner, Beck, Sall, Billy, Mingo, Winney, Burrill, Moses, Beck, Jack, Abraham, Molly, Jenny, Joe, Pat, Davey, Surrey, Pat, Molly, Silvey to brother Beverly BROWN; Doll, Judy, Hanner, Sam, Doll, Nanny to grandson William PACHAM; Lucy, James, Collin, Davey, Younker, Nat to grandson William BATTE; Harry, Robin, Phebe, Rose to daughter Elizabeth PROBY daughter of Servante PROBY

John BUTLER .... court date 13 Jan 1778, will

    Jenny, Frank, Silvey, Plats, Pool, old Ben, old Sue & her 4 children Collin, Peter, Jeffry & Aaron; young Sue, Simon, Bess, David, Cats to daughter Mary BUTLER; Hannah & her 3 sons Andrew, James, & George; little Ben, old Tom, girl Molly to daughter Sarah BATE; all negroes heretofore given to daughter Hizabeth JAMISON; old Toby, Hannah his wife, little Tom to be sold – if not sold then to daughter Sarah

Thomas BURGH .... 20 May 1751, will

    negroes to be divided between wife Mary BURGH & children Martha P. MITTO, Priscilla, James, Nath, Amy, Martha, Frederick, Woodde, Alexander, & Sara BURGH

Collin COCKE vs John S. EPES .... 7 Feb 1823, deed of trust

    James to John S. EPES

Polly M. COCKE .... 2 Jan 1809, will

    Amey, Abraham, Bet to sister Kitty WALKER; woman Maria to sister Susanna WILLCOX

Thomas P. COCKE .... 14 Dec 1831, will

    girl Betsy Bolling to half-sister Alice WYATT; boy Edward to nephew William COLE; boy Jim to nephew John COLE; girl Marsha to niece Ann WYATT; remaining slaves to brother James B. COCKE, sister Elizabeth COLE & sister Margaret WYATT

Carter H. EDLOE .... 20 Mar 1838, will

    slaves to be transported to any free state or colony as they prefer; if any slaves prefer to remain in slavery they are to be divided in two equal parts for nieces Elizabeth & Mary; the negroes under age at my death have until they are 21 to decide whether will will go or remain; to slave Harriet Barber & her children to remain on the estate & be free whenever they desire

Collin COCKE .... 7 Feb 1820, deed

    (filed under Archibald EPES, will)

    man James to John S. EPES

Peter EPES .... 17 Nov 1803, will

    negroes in his possession to son William EPES; negroes to William's sisters Martha, Sarah, & Susanna EPES; negroes in his possession to son Francis EPES; negroes in his possession to son Peter EPES; negroes on the land to son Richard EPES; Abba, Leander, Letty, Daniel, Viney, Clary, Fredrick, Charles, H__y, Almind to daughter Martha EPES; negroes in her possession to daughter Mary DO__LL; negroes in her possession to daughter Ann CONNER; Letty, Phoeby, Robin, Charles, Maria to daughter Sarah EPES; ___, Cate, Fanny, George, Isham, Minor, Ben, Harriett to daughter Susanna EPES; Annica, Eseau, Sam, David, Olive, York, Dolly to grandson William Mo_ion EPES; Charlotte, Mille to granddaughter Mary Elizabeth Poythrip DOZWELL & grandson Peter Epes DOZWELL; residue of negroes to be divided between daughters Martha, Sarah, & Susanna EPES

William EPES .... 3 July 1812, will

> negroes to wife Mary; negroes to be divided when son Spooner reaches the age of 21 – 1/3 to wife, the balance to be divided between my 3 children; girl Pat to Louisa MARTIN & at her death to her son William F.B. MARTIN; boy Isham to Ohray GREEN; Jack Cook should be sold first if necessary for payment of debt

Frances EPPES .... 6 Oct 1815, will

> Archibald, Mariah to brother Richard EPPES; woman Lily to brother Daniel EPPES

Francis EPPES .... 4 May 1843, will

> girl Mary to daughter Martha ROPER

.... 4 May 1843, codicil

> slaves may not be sold

Richard EPPES .... 27 Nov 1788, will

> 4 negroes each to sons Richard, Archibald, Thomas, & Robertson EPPES & daughters Elizabeth, Christian, & Polly EPPES; negro families to be kept together

Daniel B. FENN .... 19 Nov 1852, will

> slaves to wife Priscilla & after her death to nephew John W. GURLEY; males to be emancipated at age 28, females at age 25

Theophilius FIELD .... 13 Sept 1768, will

> girl Frank to grandson William TEMPLE; girl Bess daughter of Grace to daughter Mary TAYLOR wife of Richard TAYLOR; Jenny daughter of Belinda to daughter Sarah; all negroes at my home to be divided between sons Theophilius, James, & Thomas FIELD

James S. GEE .... 13 May 1863, will

> negroes to be hired; female slave of her choice to sister Susannah WILLIAMS; Mary age 20 to be set free; boy Henry Baugh to nephew Winfield GEE; negroes belonging to my estate to children of my dec'd brother Henry GEE after death of sister Susannah WILLIAMS

John GILLIAM the elder .... 19 Sept 1791, will

> Bess, Aggy, Beck, Hannah, Moll, old Beck, Hannah, Esther, Judy, Phillis, Beck, man Bob to wife Jane GILLIAM; Esther & Pompy,

Pompey, Suckey, Billy, Doll, Tom, Esther, Sucky & Matt, Joe, Billy, Suckey & Mingo, Ciss, Phobe, Hall, York, Manmouth, Harry, Ned, Betty & James, Moses, Bob, Mardy & Anthony, Lucy, Bristol to son Walter Boyd GILLIAM also the old negroes: Phebe, Lucy, Fanny, Pegg, Doll, Hannah; after death of wife all the rest of slaves equally divided – 1/3 to son, 1/3 to daughter Mary, 1/3 to Thomas Griffin

Peachey GILLIAM, Walter Boyd GILLIAM, & Reuben M. GILLIAM...trustees for daughter Elizabeth ARTHUR

John GILLIAM .... 15 July 1819, will

½ negroes to nephew John G. FRIEND; ½ negroes to nephew Archibald E. FRIEND; 2 boys of equal value to nephews Noth & Charles FRIEND

William GILLIAM .... 1 Nov 1799, will

negroes to wife Christian & those I received with her; boy Paul & one boy from Amelia plantation to son John; boy Tom & one boy from Amelia plantation to youngest son; negroes not before devised to son John, my youngest son, & daughters Elizabeth & Jane to be equally divided

Carter B. HARRISON .... 25 Oct 1838, decree

man Peter now in jail to be sold

George E. HARRISON .... 14 Oct 1837, will

Dolly, Jack White, Tom, Billy Buck, Anamia Buck, Richard, Francis, Fanny Griffin, Nancy Bowser, John Armistead, Nat & his wife Kate & children to wife Isabella H. HARRISON; Nat & his wife Kate & children to be free at death of my wife; Lucy & her children to sister Abby W. WALKER; girl Harriet to Ann Eliza RITCHIE daughter of Thomas & Isabella RITCHIE; old Nancy, Patty Jackson

William Allen HARRISON .... 22 May 1824, will

25 negroes to son Carter Basil HARRISON; 25 negroes to son William Allen HARRISON; 25 negroes to son John Henry HARRISON; 20 negroes to daughter Anna Martha HARRISON; negroes I got by my beloved Martha to be divide between Anna, William, & John

Michael HILL .... 26 Aug 1794, will

girl Cate to daughter Elizabeth WEEKS, to be freed at age 23

Lemuel HUNNICUTT .... 6 May 1848, will
> 1/3 slaves to wife Sarah HUNNICUTT; remainder of estate to be divided between daughters Susan E. FENN & Virginia B. HUNNICUTT

Abraham JONES Jr. .... 20 Jan 1743, will
> Jack, Sterling, Cook, Cate, Frank to wife Sarah JONES & at her death divided between children Peter, John, & Lucy JONES; Tony, Cheshire, Isham, David, Cloe, Moll to son Peter JONES; Bess, Sue, Bob, Jancy to son John JONES; Phillis, Simon, Sall to daughter Lucy JONES

Josiah M. JORDAN .... 1 Aug 833, will
> Voll, Ben, Harriett & her child Frank to son Samuel P. JORDAN; Porter, Edmund, Ma__va, Nancy & her child Winney to daughter Jane Maria; Cornelius, Henry, Polly to son Josiah M. JORDAN; Ephrain, Eliza & her 2 children, Milly, Henry, Peter, Cornelius, Lucy, Sally to wife Rebecca B. JORDAN

Stephen LEATH .... 16 Mar 1824, will
> men Lewis, Ted, Joney & a boy Tom to wife Elizabeth; boys Jim, Cook, girl Clarisy to son Eppes LEATH; girl Fanny, boy Tulor to daughter Elizabeth now Elizabeth GRANTHAM; man Peter, boy Stephen to son Truman Eppes LEATH; woman Peggy, girl Cate, child Minerva to daughter Mary Ann LEATH

Nathan LEE .... 26 Feb 1823, will
> Mason & 4 of her children Clary, Peter, Amey, & London to children of my daughter Patsey HEATH; boy Frank, girl Betty to son Pleasant LEE

David LUMSDEN .... 18 Apr 1854, will
> free woman Matilda; woman Eliza now hired by Mr. Polu STEVENSON of Petersburg to Thomas SHEDDON

Edward MARKS .... 16 Dec 1822, will
> 1/3 part of slaves to wife; equal portion of slaves to sons Edmund & John H. MARKS & daughters Eliza Ann, Mary Rebecca, & Harriet Frances

Richard MARKS .... 4 Aug 1898, will
> slaves sold as necessary; remaining slaves to children Richard E. & Elizabeth P. MARKS

Thomas MOODY .... 20 Jan 1827, will
> girl Delia, boy John to nephew Thomas MOODY

Horatio MOORE .... 21 July 1830, will
> all slaves to wife Elizabeth MOORE & emancipated at her death

Robert MUNFORD .... 8 Sept 1743, will
> Hannibal Jr., Jack, Sall, Betty, Titus, George to son Robert; Sam, Jack, girl to son Theodorick

James MURRAY .... __ 1764, will
> Harry, Hit, Jack, Lester, Jack Cooper, Joe, little Harry, Phillis, Nan, Betty, Jenny, _ab, Moll to wife Ann MURRAY & at her death to sons John, William, & Thomas; executors to purchase 4 ___ slaves for sole use of my wife & at her death to son James; 2 slaves each to daughters Anne, Margaret, & Mary & 1 other slave each for said several daughers

Thomas MURRAY .... 1 Nov 1783, will
> men Tom, Issac to mother Anne MURRAY & at her death to brother William MURRAY & sister Mary GORDON; 1 negro each to nieces Elizabeth, Anne Bolling, Susanna, & Margaret MURRAY daughters of my brother John MURRAY dec'd, Anne GORDON daughter of Thomas GORDON, & Anne Margaret daughter of Alexander GORDON dec'd; 1 negro boy to nephews James, William, & John MURRAY sons of my brother John MURRAY dec'd

Elizabeth P. POWELL nee HARRISON .... 1 Nov 1836, will
> Lucy Ann & her children George, Robert, William, & Lucy to be free, the children as they reach age 22

Robert POYTHRESS .... 24 May 1743, will
> Harry, Hunt, Tom, Jamey, George, Nilsy, Sarah, Lucy, Nick, Hannah, Matt, Nan, Penelope to wife; Jamey, Nilsy, Nan, Sarah to wife; Jamey, Nilsy, Nan, Sarah to sons as they reach age 21; remainder of slaves to be divided among children after wife's death; Tomboy, Mingo, Charles, Judy, Bett, Jenny, Sarah, George, Boatswain to son

Robert; Prince, Stirling, C__on, Jack, Sarah, Bett, Agnes, Aneky, Harry to son Peter; Phillis, Seanah, Gambia, Caesar, Pheby, Cate, Pat, Pompey to son William; negroes to daughter Elisabeth GILLIAM previously given her; boy Johnny or girl about the same age to grandson Robert GILLIAM; Abbah, Sawney, Jenny to daughter Mary Anna MINGE; girl Amy to granddaughter Tabetha HARWOOD; girl Sue to daughter Tabetha POYTHRESS; Pheby, Jack, Hannibal, Noon, Tom to daughter Susannah POYTHRESS; Phillis, Nan, Titus, Scott, Phillis to daughter Jane POYTHRESS

Richard Ryland RANDOLPH .... 11 June 1831, will
boy Archy to cousin John E. MEADE

John STURDIVANT Sr. .... 22 Mar 1815, will
Cato, George, Betty, Becky, Leeda, Hannah, Ginny, Deliah, Manah to son James STURDIVANT; Joel, Judah, Ginny, Archer to daughter Rebecca GRANEMER; Hannah & her 6 children Livy, Clarey, Doctor, Anthony, Cato, & Ginny, man Davy to daughter Elizabeth LIVESAY; Abram, Ussy, Fanny, Lucy, Pheobe, Anaca, Patience, Kisiah to daughter Sally TINNY; Ned, Lucy & her daughter Kesiah, Phoebe & her 2 children Esther & Dilsy to son-in-law Edmund EPES; man Bob to be hired out for benefit of daughter Elizabeth LIVESAY; old Beck to go to one of my children

John THWEATT .... 8 Sept 1821, will
negroes to son John James THWEATT

Richard TUCKER .... 2 May 1847, will
man Edmund to brother Abraham; girl Martha to sister Nancy ALBY; woman Maria to sister Martha NEWELL; boy Jim to brother Danny TUCKER; Charles, Hannah to Thomas TUCKER

John B. WILLIAMS .... 9 Dec 1816, will
woman Charlotte & ½ of all the negroes to wife Mary J. WILLIAMS; the residue to be equally divided between nephew Richard BARKUS & niece Julia Ann BARKUS

Richard WILLIAMS Sr. .... 7 Nov 1810, will
Frank, Billy, Colin, Peter, Jeffrey, Aron, Patty & her children, Fanny the wife of old Frank to wife Mary WILLIAMS; Plato, Nanny, George, Anky, Andrew, young Plato, Oliver, Carter, Suke, young

Davy, Moses, old Davy, Ben, Cato, big George, Bob, ½ the slaves to son John B. WILLIAMS & the other half after death of my wife; ½ the slaves after my wife's death to son John B. WILLIAMS & friend Joseph FORD in trust for grandchildren Richard & Julia Ann BARKUS children of daughter Ann BARKUS, wife of George BARKUS

Hubbard WYATT .... 5 Apr 1780, will

old Jenny & her child Parrott, James, Cretix, Tompkin, Sam, Charles, Herculas, little Amey, Pampry, Alice & her children Wills, George, Rico, Darcus, Dulcey & her children Sham, Judah, Davey, & little Milley to son John WYATT; Lilly, Critty, Henry, Milly, Amey, Kate, Stephen, Jenny, Suckey, & Amey's little child to daughter Mary WYATT; Bartley, Betty, Isaac, Aron, Charlot, Moses, Sam, Nancy, short Phillis & her children Wilson, Anaka & her little child to unborn child of wife Katherine WYATT; Nan, Africa, Sarah, Jacob, Iris, Frederick, Syrus, long Amey, Nell, Cocke, little Peter, Will, Betty, Jim, little Nan, Sam, Molly, John, great Harry, Easter, Peter, to wife Katherine WYATT & at her death to son Hubbard WYATT; remaining slaves to son Hubbard WYATT

...., codicil

Anaka & her youngest child & her son Giles may be sold

Nicholas WYATT .... 14 Apr 1720, will

girls Poll, _ett to Nicholas REEKS son of my daughter Susannah REEKS; boy Tony to Anthony WYATT; woman Moll her freedom; remaining negroes to son Edward WYATT

PRINCE WILLIAM

Prince William County was created by an act of 1730 to take effect on 1 March 1731. Many pre-Civil War records were lost, destroyed, or stolen by Union troops in 1863 during the Civil War. Sixteen deed books and five will books are missing.

Gerard ALEXANDER Sr. .... 19 Nov 1821, Deed

> Ellen, Fanny & 2 children Thornton & William, Juliet & her child Mary Anne in trust to James B. EWELL for Matilda Ann ALEXANDER; Gerard ALEXANDER Sr. to retain possession for life

William CARR .... 23 Jan 1790, will

> slaves to wife until her death then Hannah & her children to daughter Betsy TEBBS; Agga & all her children Jack & William Carr to son William CARR; Lucy & all her children Jim, Harry, & Viney to son John CARR; none of the slaves to be sold out of the family, if offered for sale they should be liberated; man Abner to be set free

Catesby COCKE .... 30 June 1763, will

> Jack to son John Catesby COCKE; slaves to be hired

Michael DERMONT .... 3 Feb 1730, will

> (found under Prince William Co but of Stafford Co)
> land left to wife Mary DERMONT & son Michael to be sold to purchase each a servant; man Charles W__ is to wife

Elizabeth GRAHAM .... 7 Apr 1791, will

> child Sukey, boy Watt to granddaughter Elizabeth GRAHAM daughter to Walter GRAHAM; Betsy to granddaughter Elizabeth Mary WIATT daughter to William WIATT; woman Lydia & her children Alexander & Nancy to daughter Jenny GRAHAM

.... 2 Sept 1791, codicil

> boy Peter, girl Prycey to granddaughter Elizabeth GRAHAM daughter of Walls GRAHAM

John GRAHAM .... 1 Mar 1783, will

> executors to purchase a girl 12-14 years of age for daughter Jean GRAHAM; man Daniel Macrae to son Dr. William GRAHAM

Alexander HENDERSON .... 24 Feb 1815, will
...farm...with all slaves in lieu of dower to wife...plus Jack & his wife Dorcus & their youngest child; Ben with his wife Clara & her child James; slaves in Fairfax made over in trust

John HOOE .... 5 Jan 1798, will
Moses, Jane, Daphne, Raphne, Solomon, George, Rose, Massey, old Ben, Hannah, Lolly, old Winney, Kitt to wife Ann HOOE; after her death to daughters Mary Ann THROGMORTON, Catherine O'LOCHLON, Sarah Burdett SWEENY, & Ann Frances HOOE; Bob, Sarah, Lucy & her children to son William HOOE; Abraham, Mingo to son Bernard HOOE; Winney, Pallas, Tom Parker, Ned, Sinah, Nelson Betsy, little Tom, Armistead to daughter Catherine O'LOCHLON wife of Cornelius O'LOCHLON; Lewis, Gilbert, Ester & her child Helen, Barey, Jesse, Joe, Nan to daughter Sarah Burdett SWEENY; Sam, Jacob, Charity, Lizzy, young Ben, Maria, Lucy, Syller, Rachel to daughter Ann Frances HOOE; Sarah, Aggy, Eliza, Beck, Frank, Ann, John, Felicia, Matilda, Virgin to daughter Susanna Fowke HOOE; Tommy to grandson John THROGMORTON

John LEE .... 15 June 1848, will
woman Luend & her children to Jane Matilda MATTHEW, wife of Henry P. MATTHEW; boy Polk to Mary CLARK; an equal distribution of remaining slaves to Mary CLARK's children: Richard A. CLARK, Thomas O. CLARK, Solomon CLARK, John CLARK, William H. CLARK, Mary E. wife of Matthew A. LEE; Anthony to remain with Richard A. CLARK; Sukey & her daughter Henny to James ROBINSON; woman Henny wife of Nathaniel Harris be set free; Jamima & her 2 children Dianer & Pendelton is at liberty to live with James Robison her father

RICHMOND CITY

All county court records prior to 1655 and almost all prior to 1677 are missing. Many records were destroyed by British troops during the Revolutionary War. Post-Revolutionary War county court records exist. Almost all circuit superior court of law and chancery and circuit court records were destroyed by fire during the evacuation of Richmond on 3 April 1865 in the Civil War. The county's circuit court held its sessions at the state courthouse in Richmond.

Richard ADAMS .... 30 Jan 1800, will

12 negroes of her choice to wife Elizabeth; all the negroes in his possession to son John GRIFFIN; all the negroes in his possession to son Samuel GRIFFIN; 10 negroes to daughter Tabitha; 10 negroes to daughter Elizabeth GRIFFIN; all the negroes in their possession to daughters Ann, Sarah, & Ailice; 10 negroes to son Richard GRIFFIN; remainder of negroes to be divided among my 8 children: Richard, John, Samuel GRIFFIN, Tabitha, Elizabeth GRIFFIN, Ann, Sarah, & Ailice

Gerard Thomas ADAMS .... 14 July 1851, will

woman Patty, boy Temple to wife Elizabeth ADAMS; boy Lewis to son Bartlett P. ADAMS; boy Bob to son William N. ADAMS; boy Jim, girl Margaret to daughter Ann Elizabeth CHANDLER; man John, woman Sarah & her daughter Caty to daughter Virginia Frances ADAMS

Robert Bee .... 22 May 1846, free negro regis

Age 23, 5 ft, 5" and identifying marks

Campbell BLADES .... 3 Aug 1835, will

7 negroes to daughter Maria AYRES held in trust by M.C. LACKLAND executor & trustee

Lewis BURWELL .... 10 Nov 1802, will

man Cyrus to sister Miss Eliza PAGE & at her death to be sold; man George, brother to Cyrus, to choose his master; girl Abby to niece Frances T. BURWELL; woman Polly to be made free

Louisa Johnson .... 12 July 1848, cert of freedom

age 40, 5 ft 2" and identifying marks; born free by testimony of C.C. BURTON

Ann A. LANKFORD etc to Sarah TEASLEY .... 3 Apr 1835, deed

Rose & child Sally to Sarah TEASLEY

Dorcas LANKFORD .... 29 Apr 1834, will

Rose & her child Tulip to daughter Sarah TINSLEY; woman Charlotte to be sold; woman Lavinia to unmarried daughters

William MARSHALL .... not dated, will

all the slaves & their increase received in consequence of my intermarriage with their mother to son John, Jaquelin, & his youngest sister after the death of their mother; the residue of my slaves to my sons William, Thomas Griffin, & daughter Eliza

William MARSHALL vs Admr of Lewis LEATH Admr of John WALTHALL .... 22 Nov 1831, in Chancery
.... 17 Aug 1836

...to sell at public auction...all the slaves now remaining of the estate of the said John WALTHALL dec'd...

.... 15 June 1837

Betsy & children Randolph & Henry, Granderson, John, Sylvia to Lewis LEATH; Garrison to John T. BOTTOM

Joseph MARX .... 12 Sept 1836, will

all slaves to wife Richa MARX; slaves purchased from Moses M. MYERS to Catharine, Harriet, & Julia MYERS

MASON & COCKE vs Admr of Daniel BOISSEAU ....
.... 29 June 1836, in Chancery

China, Sylvia, old & infirm, sold 15 Oct 1833 to Samuel Madison FARMER; Ned a runaway slave to be sold

Francis G. MORRISON, etc vs James SCOTT Jr. ....
.... no date, in Chancery

many negroes in Robert GOODE the elder's estate & Robert R. GOODE

Samuel OVERTON & wife vs admr of Thomas P. OVERTON ....
.... 1 Nov 1831, in Chancery

11 negroes sold

....24 Nov 1796, inv & appr

 man Daniel, women Abby, Clary, Betty, child Anne, boys Pleasant, Ives, girls Aggy, Phillis, man Jack, woman Tabby

John RANDOLPH..5 Dec 1821, will

 all slaves to be freed; old servants Essex & his wife Hetty, woman Nancy daughter of Juba (alias Jupiter), Queen, Johnny; confirm to brother Beverly the slaves I gave him; not included my mother's descendants...profits of my late father's estate...the slaves given by my grandfather Bland as her marriage portion inventoried at my father's death...1/2 of them now scattered from Maryland to Mississippi were entitled to freedom at my brother Richard's death

....3 Jan 1826, codicil

 same provision for servant John, sometimes called John White, as for his father Essex, same for John's wife Betsy, Juba & his wife Celia, Archer's wife Nancy

Robert RIVES vs William GILLIAT, adm of Seymour SCOTT.................
....31 Oct 1832, in Chancery

 ...question that slaves mentioned in the deed of trust...are liable to be sold; William G. PENDLETON required to deliver the said slaves to the said Herbert A. CLAIBORNE for the purpose of the sale

....17 Feb 1834, inv & appr

 man James & Mary his wife, Aggy & daughter Willianna, Letty & children Jilina & infant Caroline, Caroline & children Eliza, Amanda, Martha, & Charles

Joseph SCOTT & wife vs William M. BOOKER...
....22 June 1847, in Chancery

 ...hires & profits of the slaves...

....29 Mar 1843, in Chancery

 ...division of the slaves...the said Nathaniel HARRISON as trustee is entitled to receive...the slaves personal property...sustaining the exception of the defendant William M. BOOKER; slaves aloted as follows: Burg, Ussy, Caroline, John, Rose & her child Suckey to Joseph SCOTT administrator of Caroline M. SCOTT dec'd also Henry, Elam, Lucy reisdue of slaves belonging to the estate of William M. BOOKER Sr dec'd; Robert, Polly, Cyrus, Nancy, to John

ROBERTSON & his wife Elizabeth, Gabriel, Zephamiah, Kate & her child Richard, old Nancy reisdue of slaves belonging to the estate of William M. BOOKER Sr. dec'd; Jackson, Jim, Polly (the last sold by him) to William M. BOOKER the son as his ¼ part reisdue of slaves belonging to the estate of William M. BOOKER Sr. dec'd; George, Everand, Miles to Nathaniel HARRISON as his ¼ part reisdue of slaves belonging to the estate of William M. BOOKER Sr. dec'd

Daniel P. Vanderwall .... 31 Aug 1829, free negro regis
age 17, 5 ft 7", born free

John WALKINS .... 22 June 1817, will
Charles (called Sussex) with his wife & all his children be sold, also man Dick if wife does not take

ROCKINGHAM

Rockingham County was created in 1778. A courthouse fire in 1787 destroyed primarily wills and estate records. In June 1864 during the Civil War, court records (mostly volumes) were removed from the courthouse and loaded on a wagon to be taken to place of safety on or beyond the Blue Ridge. The wagon was overtaken by Union troops near Port Republic and set afire, which was put out by local citizens. Many order books, deed books, will books, and fiduciary books, however, were lost or severely damaged by the fire. The loose records that remained at the courthouse were undamaged. Pre-1865 records including deeds and wills were rerecorded following an act of assembly passed in November 1884.

James BEARD .... 11 Sept 1790, will

> negroes to work plantation as long as wife and children continue together

Elizabeth CHANDLER .... 19 Apr 1847, will

> man Joshua to grandson David CHANDLER Jr., David CHANDLER Sr. to manage slave

Peter CONRAD .... 22 June 1800, will

> boy George, girl Judith to wife Mary Eve

Robert DAVIES .... 11 Sept 1804, will

> woman Anny, man Harry to wife Nancy DAVIES; man Tom to be sold

John DUNCLE .... 22 May 1782, will

> fellow Tom to wife Margaret DUNCLE & at her death divided between son John & daughter Mary DUNCLE

Thomas FULTON .... 14 Feb 1800, will

> girl Lucy, big London, Polly to wife Elizabeth FULTON, at her marriage or decease Polly to daughter Martha FULTON, big London to son James FULTON

Jacob HARNESBERGER .... 25 Mar 1852, will

> slaves are not to be sold

Jesse HARRISON .... 18 Jan 1826, will
> men Simon, Stephen to choose own masters; girl Peggy to wife Polly to be sold at wife's death

John HARRISON .... 6 May 1815, will
> Rachel & her child, man Ben to wife Grace HARRISON; if Ben lives longer than my wife or me he is to be free; girl Janny, woman Hannah to daughter Lidda TAULMAN & husband Benjamin TAULMAN; my boy Isaac commonly called Buck to son-in-law Benjamin until he is 18, 6 years from now...then free...

Thomas HARRISON .... 4 June 1799, will
> yellow woman Patty to be free, her daughter Barbara to be free at age 18; yellow George & his sister Liddy to wife, George to be free at age 21 & Liddy at age 18; black George to be free 1 year from this date

Silas HART .... 19 Dec 1791, will
> fellow Ambrus, wenches Pheby, Poll to wife; Moses, James, Jack to be sold?

John HERDMAN .... 28 Jan 1826, will
> ...claims held on John LONG with the negroes given to him some years ago...

.... 28 Jan 1826, codicil
> boy Moses to be free

Peter HOG .... 5 Oct 1773, will
> slaves, servants to wife Elizabeth HOG; slaves in Augusta County to be sold at wife's death

.... 10 Nov 1777, codicil
> ...Duncan Furguson my servant...enlisted as a drummer in my company...

WHERE DID I FIND THE FOLLOWING?

(Not in Peter HOG's will.)

George to son James HOG; Elce to son Peter HOG; Lucy to daughter Betsy; girl Milly to be free at age 31, to daughter Nancy all after wife's death

---

164

John HOOVER .... 9 July 1829, will

> man Robin to work for my estate until 1 Jan 1833 and then be free; boy Granason to work for my estate until 1 Jan 1845 and then be free; boy Benjamin to work for my estate until 1 Jan 1851 and then be free; girls Carlina, Milly, Rachel, Julian to work for my estate until age 28 and then be free

Henry HOTTEL .... 16 Dec 1815, will

> girl Milly, woman Nan to wife Climitena; slaves not disposed in this will to be sold; boy Tom to son Joseph HOTTEL

John KRING Sr. .... 16 Feb 1802, will

> (Listed under John KING Sr.)
>
> women Jude, Hannah to wife Catherine KRING

.... 5 July 1802, codicil

> woman Jude not be sold but maintained among my children

William KRING .... 3 Mar 1806, will

> ...slaves...I Mary KRING widow of the said William KRING dec'd...will not take or accept the provision made for me by the said will...

Thomas LEWIS .... 10 Oct 1789, will

> negroes, lad Solomon to wife, at her death ½ the negroes to son Charles the other half to son William Benjamin; wench to granddaughter Elizabeth given some 2 years ago

Henry LONG .... 16 Jan 1779, will

> man to wife

John MACKALL .... 20 Jan 1799, will

> Bob, Sarah & her 2 children Frank & Caesar, Hainy & her 2 children Bob & Christopher, Joan, Dick, Sall, Tom to son John James MACKALL; wife to have maintenance from negroes; young Isaac & wife Dina & their 5 children Darky, Frank, Henry, Nelly, & Peggy, girl Polly, boy Ben son of Nan Therman to daughter Frances Holland MACKALL; Fanny & her 3 children Charles, Abraham, & Mary, Hannah & her children Winney, James, & Daniel to sons Edward & Richard when Richard reaches age 21

John McCUNE .... 11 Aug 1819, will
    girl Cate to be free

Thomas McKINZIE .... 3 Mar 1812, will
    boy Bill, woman Delph & her offspring to wife Margaret; Delph & her offspring to be free at wife's decease

Gasper MEFFORD .... 8 Dec 1805, will
    woman Rachel to daughter Leaney Hannah; girl Hannah to daughter Caty Kyle

Samuel MILLER .... 17 Apr 1811, will
    Kitty & her youngest child to be sold; Sal to daughter Peggy; Phebe to daughter Jane; boy Joe to son William

John NICHOLAS .... 10 Apr 1794, will
    1/3 negroes including Bill & his mother Peg to wife; young fellow Giles & his sister Betty to son John; Hannah & her children, Sukey, girl Polly to daughter Mary Rose; choice of girls except Lydda to daughter Elizabeth; choice of girls & Lydda to daughter Martha; slaves to be divided among sons Robert, Joshua, & George & daughters Elizabeth & Martha

Jacob PERKEY .... 11 May 1809, will
    Hannah, Lucy, Polly to wife Elizabeth; Harry, Jim, Patty to son Henry; wife's slaves to be divided among my 7 children at her death

John PERKEY .... 30 Nov 1794, will
    Gabriel, Jude to be sold

Jennet POWELL .... 16 Mar 1803, will
    Cesar, Moses, Diner, Mary, Phillis, Wiggin to be sold

John REEVES .... 5 May 1799, will
    5 children Reuben, Pheby, Lidya, John, Tom to William REEVES

Zachary SHACKLEFORD .... 27 Apr 1822, will
    Bauston, Sela, Sarah, Samuel, Daniel son of Sela, Benjamin to be set free; Daniel's siblings Samuel, Benjamin, & Sarah

Nicholas SHAFFER .... 10 Feb 1790, will
    wench Jane & all 5 slaves to wife Modena until son John SHAFFER; turns 21; Charles to John SHAFFER

Lewis ZIRCHEL/ZIRKLE .... 18__, will
    slaves which are not herein willed to be sold

Ludwick ZIRCLE .... 25 Feb 1800, will
    girl Margaret to wife & at her death to be sold; man George to be free

Ludwich ZARKLE .... 5 May 1812, will
    boy Daniel to wife Mary Magdalene; slaves except Daniel to be sold

SPOTSYLVANIA

Created by an act of 1720 to take effect on 1 May 1721. Many loose county court papers prior to 1839, when the courthouse moved from Fredericksburg to Spotsylvania Courthouse, are missing. Volumes that record deeds, court orders, and wills exist. The district court, superior court, and circuit court records of Spotsylvania County from 1813 to 1889 are in Fredericksburg.

Edward CARTER ...._ Feb 1792, will
slaves to wife Sally CARTER; slaves to sons Charles & Howard CARTER in trust for John CARTER & his wife Apphire; slaves to son Charles CARTER; slaves to son Edward CARTER; profits of slaves to maintenance of daughter Jane BRADFORD wife of Major Samuel K. BRADFORD; 4 male & 4 female slaves to daughter Sally CARTER wife of M. George CARTER; Stepney, Charles Quash, Phill, Seth, old man Bill be liberated; remaining slaves to be divided among youngest sons William Champ CARTER, George, Robert, Whitacre, & Hill

STAFFORD

Stafford County was created in 1664. Many pre-Civil War court records were lost to vandalism by Union troops during the Civil War. A few volumes that record deeds, court orders, and wills exist.

Enoch BROWNE ....20 Oct 1804, marriage settlement
> Lucy, Nan, Rose, Times, Congo, Dennis, Lucinda, James, Yarrow, Alcy, Harlow in possession of Elizabeth DENT widow of George DENT; ...daughter Judith A. DENT...

Edward BURGESS .... 1783, inv & sale
> Winny to John FRENCH; Bristol, Lucy to Garner BURGESS

Edward BURGESS .... 9 Jan 1759, will
> negroes to be sold

Sally CARTER .... 18 Oct 1807, will
> slaves to mother Sally Carter CUTTING

Thomas ELSEY .... 19 May 1698, will
> negroes to be divided between wife Jane & my 4 children Thomas ELSEY, John ELSEY, William, & Sarah

Miss E.H. FRENCH .... no date, will
> (filed under J.E.H. FRENCH)
> boy Lucien to brother William's son Howard, I desire he should not be sold; man Jered to my mother; servant Thornton to hire out for 4 years to L. HANSBERGER, Jr., then hire out for brother Stephen; Eliza Jane & her child to sister Martha, at her death said child to L. HANSBERGER, Jr. son of my sister Martha, & Eliza to choose for herself; boy Ira to William F. HANSBERGER; boy George to sister's son Henry HANSBERGER; girl Fanny to Louise F. HANSBERGER

Jane GREGG .... 2 Feb 1720/1, will
> boy Joseph to granddaughter Jane ELZEY; boy Robert to grandson Thomas ELZEY; woman Susannah to Lewis ELZEY; girl Susannah to grandson Lewis ELZEY; boy Jack to son John ELZEY; boy William to daughter Sarah THOMASON

John HOOE .... 8 Oct 1763, will
> girl Milly Thomas, Mary Thomas, Lenny to daughter Mary HOOE; 1/3 part of slaves not given to wife Anne HOOE; residue of slaves to be divided among sons Gerrard & Seymour & daughters Anne, Sarah, & Susannah after death of their mother; son Gerrard to have no other part of my slaves; girl Frank, Winney Thomas to daughter Anne HOOE, girl Lydia to daughter Sarah, & girl Sukey to daughter Susannah

Matthew KEENE.. 10 May 1732, inv & appr
> man Matt, 2 years of a servant woman

Matthew KOON .... 21 July 1723, will
> boy Matt to wife Bridgett

John MERCER to Gerard FOWKE............................. 15 Nov 1751, deed
> Wench _allas to Capt. Gerard FOWKE

William MOUNTJOY .... 16 Sept 1777, will
> boy Joseph to son Alvin MOUNTJOY; girl Sal, boy Will to daughter Mary ALLEN; girls Jude, Sarah, boy James to daughter Elisabeth GANARD; Henry, Charles, Sue, Hannah to son George MOUNTJOY; Jerry, Will, Con, Frank, Tom to son Edmund MOUNTJOY; Sarah, Peter to granddaughter Mary MOUNTJOY daughter of Edward MOUNTJOY

Anthony MURRAY .... 24 Oct 17_8, will
> fellow Waggery to be hired out to support son John

.... 9 Apr 1751, appr & inv
> Waggery, wenches Phillis, Jane, boy Gerrat, girl Indio, man John Brown, boy Harry, boy Jacob, girls Betts, Dinah

Aaron PATES to Jonas PATES .... 30 July 1786, deed
> boy Will alias Bob to Jonas PATES

STAFFORD COUNTY ORDER BOOK .... pg 1 – 11
(NOTE: the first page noted is the digital page number, the second page is the Order Book number)

John THOMAS .... pg 1/1, Aug 1749
    releases servant Alosis Walker

Mary Mason .... pg 4/6, Sept 1749
    ...brought her indenture...master Jacob WILLIAMS & wife

Gerrard JENKE vs Chandler FOWKE dec'd .... pg 4/7, Oct 1749
    ...against the servant Orphus of Chandler FOWKE dec'd

Ann Gray vs Edward RALLS .... pg 4/7, Oct 1749
    servant to Edward RALLS urged court to quit her master her Freedom dues

John HAMILTON .... pg 5/8, Oct 1749
    servant Mathew McEntire ran away

Margaret Cocklin .... pg 5/8, Oct 1749
    servant girl belonging to William MOUNTJOY

John SHORTS .... pg 6/11, Dec 1749
    servant boy Thomas Williams adjudged to be 11 years old

George JAMES .... pg 5/9, Nov 1749
    boy Robert adjudged to be age 13; girl Lucy 13

Joanna Campbell .... pg 5/9, Nov 1749
    to serve her master John WASHINGTON the term she has to serve

STAFFORD COUNTY ORDER BOOK .... pg 12 – 29
(NOTE: the first page noted is the digital page number, the second page is the Order Book number)

Sarah Lucas .... pg 3/15, Mar 1749
    petitioned for her freedom from Thomas MASSEY

Ann MASON, widow .... pg 4/17 – 9/27, Mar 1749
    ...George MASON...slaves...devises to his sons Francis &Thomas & daughter Sarah (dec'd) children of his first wife...Sarah MASON married Thomas BROOKS...; Jenny & Kate children of Walker; Bess, Maddy, Moses, Leonard, Nan, Harry, Ben, Nice, Will, Nell, man, Bess; Moses, Leonard, Nan, Harry, Ben, Nice, Will, Nell, man

are the children & increase of Bess; Bess & Maddy the said George MASON the father by his last will (?); Bess, Moses, Leonard, Nan, Harry the children & increase of Bess sold

STAFFORD COUNTY ORDER BOOK............................pg 30–49
(NOTE: the first page noted is the digital page number, the second page is the Order Book number)

William MILLS ....pg 1/31, Apr 1750
    Honour Early to serve her master for having a bastard child, 25 lashes to her bare back

Sarah Bredwell .... pg 3/34, Apr 1750
    to pay the Church Wardens for having a bastard child

Judith Lunsford .... pg 3/34, Apr 1750
    to pay the Church Wardens for having a bastard child

Elizabeth Iycer .... pg 3/34, Apr 1750
    to pay the Church Wardens for having a bastard child

Church Wardens... pg 9/44, May 1750
    to bind Jusanna Simpson to such peson as they shall think proper

Randall Daves .... pg 10/47, June 1750
    to serve his master John HAMILTON till the _th day of July net; that the said HAMILTON then discharges him

Grace Jackson... pg 11/49, June 1750
    to pay the Church Wardens for having a bastard child

STAFFORD COUNTY ORDER BOOK ....pg 50 – 79
(NOTE: the first page noted is the digital page number, the second page is the Order Book number)

John RALLS ....pg 1/50, 1750
    boy Orson adjudged to be 10 years old

John PAYTON ....pg 1/50, 1750
    servant boy John Pebbles adjudged to be 15 years old

John HAMILTON .... pg 1/51, July 1750
    discharged his servant Randall Davis

Joseph Lane .... pg 10/66, Aug 1750
    to serve his master John HOOE for runaway time

Peter DANIEL .... pg 10/66, Aug 1750
    Nell, Lucy, Dinah, Beck, Judy adjudged to be 9 years old, Sue 10

James HANSBROUGH .... pg 10/66, Aug 1750
    boy Jack adjudged to be 10 years old

Edward BURGESS .... pg 10/66, Aug 1750
    servant boy James Regan adjudged to be 12 years old

Jane Osborne .... pg 10/67, Aug 1750
    George ASBURY agreed to her freedom

STAFFORD COUNTY ORDER BOOK .... pg 80 – 107
(NOTE: the first page noted is the digital page number, the second page is the Order Book number)

Nathaniel HARRISON .... pg 1/80, Sept 1750
    Jack adjudged to be 8 years old, Juno 8

John ALEXANDER .... pg 1/80, Sept 1750
    Ben adjudged to be 9 years old, Chloe 7

Thomas BARBY .... pg 1/80, Sept 1750
    Rose adjudged to be 9 years old

Gardiner BURGESS .... pg 1/81, Sept 1750
    Dinah adjudged to be 11 years old

John ALEXANDER .... pg 1/81, Sept 1750
    Barnaby Riley to serve his master for runaway time

John RALLS .... pg 1/81, Sept 1750
    George adjudged to be 15 years old

James KENNY .... pg 1/81, Sept 1750
    gift of girl to son James KENNY

Murdy M. COY .... pg 1/81, Sept 1750
    servant boy James Crose adjudged to be 14 years old

John HOOE Jr. .... pg 1/81, Sept 1750
    Winny adjudged to be 9 years old; Frank 12

Alexander JEFFRICE .... pg 1/81, Sept 1750
    Jenny adjudged to be 14 years old

Nathaniel OVERALL & George ALLEN .... 5/87, Sept 1750
    "We of the jury find the negro man mentioned...Edward HERNDON foreman...

Henry SMITH .... pg 8/93, Sept 1750
    Lucy adjudged to be 9 years old

Thomas NORMAN .... pg 8/93, Sept 1750
    Moll adjudged to be 8 years old

William GEORGE .... pg 8/93, Sept 1750
    Jack adjudged to be 12 years old

Richard FOOTE .... pg 9/95, Nov 1750
    servant boy Joseph Park adjudged to be 11 years old

John STUART .... pg 9/95, Nov 1750
    servant boy John Ash adjudged to be 11 years old

William KING .... pg 9/95, Nov 1750
    Jenny adjudged to be 7 years old, Venus 8

James STARK .... pg 9/95, Nov 1750
    Jack adjudged to be 7 years old

Joseph SMITH .... 10/97, Nov 1750
    Tom adjudged to be 12 years old

Richard BRISTOE .... pg 15/106, Dec 1750
    John Turner to serve his master for runaway time

STAFFORD COUNTY ORDER BOOK .... pg 108 – 125
(NOTE: the first page noted is the digital page number, the second page is the Order Book number)

William JOHNSON .... pg 3/110, Apr 1751
    servant boy Thomas Philip adjudged to be 14 years old

Mary Grace .... pg 3/111, Apr 1751
    to serve her master John HUGHS for having a bastard child; to receive 25 lashes on the bare back well laid on

John Holt .... 9/123, June 1751
    runaway servant belonging to Moses GRIGSBY

William ETHERINGTON .... pg 10/125, Aug 1751
    London adjudged to be 11 years old, Davy 10 years old

STAFFORD COUNTY ORDER BOOK .... pg 126 – 156
(NOTE: the first page noted is the digital page number, the second page is the Order Book number)

Carty WELLS .... pg 2/128, Aug 1751
    Harry adjudged to be 8 years old

Richard BERNARD .... pg 9/141, Oct 1751
    slave Coffee not guilty of felonies, burglary & to be discharged to estate

Ann ALLENTHORP .... pg 12/147, Nov 1751
    servant boy Thomas Whitehouse adjudged to be 13 years old

Margaret Young .... pg 13/148, Nov 1751
    to serve her master William THORNBURY

William Darby .... pg 17/156, Feb 1752
    to serve James YELTON for runaway time

Padie Wheeler .... pg 17/156, Feb 1752
    serve Elizabeth McABOY for runaway time

Sylvester MOSS .... pg 17/156, Feb 1752

> Sylvester MOSS produced certificates for Phil belonging to John BALLENTINE, servant man John Anderson belonging to Edward RANDALL, & servant man William Butler belonging to S__dele HORTON

William DYE.. pg 17/156, Feb 1752

> produced certificate for man William Pu__

STAFFORD COUNTY ORDER BOOK .... pg 157 – 180
(NOTE: the first page noted is the digital page number, the second page is the Order Book number)

William JONES & Thomas FLETCHER .... pg 1/157, Mar 1752

> produced certificate for taking up Michael Storm, a servant belonging to Moses GRIGSBY

William CORBIN .... pg 1/157, Mar 1752

> produced certificate for taking up fellow Tom belonging to James MAXWELL

John CANADY .... pg 1/157, Mar 1752

> produced certificate for taking up William Darbey a servant belonging to James YELTON

George PILCHER .... pg 1/157, Mar 1752

> produced certificate for taking up John Holt a servant belonging to Moses GRIGSBY

William Elliott... pg 3/161, Apr 1752

> petition of his freedom; ordered that he be discharged from Philip ALEXANDER who had detained him as a servant by purchase from George CLARK

Thomas Pairinain.. pg 3/161, Apr 1752

> late servant to Benoni STRATTON dec'd, petition against John ADDISON & Ann his wife

John FOUSHEE vs Samuel EARL........................... pg 5/165, Apr 1752

> negroes were valued

William KENDALL .... pg 9/172, May 1752

    servant John Coleman adjudged to be 11 years old

Peter DANIEL .... pg 13/180, June 1752

    Robert alias Tubby - Alexander ROSE to enquire into allegations of his petition for freedom

Peter ROUT .... pg 13/180, June 1752

    Rose Lynaugh to serve her master for having a bastard child; to have 25 lashes on the bare back well laid on

STAFFORD COUNTY ORDER BOOK .... pg 181 – 204
(NOTE: the first page noted is the digital page number, the second page is the Order Book number)

Thomas WEATHERS .... pg 1/181, July 1752

    Church Wardens ordered to bind child Catharine now in Thomas WEATHERS' possession to Thomas WEATHERS

Geoffrey Box .... pg 1/181, July 1752

    servant boy of Edward RALLS was whipped; an orphan child belonging to Edward RALLS who purchased him from his brother John RALLS to whom he was bound by the Church Wardens to be indentured with Adam PAVEY

John GREGG .... pg 1/181, July 1752

    Harry adjudged to be 8 years of age; Charles 15

William Kelly .... pg 1/181, July 1752

    to serve his master William KENDALL for runaway time

John Bryan .... pg 2/182, July 1752

    to serve his master Darby OCAIN for runaway time

John MERCER .... pg 4/187, Aug 1752

    Chloe adjudged to be 12 years old, Seraphina 12, Sylvia 12, Dorinda 12, Essex 15

Joseph COMBS .... pg 4/187, Aug 1752

    Tom adjudged to be 6 years old

Elizabeth PARANDINE .... pg 4/187, Aug 1752
 Cate adjudged to be 8 years old, Matt 7

George JEFFERICE .... pg 4/187, Aug 1752
 Angelah adjudged to be 12 years old

John RALLS Sr. .... pg 4/187, Aug 1752
 Nalanline adjudged to be 10 years old, Rose 10

Jacob WILLIAMS .... pg 4/187, Aug 1752
 Lucy adjudged to be 9 years old

John SHORT .... pg 4/187, Aug 1752
 Chloe adjudged to be 11 years old

Francis Neighing .... pg 4/187, Aug 1752
 to serve his master William PATTEN for runaway time

Carty WELLS .... pg 4/187, Aug 1752
 Chloe adjudged to be 8 years old

John NORRIS .... pg 4/187, Aug 1752
 who intermarried the widow of John TURNER..having the negroe's work...

Benjamin ROBINSON .... pg 4/187, Aug 1752
 Peg adjudged to be 8 years old, Juda 8

John MAUZY .... pg 5/189, Aug 1752
 Will adjudged to be 9 years old

John THORNBURY .... pg 6/190, Oct 1752
 girl Frank adjudged to be 8 years old, Ned 10

Henson HOOE Jr. .... pg 6/190, Oct 1752
 Chloe adjudged to be 9 years old

Nathaniel HARRISON .... pg 6/191, Oct 1752
 Wasefield adjudged to be 11 years old, Stafford 12, London 12, Hampshire 11, Braughton 12, Brandon 13

Thomas I_ONROE .... pg 6/191, Oct 1752
    Scipio adjudged to be 10 years old

Samuel BREDWELL .... pg 6/191, Oct 1752
    Dick adjudged to be 10 years old, Phillis 11

Even PAYTON .... pg 6/191, Oct 1752
    Charles adjudged to be 10 years old

Margaret BARBEE .... pg 6/191, Oct 1752
    Cupid adjudged to be 9 years old

William MATTHEWS Jr. .... pg 6/191, Oct 1752
    Lucy adjudged to be 10 years old

Hugh Bowen .... pg 7/193, Sept 1752
    to serve his master John PEYTON for runaway time

James Pepples .... pg 7/193, Sept 1752
    to serve his master John PEYTON for runaway time

Thomas FITZHUGH vs John PEYTON .... pg 11/200, Nov 1752
    for not receiving runaways sent him

William CUNNINGHAM .... pg 12/202 Dec 1752
    Glasgow adjudged to be 11 years old

James JEFFRICE .... pg 12/202 Dec 1752
    Hannah adjudged to be 10 years old

John MERCER .... pg 12/202 Dec 1752
    Daniel Shehon to serve his master for runaway time

STAFFORD COUNTY ORDER BOOK .... pg 205 – 227
(NOTE: the first page noted is the digital page number, the second page is the Order Book number)

Burkett PRATT .... pg 1/205, Feb 1753
    man Bob on trial for theft, to be hung until dead

Ann MASON .... pg 2/206, Feb 1753
    Limbrick adjudged to be 12 years old

Margaret Cornwall. .... pg 2/207, Feb 1753
    to serve her master John FOLEY Sr for runaway time & having a bastard child

Henry Pooley .... pg 3/209, Mar 1753
    to serve his master Henry FITZHUGH for runaway time

Peter Crann .... pg 3/209, Mar 1753
    to serve his mistress Ann MASON for runaway time

Francis Bolling, servant .... pg 3/209, Mar 1753
    to serve his master William ROSS Sr. for striking him

John PETYON... pg 4/210, Apr 1753
    Will adjudged to be 10 years old, Peter 8, Titus 8

Jane Thompson .... pg 4/210, Apr 1753
    to serve her master Thomas SMITH for having a bastard child

Jamima Mills .... pg 4/210, Apr 1753
    to serve her master William MILLS for runaway time

William Cove .... pg 4/211, Apr 1753
    to serve his master Darby OCAIN for runaway time

Joseph Neale .... pg 4/211, Apr 1753
    serve his master John FITZHUGH for runaway time

Mary _nvest.. pg 5/212, May 1753
    for bearing a base born child

William... pg 5/212, May 1753
    Rachel adjudged to be 10 years old

Church Wardens... pg 5/212, May 1753
    Francis ___, an orphan left by his mother, likely to become a Parish Charge

Gerard FOWKE.. pg 5/212, May 1753
    man Joe on trial for theft, to be burnt in his right hand & one of his ears nailed to the pillory for one quarter of an hour & then cut off

John ALEXANDER .... pg 6/214, May 1753
   Hannah adjudged to be 12 years old

Alexander BROWN vs estate of Solomon HARDWICK ....
.... pg 8/218, May 1753
   2 negroes to be sold

Alexander BROWN vs estate of Solomon HARDWICK ....
.... pg 8/219, May 1753
   2 negroes, an orphan girl

Robert ASHBY (the elder) .... pg 8/219, May 1753
   to pay the freedom dues for Margaret Smith's indenture

John THOMAS .... pg 9/220, May 1753
   John Walker to serve his master for runaway time

John BAYLIS .... pg 9/221, May 1753
   George, Juda, Coffee possessed by Hannah BAYLIS, dec'd; bill of sale from nephew John BAYLIS to John FOUSHEE who said he never received them

John FRENCH .... pg 10/222, June 1753
   Ben adjudged to be 13 years old

John PEYTON .... pg 10/222, June 1753
   London adjudged to be 9 years old, Jack 9, Winny 9

Gerard FOWKE .... pg 10/223, July 1753
   Joe is not guilty & he is discharged

Church Wardens .... pg 12/227, Aug 1753
   Mary Duas had a bastard child

STAFFORD COUNTY ORDER BOOK .... pg 228 – 241
(NOTE: the first page noted is the digital page number, the second page is the Order Book number)

John TYLER .... pg 1/228, Sept 1753
   boy Daniel adjudged to be 12 years old which is ordered to be certified

Sarah WHITECOTTON .... pg 1/228, Sept 1753
    girl Jugg adjudged to be 12 years old which is ordered to be certified

William GERRARD .... pg 1/228, Sept 1753
    Gray adjudged to be 12 years old which is ordered to be certified, Sylvia adjudged to be 11 which is ordered to be certified

Michael BLACK .... pg 1/228, Sept 1753
    Isbell Frazier to serve her master for runaway time

Diana SIMPSON .... pg 2/229, Sept 1753
    Joe adjudged to be 11 years old which is ordered to be certified

George HARDING .... pg 6/236, Oct 1753
    Venus adjudged to be 12 years old

William HORTON .... pg 6/236, Oct 1753
    Lewis adjudged to be 12 years old

John HORTON .... pg 6/236, Oct 1753
    Milly adjudged to be 13 years old

John STUART .... pg 6/236, Oct 1753
    made oath against Isabell Moore for runaway time, the lash to be discharged in tobacco; Isabell Moore confessed she had 5 years to serve

Dr. Michael WALLACE .... pg 6/236, Oct 1753
    girl Sapho adjudged to be 10 years old, Miranda 10

Daniel CHAMBERS .... pg 6/236, Oct 1753
    produced certificate for Will, a runaway man belonging to John TAYLOE

John HOLLAND .... pg 6/236, Oct 1753
    produced certificate for Dick, a runaway boy belonging to Joseph SMITH

John EATON .... pg 6/236, Oct 1753
    produced certificate for Mary Williamson, a runaway servant woman belonging to John ROSE

William GERRARD...pg 6/236, Oct 1753
    produced certificate for man Sam belonging to Sampson DEMOVALL

John SMITH...pg 6/236, Oct 1753
    produced certificate for man servant John Smith belonging to Richard COBB

William Watson..pg 8/241, Dec 1753
    to serve his master Peter ROUT 2 years after his time by indenture is expired

STAFFORD COUNTY ORDER BOOK ....pg 242 – 272
(NOTE: the first page noted is the digital page number, the second page is the Order Book number)

Matt DONIPHAN..pg 1/242, Mar 1754
    Peter adjudged to be 13 years old which is ordered to be certified

Adam STEPHEN..pg 2/245, Mar 1754
    discharged his servant Thomas Page from his service

John INGLISH ....pg 14/267, Apr 1754
    Harry adjudged to be 14 years old which is ordered to be certified

STAFFORD COUNTY ORDER BOOK ....pg 273 – 316
(NOTE: the first page noted is the digital page number, the second page is the Order Book number)

William GARRARD..pg 1/273, June 1754
    servant Rachael Whitaker to serve for runaway time

Mary Frazier ....pg 2/274, June 1754
    to serve her mistress Mary SUDDUTH for having a bastard child

Mary SUDDUTH ....pg 2/274, June 1754
    Isabell Smith agreed to quit her mistress' her freedom dues

Church Wardens .... pg 4/277, June 1754
    Ann Dillon for having a bastard child

Church Wardens .... pg 4/277, June 1754
    Ann Lowry for having a bastard child

STAFFORD COUNTY ORDER BOOK .... pg 317 – 345
(NOTE: the first page noted is the digital page number, the second page is the Order Book number)

Patrick GRADY .... pg 1/317, Sept 1754
    servant Frances Price agreed to quit her master her freedom dues

Andrew HENNY .... pg 1/317, Sept 1754
    Jane Elliott serve her master for runaway time

James HENNY .... pg 3/321, Oct 1754
    discharged his servant Daniel Harvey

Adam STEVEN .... pg 3/321, Oct 1754
    James Campbell to serve his master for runaway time

Alexander STEPHEN .... pg 3/321, Oct 1754
    Mardin Owens to serve his master for runaway time

William DAVIS .... pg 7/326, Oct 1754
    Elizabeth Waller to serve her master for salivating her

Robert YATES .... pg 10/332, Oct 1754
    produced certificate for servant man Joseph Jefferson belonging to James SEBURN

Edward BEGTHILL .... pg 10/332, Oct 1754
    produced certificate for boy John Williams belonging to Thomas HAMPTON

Thomas JOHNSON .... pg 10/332, Oct 1754
    produced certificate for servant boy Joseph Basset belonging to Henry ASHTON

William DIE ....pg 10/332, Oct 1754

   produced certificate for 2 runaway men Jacob & Dick belonging to William ROBINSON

George WHITE ....pg 10/332, Oct 1754

   produced certificate for runaway woman Flora belonging to John SKINKER

John SYLVY ....pg 11/333, Nov 1754

   produced certificate for runaway servant man William Coo belonging to Darby OBAIN

William BURTON & Derrik MONNON ....pg 11/333, Nov 1754

   produced certificate for runaway servant man John Brown belonging to John BROWN

STAFFORD COUNTY ORDER BOOK ....pg 346 – 374
(NOTE: the first page noted is the digital page number, the second page is the Order Book number)

John RALLS ....pg 2/347, Mar 1755

   Agnes McCollister to serve her master for runaway time

Gerard FOWKE..pg 8/357, Mar 1755

   man Joseph on trial for arson

Gerard FOWKE..pg 8/358 & 9, Apr 1755

   man Joseph said he is guilty, to be hanged until dead

Catherine OVERALL...pg 9/360, Apr 1755

   Jane English serve her mistress for having a bastard child

Aaron PATES to Jonas PATES..30 July 1786, deed

   boy Wile also called Bob to Jonas PATES

Alexander F. ROSE..29 Oct 1831, will

   negroes formerly held by John ROSE dec'd; Joe, Lucy & children, Fanny, Sukey, Dolly & children, young Maria & children conveyed to my by my dec'd brother Patrick ROSE to be sold? Negroes except those to be sold to wife Sarah Fontaine Hampstead; Fanny, William,

John, a little girl now in the possession of Nathaniel ANDERSON to Doctor Samuel SCOTT in trust for sister Eliza WOODS

David STUART to Joshua DODSON .... 16 June 1747, deed

Joshua DODSON agrees...not to work above 3 servants or slaves...

George WILLIAMS .... 31 Jan 1749/50, will

Tom, Dublin, Jerry, Jenney to son Nathaniel WILLIAMS; wife Jane to have right to Tom; woman Cillar to son Benjamin WILLIAMS; wench Lucy to son George WILLIAMS; women Bess, Grace, Lydia to daughter Margaret RALLS; boy Will to son John Pope WILLIAMS; boy Godby to son Jesse WILLIAMS; girl Maryann to son Charles WILLIAMS; girl Winney to granddaughter Lydia Beck RALLS; slaves to be purchased for wife Jane

James WITHERS .... 12 Aug 1746, inv & appr

men Ned, Rodger, Harry, Dick, Matt, boy Daniel, girls Sue, Hannah, Nan, man Ben, wench Pegg & her child Dinah, wench & child Tamsend, Esther, boy Cesar, girls Phillis, Winney, Priss, wench Bess, men Tom, Bricky

.... Prince William, 1746

men George, Dembo, women Flora, Jane, girl Moll, man Peter, woman Sarah, boys James, Frank, girl Kate, men Sam, Jack, Will, girl Sarah, boy Robin, girls Nan, Lydia

James WITHERS & wife Elizabeth .... 8 Oct 1767, inv & appr

wench Phoebe

SURRY

Surry County was created in 1652. Deed Book 10 (1835–1838) is missing, and order books for 1718–1741 and various other early volumes are fragmentary. Most pre-Revolutionary War–era loose records are missing. Courthouse fires in 1906 and 1922, however, did not result in loss of records, which were then housed in a separate clerk's office

Moses .... 10 Jan 1800, cert of freedom
    age 24, 5 ft, 5" and identifying marks; liberated by Anselm BAILEY

Rebecca EVANS vs William EVANS .... Mar 1857, decree
    Jim, Hannah, Belah, Dedan, Charlotte, Anthony allotted dower of Rebeca EVANS widow of William EVANS dec'd; Moll, Peter allotted to Rebecca EVANS

SURRY COUNTY COURT MINUTES 1718

    boy Harry belonging to Thomas COLLIER is judged to be 10 yrs old

WARWICK

Recognized as Warwick River County, one of the original shires, in 1634; the name was shortened to Warwick in 1643. County court records were destroyed at several times with most destruction occurring during the Civil War. The clerk's office was burned on 15 December 1864. County court minute books and loose records from 1787 to 1819 were destroyed by the fire. Additional records were burned in Richmond on 3 April 1865, where they had been moved for safekeeping during the Civil War.

Rev. Thomas CURTIS .... 5 May 1837, will

(listed under CARTER)

1/3 negroes I may be entitled to at the death of my sister Sarah PRESSON which is her 1/3 of Nicholas PRESSON's estate; the other 2/3 to sons Christopher & Edmund CURTIS; Hannah's child Zinea, old man Jack to son Christopher CURTIS; man Lewis to son Edmund CURTIS; man Harrison to son Thomas Crandol CURTIS; boy Peter to daughter Jane HAYNES; boy Joe to daughter Elizabeth TOPLAY; boy Adrian to daughter Nancy Drewey CURTIS; boy Phil to son Samuel Gray CURTIS; boy Robin to son William Henry CURTIS; girl Lucy to son Robert Gray CURTIS; Paul, Hannah, Sarah, Mary, Aceaner & the 2 young children to wife Nancy CURTIS; slaves to son Daniel CURTIS at death of his mother

Henry CARY .... 27 Jan 1716, will

negroes to be divided between sons Henry CARY & Miles CARY, & daughters Anne STUCKEY, Elizabeth TEASBROOK, & my late daughter Indith BARBAR's 2 sons Thomas & William BARBAR except girl Rachel to son Henry CARY

William COLE .... 1 Nov 1729, will

Will, Sarah to wife Mary COLE; boy Lewis to son William COLE; money for negroes to son John COLE bequeathed to him by late brother James ROSCOW Esq, boys Gaby, Bob, girls Moll, Betty; remaining negroes to children William, John, Roscow, James, Mary, Martha, Jane, & Susannah COLE

John CRAFFORD .... 4 Jan 1803, will

negroes to wife Patsy Cany CRAFFORD

Susannah GODWIN .... 12 Sept 1781, will
negroes to be kept together & worked on the plantation for the benefit of my 2 granddaughters Mary & Susanna PRENTIS

William HARWOOD .... 1780, in Chancery (listed under will)
I give all my slaves that I have not mentioned, to be equally divided between my daughters Mary, Margaret, Anne, & Dorothy, & my granddaughter Dorothy Harwood HEWIT

John HUGHES .... 20 Jan 1823, will
girl Sarah to daughter Margaret HUGHES ; Phoebe & her youngest child John to son-in-law Augustine MOORE; remaining slaves to be hired out; 11 slaves each except those negroes named to sons James, Thomas, & George when James or Thomas reaches the age of 16; the residue to be divided among sons-in-law William YOUNG, Richard W. INTOSH, & Augustine MOORE, & daughter Margaret HUGHES

Capt. Scervant JONES .... 11 July 1782, estate sale
Hanner to George BOSOMEWORTH

Scervant JONES .... 20 Nov 1772, will
slaves to be sold

William JONES Sr. .... 13 June 1824, will
Fanny, Julius, Bob, William, Lucinda to son John JONES

William LANGHORNE .... 3 Nov 1796, will
all slaves conveyed to me by George LANGBY to sons Maurice & William LANGHORNE except wench Lettice in trust for daughter Mary LANG wife of George LANG & at her death to daughter Ann LANGHORNE; Phillis & her 2 children to daughter Lockey CURLE; man Anthony to son Maurice LANGHORNE; wench Venus to daughter Ann LANGHORNE; Nanny & her child to daughter Martha Cary LANGHORNE; boys James, Read, Bedford to son William LANGHORNE; girl Lucy to daughter Sarah DIGGES; boy Harry to grandson John LANGHORNE; negroes to wife Elizabeth LANGHORNE

Robert LUCAS .... 20 May 17_1, will
> Stepney, Venus to son Tom LUCAS; slaves to be divided among children Sally, Nancy, Robert, Gervase, Lucy, Eliza, & John

Thomas MALLICOTE .... 5 Dec 1725, will
> boy to Mary MALLICOTE; man Quashey to son John MALLICOTE; girl Judy to daughter Frances MALLICOTE; girl Dianer to daughter Mary MALLICOTE; the child that my negro woman Betty...Tomboy a negro man to son Thomas MALLICOTE; wife Mary MALLICOTE to have worth of son's negroes till they come of age
> ....codicil
> woman Betty & her increase to wife & at wife's decease to be equally divided among by children

Thomas MALLICOTE .... 6 June 1814, will
> girl Pheby to granddaughter Eliza Ann MALLICOTE daughter of son George MALLICOTE

Thomas MALLICOTE .... 17 Mar 1831, will
> Hannah to be supported by the estate; choice of negroes to wife Maria D. MALLICOTE & at her death to be divided among the children

Samuel SELDON vs John LUCAS .... 9 Mar 1718, judgment
> excuted one a woman Combo

SMITH assignee vs HARWOOD, etc .... 16 Nov 1837, Fifa
> man slave property of Robert M. HARDWOOD...is liable to satisfy execution previously levied on Samuel SHIELD...

WARWICK CO. DIVISION OF REAL & PERSONAL PROPERTY .... 1656 – 1676
(D = digital page, R = right page, L = left page)

> D/3 R: 3 negroes & __ negro children belonging to the children
>
> D/3 R: amount of the orphan & estate Capt. Thomas HARWOOD: 2 men & 1 woman, 2 children

WARWICK CO. MISC. COURT RECORDS .... 1701 – 1728

D/13: Miles CARY against Toby a negro slave belonging to Thomas CARY & Capital Harry a negro slave belonging to Mary CARY...order the sheriff the body of this negro into his custody to reappear at the next Court ....(7 Apr 17__)

WARWICK CO. ORDER BOOK.. 1697 - 1698

D/2: sale of negro to Major Lord BUNSOLL from deed of David CONDON (26 May 1697)

WARWICK CO. ORDER BOOK..1713 – 1714

D/4 R: Mary CARY widow, Jonathan DICKINSON & Joanna his wife...render unto them 8 negroes: Michel, Winefred, Moll, Hannah, Jinny, Harry, Jack, Tenh... (2 Apr 1713)

D/9 R: Thomas HAY ordered to pay any County Levies for old woman Venus for the future (7 May 1713)

D17 R: William CHAMESY for taking up...boy belonging to John DOWCHER (_ Oct 1713)

D/32 L: Abraham COLE, William Harwood COLE; boy Robin (3 June 1714)

D/43 R: Willy CARY certificate for taking up 2 runaway negroes belonging to Mr. James BATES of York County (9 Nov 1714)

D/43 R: William HOOKER certificate for taking up 2 runaway negroes belonging to Richard RATELIS & Thomas __MAN (9 Nov 1714)

D/43 R: Seamer POWELL certificate for taking up Lymon Harding a runaway servant belonging to ___ WHITHEAD of James City County (9 Nov 1714)

D/43 R: William HAWOOD certificate taking on Jack an Indian boy belonging to James BRITTELL of Elizabeth City County (9 Nov 1714)

D/44 L: John WILLS certificate for taking up Betty a runaway slave belonging to Col. David BRAY of James City County (9 Nov 1714)

WARWICK CO. ORDER BOOK .... 1650 – 1651

D/8: ...bill from Thomas HOLMES & the malato girl with...

WARWICK CO. ORDER BOOK 1685

D/2 L: divided between widow & 3 children Charles, Phillip, & George; boy Robert to Phillip MOORY (23 July 1685)

WARWICK CO. ORDER BOOK 1688

D/1: a negro man _enoy to John DODMAN

WARWICK CO. ORDER BOOK 1701

D/1: ____, Guy to have their ages adjudged at 8 years of age, owned by Matthew ____

Edmund WASH .... 8 Mar 1858, will
slaves to be divided after wife Nancy WASH's death, 1 share to exectors in trust for the children of dec'd daughter Emily D. GRAMMON; 1 share to exectors in trust for the children of dec'd son Richard WASH including widow Lucy Ann WASH; 1 share to son William WASH; 1 share to son James C. WASH; 1 share to exectors in trust for daughter Susan M. CHICK; 1 share to daughter Sarah A. WALTON; 1 share to the children of dec'd daughter Ellen V. WILLSHIRE, husband William B. WILLSHIRE

Lucy Ann left 4 children & GRAMMON has 3 children

Elizabeth WILLS .... 21 Oct 1773, will
Hannah & her child Cate to daughter Elizabeth WILLS; woman Betty to daughter Mary WHEADON; boy Tom, child of Betty, to grandson John WILLS

Mary WILLS .... 10 Apr 1751, will
girl Priscilla to daughter Susannah COLE; old Will to choose his master

Thomas WILLS the elder .... 20 Dec 1763, will
Fanny & her child Betty to daughter Anne WILLS; man Jammey to son John WILLS & at death of my wife also Billy, Nanny & her children Dick, Frank, & Pat; Mirti__ & her children Roger & Phillis to daughter Elizbeth WILLS & at death of my wife also man great George, boy little Billy; girl Nanny to daughter Mary & at death of my wife also man little George, Amy, Body, little Jamey; woman Betty, girl Hannah to wife Elizabeth WILLS; Pompey, Moll to son John WILLS for use of daughter Dorothy WILLS; girl Sarah to daughter Mary WILLS

Willis WOOTEN .... 24 Apr 1___, will
 Daniel, Milly to granddaughter Sarah CHARLES now in the possession of her father Henry H. CHARLES; man Tom to son Willis WOOTEN; 1/3 slaves to grandsons Willis & Thomas WOOTEN sons of deceased son William WOOTEN

Humphrey H. WYNNE .... 27 July 1822, will
 slaves to daughters Elizabeth & Mary WYNNE; slaves sold
.... 1828
 negroes to John A. JONES; remaining negroes divided into 4 parts

Nathaniel WYTHE .... 5 Feb 1750, will
 all slaves to wife Elizabeth WYTHE

WASHINGTON

Created by an act of 1776, court first met on 18 January 1777. Minute books for the periods 1787–1819 and 1821–1837 and many loose papers were lost in a courthouse fire set by Union soldier James Wyatt on 15 December 1864 during the Civil War. Wyatt, who was raised in Washington County, sought revenge for what he claimed was a wrong done against him by a county court judge before the war.

John BEATIE .... 18 Aug 1790, will
  woman Anogh to wife Elenor; men Peter, Joshua to son William

Lilly BOWEN .... 4 Apr 1780, will
  wench Jean to son Henry BOWEN; lad Wyatt, fellow Jack left him by his father & of which he is now wrongfully dispossessed to son Charles BOWEN

William CAMPBELL .... 28 Sept 1780, will
  John, Aggy to son Charles Henry CAMPBELL; Isaac, Milly to daughter Sarah Buchanan CAMPBELL; woman Liddy to wife Elizabeth CAMPBELL

Stephen CAWOOD .... 6 Nov 1810, will
  Nell, Jacob, David to wife Esther, to be free at age 45

Robert EDMONDSON .... 23 Mar 1779, will
  2 negroes to wife

James KING .... 21 Oct 1809, will
  woman Hannah, boys Samuel, Joe, girl Mary, boy Alexander to wife Sarah KING

William KING .... 20 Mar 1809, statement
  Mary KING renounced the provision made for her by the last will & testament of William KING dec'd – my dower in real estate & slaves

Humbeson LYON .... 11 Oct 1783, will
  Dick, Ra_h to wife

William TRIGG .... 11 June 1813, will
  Sally & her children to wife Rachel

WESTMORELAND

Many loose papers were burned during both the Revolutionary War and the Civil War. Volumes that record deeds, court orders (except for an order book for the period 1764-1776), and wills exist.

John LEE .... 23 Sept 1765, will
  (will lists Essex Co but probated under Westmoreland Co)
  1/3 negroes to brother Richard LEE; 1/3 slaves to brother Henry LEE; 1/3 slaves, fellow Peter to Hancock LEE son of John LEE Jr.

John NEWTON .... 19 Aug 1695, will
  Joseph, Newton, Benjamin & their widows free after 7 years after my death to eldest son John NEWTON; Harvey then to be no longer to be free; Tim, Narmo Will, Sarah to son Garret NEWTON; boy Wappier, girl Betty to my daughter; girl _oase at the death of my wife to daughter; ...to the other 4 of my grandchildren of Joseph children daughter of Benjamin as is before devised & my 3 sons John, Joseph, & Benjamin & their widows shall be free as above & also payments to my loving wife his mother...Cuffey Pegg, Jack, Mall to son Thomas; girl, Frank, Jew to wife
  .... 21 Dec 1696, codicil
  son Garret not to have negro Will; Jack, bought of Wm BOLTON? to son John; negro Will to wife; ...but the negro I give to my 3 English sons...; Frank, Sue to be divided

Samuel RUST .... 2 Mar 1798, will
  men Will, Solomon to daughter Elizabeth CRABB; London, Joane to Hannah ATTWELL daughter of Mary BEALE; boy George to Richard ATTWELL son of William ATTWELL; boy Daniel to Nancy ATTWELL; boy Frederick to Molly ATTWELL daughter of William ATTWELL; girl Molly to Sharlotte ATTWELL daughter of William ATTWELL; the hire of fellow Daniel to sister Hannah BAUGNS, Daniel to choose his master yearly; men Jerre, Job to grandson Thomas RUST

Martin TAPSCOTT .... 21 Oct 1800, will
  Milly & her children to be sold; my estate to son Henry Breeton TAPSCOTT...& if no heirs all the negroes herein given him can be

emancipated; 4 or 5 negro boys about the age of son Henry Breeton TAPSCOTT be bound to him until they are 21; women Lavinia, Sally to be free after my decease; inventory to have ages of negroes

WILLIAMSBURG

It was declared a "city Incorporate" by a royal charter in 1722, although its actual status was that of a borough. Records were transferred to Richmond during Civil War for safekeeping but were destroyed by fire there on 3 April 1865.

Mary Blair ANDREWS...15 Oct 1819, will

slaves in Albermarle to John Blair PEACHY youngest son of my father's niece Mary M. PEACHY & negroes by my husband's will
....25 Oct 1819, codicil

negroes to be divided at my death shall be between Fanny EGGLESTON, William BLAIR 3rd son of Archibald BLAIR, & Margaret BLAIR oldest daughter of John N. BLAIR

...I have credited myself with the price Ben sold...

John BLAIR .... 4 June 1799, will

slaves of Albemarle County to daughters Mary wife of Robert ANDREWS & Jane wife of James HENDERSON

James HENDERSON ....8 Aug 1818, will

I give to my step-son Iinnus K. HORSBURGH all right & claim...to slaves in the possession of Martin BAKER...; slaves in Albemarel to son James Peter; some negroes to be hired out, others sold; Davie Lia_, man Tom Thandy to be freed

Robert McCANDLISH.. 1 Oct 1857, codicil

slaves which I derived from the estate of my wife's father to my wife Rebecca McCANDLISH

INDEX

___WOOD: William B., 123
__MAN: Thomas, 194
_ames, 68
_asso, 113
_aues, 92
_egut, 64
_eleaner, 12
_elere, 60
_enoy, 195
_inny, 63
_nvest: Mary, 182
_oase, 199
_omund, 90
_outer: Royal, 143
_usery, 144
Aaron, 17, 35, 39, 40, 43, 59, 61, 68, 81, 82, 83, 87, 90, 93, 97, 123, 125, 136, 148
Abba, 149
Abbah, 154
Abbe, 69
ABBET: Catherine, 101
Abbey, 12, 75, 77, 94
ABBITT: Benjamin, 21; Jane, 21
ABBOTT: John, 74
Abby, 41, 72, 113, 141, 159, 161
Abe, 82
Abel, 25
Aberdeen, 87, 97
Abigail, 36, 53, 69
Able, 45
Abner, 157
Abraham, 18, 47, 54, 56, 59, 65, 67, 70, 71, 92, 97, 102, 109, 113, 117, 141, 148, 149, 158, 165

Abram, 10, 12, 13, 15, 20, 25, 35, 45, 61, 67, 77, 83, 87, 114, 119, 126, 128, 145, 154
ABRAM: Capt, 87
Absalom, 65, 101, 134, 135
Aceaner, 191
Achilles, 26
ACKRAN: Richard, 118
ACRILL: Hannah, 31; William, 134
Adain, 62
Adalaney, 126
Adam, 1, 14, 18, 42, 56, 57, 66, 70, 78, 80, 84, 88, 96, 102, 118, 119
ADAMS, 59; Bartlett P., 159; Elizabeth, 159; Gerard Thomas, 159; James, 34; Richard, 159; Virginia Frances, 159; William N., 159
Addin, 94
Addison, 29, 115
ADDISON: Ann, 178; John, 178
Addy, 90
Adeline, 39, 115, 119, 128
Aden, 141
Adrian, 191
Africa, 40, 45, 155
Agg, 14, 38, 62
Agga, 43, 65, 103, 128, 157
Agge, 31, 36, 56, 76, 86, 130
Aggey, 68
Aggy, 11, 19, 26, 35, 42, 44, 47, 60, 61, 72, 74, 78, 79, 83, 84, 85, 87, 88, 93, 94, 95, 97, 102, 104, 105, 106, 111, 114,

203

116, 118, 133, 137, 139, 141, 142, 144, 147, 150, 158, 161, 197
Agnes, 10, 19, 24, 44, 47, 53, 60, 65, 135, 143, 154, 187
Ailey, 100
Ailsey, 26, 52, 60
Alarny, 119
Albert, 41, 66, 71, 126, 130, 133, 142
ALBRIGHT: Ann, 101; Lucy Ann, 107
ALBY: Nancy, 154
Alcey, 12
ALCOCK: Ann, 28; Patsy, 38
Alcy, 171
Aldren, 85
Aleck, 8, 15, 43
Aleena, 100
Alek, 15
Alert, 71
Alex, 80
Alexander, 19, 42, 78, 88, 89, 157, 197
ALEXANDER: John, 175, 183; Matilda Ann, 157; Philip, 178
ALEXANDER Sr.: Gerard, 157
ALFORD: Charity, 133; Elizabeth, 133; John, 133; Unity, 133
Alfred, 111
Alice, 54, 60, 65, 78, 82, 84, 87, 92, 97, 100, 103, 104, 114, 116, 143, 155
ALL___AN: Mary, 53
Allen, 12, 14, 21, 126, 139, 141, 144
ALLEN: Ann, 40, 47; Anna, 31; Anne, 31; Anthony, 47;
Archer, 78, 88; Archibald, 125; Armistead, 71; Baller C., 11; Benjamin, 31; Capt. James, 87; Charles, 31; Cornelius Edward, 125; Edward, 125; Elenor, 47; Elizabeth, 11, 47, 78, 88; George, 11, 176; Hannah, 11; Henry Jno, 125; James, 31; Jesse, 11; John, 11, 78, 87, 88; Jones, 78, 88; Julius, 78, 88; Lucy, 11; Mary, 78, 172; Roy C. Richard, 78; Samuel, 11; Samuel Hunt, 11; Sarah, 31, 47; Sutton Farras, 11; Thomas, 47; Thomas William Gilbert, 125; Walter C., 11; William, 11, 47, 78, 87, 88; William F., 88; William Flounce, 78; William Hunt, 11
ALLEN Jr.: William, 88
ALLEN Sr.: Christian, 71
ALLENTHORP: Ann, 177
Alley, 61, 78, 82, 87, 92, 136
Ally, 16, 85, 95
ALMAND: John, 27
Almind, 149
Alosis, 173
Alrina, 100
Amanda, 74, 114, 161
Amania, 116
AMBLER: John, 78, 87
Ambrose, 7, 15, 26, 78, 86, 88
Ambrus, 164
Amby, 13
Amelia, 128, 145
Amer_, 86
America, 81, 92
Amery, 127

Amey, 10, 16, 36, 42, 45, 64, 71, 79, 80, 82, 83, 84, 85, 87, 89, 90, 91, 93, 94, 95, 97, 107, 108, 109, 127, 136, 145, 149, 152, 155
Amica, 145
Amis, 16
AMISTEAD: Francis, 121; Sarah F., 121
AMMONETH: John, 83
AMORY: William, 78
Amos, 102, 115, 145
AMOS: Clough T., 20
Ampy, 12, 78, 87
Amy, 9, 13, 14, 40, 42, 43, 67, 80, 104, 108, 115, 128, 133, 134, 147, 154, 196
Ana, 141
Anabella, 45
Anaca, 14, 154
Anaka, 65, 155
Anakey, 10
Anaky, 71, 86
Anamia, 151
Ancy, 61, 140
And__, 119
Anderson, 3, 15, 21, 24, 41, 60, 102, 103, 104, 126, 128
ANDERSON: Charles, 32, 59; Dabney, 23, 29; Dorothy, 113; Elizabeth, 106; Esther, 16; Fanny, 60; Henry, 59; James Spencer, 106; Jane, 59; John, 59, 68; John B., 59; Mary, 67, 68; Matthew, 34; Mitchel, 59; Nathaniel, 188; Patsey A., 59; Robert, 59, 68, 78, 88; Sarah, 59; Sarah Elizabeth, 106; Secelia, 59; Stephan, 59; Thomas, 60; William, 59, 113
Andren, 19
Andreus, 65
Andrew, 14, 42, 65, 87, 96, 102, 106, 114, 115, 121, 148, 154
ANDREWS: Ann, 103; Elizabeth, 5; Mary, 201; Mary Blair, 5, 201; Robert, 201
Anebellar, 45
Anecy, 96
Aneky, 154
Aney, 118
Angelah, 180
Angelina, 16
Angeline, 126
Angello, 61
Angelo, 113
Angillo, 61
Anica, 21, 40
Anky, 154
Ann, 19, 24, 54, 61, 68, 71, 103, 128, 130, 133, 141, 142, 158, 173, 186
Anna, 19, 26, 44, 47, 100
Anna Frances, 14
Annaka, 134
Annanias, 67, 114, 118
Anne, 59, 67, 72, 115, 161
Annica, 41, 149
Annis, 18, 31, 44, 116
Anny, 27, 66, 163
Anogh, 197
Anora, 115
Anthony, 7, 17, 18, 19, 22, 36, 40, 43, 44, 47, 53, 61, 73, 79, 81, 82, 89, 92, 104, 106, 109,

128, 145, 151, 154, 158, 189, 192
Antony, 87, 97, 106
APPERSON: George, 78, 88; James, 78, 88; John, 85
Arch, 29
Archer, 11, 12, 17, 42, 65, 66, 73, 103, 141, 154, 161; John, 142
ARCHER: Anna, 103; L., 103
Archibald, 26, 150
Archy, 112, 154
Arclin, 61
Ardinia, 3
Armistead, 17, 26, 55, 78, 79, 88, 89, 127, 142, 143, 158; John, 151
ARMISTEAD: Armistead, 133; Elizabeth, 51; John, 51; Robert, 23, 60
Armstead, 16, 65, 66, 115
ARNETT: David, 113; James, 113; Martha, 113; Mary, 113; Robert, 113
Aron, 21, 57, 154, 155
Arter, 46, 147
Arthur, 46, 82, 86, 92, 96, 113, 147
ARTHUR: Elizabeth, 151
Arthura, 3
Asa, 141, 144
Asabell, 139
ASBURY: George, 175
Aser, 143
ASHBURN: John, 29; Sarah, 29
ASHBY the elder: Robert, 183
Asher, 25
Ashley, 113
ASHLOCK: John, 85, 95

ASHTON: Henry, 186
Aston, 83, 93
ATTHISON: Elizabeth, 62
Attiony, 61
ATTWELL: Hannah, 199; Molly, 199; Nancy, 199; Richard, 199; Sharlotte, 199; William, 199
Atwater, 79
Austin, 59, 60, 91
AUSTIN: Charlotte, 60; Constance, 60; Thomas, 60; William Smith, 60
AUSTIN Jr.: John, 60
Avery, 136
AVERY: John, 147; Mary, 147
AYLETT: Benjamin, 113; Elizabeth, 113; Jane, 113; John, 113; Philip, 113; William, 113
AYRES: Catharine, 13; Maria, 71, 159
B_in_y, 87
BABER: George, 23; James, 23
Baccus, 37
Backus, 113
BACON: Edmond, 79, 89; Mary, 135
BACON Jr.: Edmond, 89
BAGBY: Richard, 99
Bailey, 131
BAILEY: Anselm, 189; John, 79
BAILEY Jr.: Jon, 89
BAIRD: John, 147
Baker, 94, 113
BAKER: Abraham, 16; Benjamin, 125; Benjamin Blake, 125; Elizabeth, 125; Emela, 125; Julianna, 125;

Martin, 60, 201; Mary, 16, 125; Richard, 125; Samuel, 16; William, 125; William H., 125; William Henry, 125
BALL: Rebecca, 16
Ballard, 119
BALLE: John, 33
BALLENTINE: John, 178
Ballock, 27, 28
BANKS: Andrew, 79, 89; Joseph, 89; Townley, 99; William, 79
BARBAR: Indith, 191; Thomas, 191; William, 191
Barbara, 56, 128, 164
Barbary, 134
BARBEE: Margaret, 181
Barber: Harriet, 149
Barberry, 79, 89, 94
BARBY: Thomas, 175
BARCH: John H., 114
Barco__, 102
Barey, 158
BARHAM: Frances, 133; John, 79, 88; Robert, 79, 88; Thomas, 79, 88
Barker, 123
BARKER: Garinter, 62, 71; Mary H., 62, 71; Sarah, 89
BARKUS: Ann, 155; George, 155; Julia Ann, 154, 155; Richard, 154, 155
Barnaby, 59, 175
BARNES: Charles, 37; Henry, 37; Richard, 104
BARNES the elder.: Leonard, 37
Barnet, 70
Barnett, 28
Barret, 64

BARRET: William, 75
BARROM: William, 89
Bartlet, 68, 96
Bartlett, 60, 111, 115
Bartley, 14, 155
BARTON: Martha, 45
Bash, 3
BASHIR: Sarah, 79
BASS: Jane, 42
Basset: Joseph, 186
Bat, 82
BATE: Sarah, 148
BATERSBY: Elizabeth, 12
BATES: Frances, 86; James, 194
Batt, 92, 96
BATTALIE: Lawrence, 24; Sarah, 24
BATTE: Elizabeth, 33; Henry, 33; John, 33; Mary, 33; Robert, 147; William, 33, 148
Baugh: Henry, 150
BAUGNS: Hannah, 199
Bauston, 166
BAXTER: John, 34
BAYLIS: Hannah, 183; John, 183
Baylor, 24, 118
BAYLOR: Mr., 26
BEAL: John, 60, 67
BEALE: John, 7; Mary, 199; Peggy, 8
BEALL: Samuel, 79, 88
BEARD: James, 163
BEATIE: John, 197
BEAZLEY: Bridget, 12; Fuqua, 12; Hyram, 12; John, 12
Becca, 12

Beck, 7, 25, 39, 42, 43, 45, 46, 51, 53, 54, 56, 69, 74, 78, 82, 83, 84, 85, 86, 87, 90, 92, 93, 94, 95, 96, 101, 107, 108, 109, 113, 129, 148, 150, 154, 158, 175
BECK: Marablis, 56
Becker, 54
Becky, 20, 35, 82, 111, 115, 144, 147, 154
Bedford, 192
Bee: Robert, 159
Beechy, 9
BEGTHILL: Edward, 186
Beit, 130
Belah, 189
Belfield, 39
Belinda, 80, 86, 96, 150
BELL: Alfred, 44; Benjamin H., 12; George, 61; Henry, 12, 13; Henry Cary, 12; Jane, 44; Mary, 13; Mary Ann, 44; Mary Anne, 44; Moor, 61; Nathan, 61; Rebecca, 12, 13; Virginia, 13; William, 44
Ben, 1, 10, 11, 16, 17, 18, 21, 26, 28, 36, 38, 39, 41, 43, 45, 55, 59, 60, 63, 65, 78, 79, 80, 81, 82, 83, 84, 85, 86, 87, 88, 89, 90, 91, 92, 93, 94, 95, 96, 97, 100, 102, 111, 113, 115, 116, 118, 128, 130, 141, 145, 147, 148, 149, 152, 155, 158, 164, 165, 173, 175, 183, 188
Benjamin, 11, 65, 67, 165, 166, 199
BENNETT: Richard, 126
Benson, 85
BENTON: John, 129; Pleasant, 129

BERGLEY: Ann, 79
Berkeley, 118
BERNARD: Richard, 177
Beshley, 87
Bess, 1, 25, 32, 34, 35, 45, 56, 68, 69, 74, 83, 86, 93, 106, 113, 131, 133, 135, 148, 150, 152, 173, 188
Bet, 55, 62, 90, 149
Beth, 84, 88
Betsy, 11, 15, 26, 35, 36, 41, 42, 57, 67, 68, 69, 72, 73, 77, 85, 87, 94, 100, 105, 116, 133, 143, 149, 157, 158, 160, 161
Betsy Ann, 14
Bett, 31, 36, 40, 84, 94, 153, 154
Bette, 102
Betts, 172
Betty, 1, 9, 11, 12, 13, 16, 19, 20, 21, 27, 35, 36, 39, 41, 42, 45, 47, 60, 61, 65, 69, 72, 73, 77, 78, 79, 80, 81, 82, 83, 84, 85, 86, 87, 88, 89, 90, 91, 92, 93, 94, 95, 96, 97, 100, 101, 102, 103, 109, 113, 118, 119, 123, 125, 127, 133, 136, 140, 145, 147, 148, 151, 152, 153, 154, 155, 161, 166, 191, 193, 194, 195, 196, 199
Betty Jane, 119
Beverly, 115, 133
Bib, 21, 91
Biddy, 73
BIDGNAY: Phebe, 119
BILBA: Harriet, 16
Bill, 19, 102, 166, 169

BILLUPS: Alfred, 121; Austin, 39; Joice, 121; Mary, 39; Octavia, 121
Billy, 12, 13, 14, 16, 17, 18, 19, 21, 26, 28, 29, 40, 41, 42, 43, 53, 54, 55, 61, 65, 67, 76, 80, 85, 88, 89, 90, 94, 95, 100, 101, 102, 104, 107, 108, 109, 113, 114, 115, 116, 118, 127, 128, 135, 147, 148, 151, 154, 196
BINFORD: Madgelena S., 61; William A., 61
BINGLEY: Ann, 89; James, 89; Lewis, 79, 89
BINNS: Charles, 133; Charles H., 133; Martha E., 133; Matilda, 136; Otway P., 133
BINS: Martin, 89
Bit, 104
BIX_OM: William, 79
BLACK: Augustine A., 114; Michael, 184
BLACKNELL: Charles, 51; Mary, 51
BLADES: Campbell, 71, 159
BLAIR: Ann, 147; Archibald, 147, 201; Henrietta Maria, 147; James, 147; John, 79, 88, 147, 201; John N., 201; Margaret, 201; Marion, 147; William, 201
Blake, 3
BLAKE: Augustine A., 114
Blanche, 3
Bland, 104
BLAND: Richard Y., 141; Roderick, 99
BLAND Jr.: John, 99

BLAND/BLUND: Mary, 147; Theodonick, 147
Blue, 90
BLUNKER: James, 33
BLUNT: Thomas, 125
Boatswain, 79, 95, 114, 116, 140, 153
Bob, 1, 3, 9, 12, 16, 18, 20, 21, 25, 26, 37, 39, 41, 42, 43, 45, 46, 53, 54, 55, 56, 59, 60, 63, 65, 68, 69, 74, 76, 78, 80, 81, 85, 87, 89, 90, 94, 97, 102, 103, 104, 105, 109, 114, 125, 127, 129, 133, 140, 148, 150, 151, 152, 154, 155, 158, 159, 165, 172, 181, 187, 191, 192
BOCKIUS: Samuel M., 63
BOCOCK: William B., 15
Body, 196
BOHANNON: Ambrose, 51; Mary, 63
BOHANON: James, 37
BOISSEAU: Daniel, 72, 160; Elizabeth, 44, 47; Nancy B., 44, 47; Sarah M.C., 72
Boler: Elnora, 143; George, 143
Boller, 131; Billy, 135
Bolling, 12, 144, 149; Francis, 182
BOLLING: Mary, 15; Philip, 18; Robert, 39; Susanna, 39
BOLTON: Wm, 199
BOND: Joseph, 89; Thomas, 49
BONNER: Jesse, 39; Rebecca, 39; Robert, 147
Booker, 96, 141
BOOKER: Ann, 100; Isaac, 99; Lewis, 83; William M., 161, 162
BOOKER Sr: William M., 161

BOOKER Sr.: William M., 162
Boon: Moses, 129
BOON: George Green, 111; William, 111
BOOTEN: Judith, 37
BOOTH: James, 79; Robert, 39
BOOTON: Ambrose, 37; Lewis, 37; William, 37
BORUM: Benjamin, 121; Edmond, 121; John, 121; Sterling, 121
BORUM Sr.: John, 121
Bosen, 85
BOSOMEWORTH: George, 192
Boson, 89
Boston, 26
BOSWELL: Thomas, 51, 57
BOTTOM: John T., 72, 160
BOWEN: Charles, 197; Henry, 197; Lilly, 197
Bowler, 113
Bowser, 66; Nancy, 151
BOWYER: Henry, 7; Major Thomas, 7
BOYD: Andrew, 7; James, 7; John, 113; Luis, 7; Lydia, 113; Mary B., 7; William Watson, 7
BRACH: Mary, 89
Bradberry, 87
Bradbury, 90
Braddock, 78, 88
BRADFORD: Elizabeth Landon, 111; Jane, 169; Maj. Samuel K., 169
Bradley, 86
Branch, 141, 142; Edward, 142; Ned, 51

BRANCH: Bolling, 13; Henry B., 13; Rebecca, 12, 13; Virginia, 13
Brandon: Randolph, 148
Brandon, 180
Brannum, 144
Brass, 113
Braughton, 180
Braxton, 66
BRAXTON: Betsy, 57; Betty, 114; Carter, 114; Corbin, 114; Elizabeth, 57; Fanny C., 114; George, 99; Lucy, 114; Tomlin, 114; William A., 114; William P., 115
BRAY: Col. David, 194
Bredwell: Sarah, 174
BREDWELL: Samuel, 181
Breeches, 45
BREEDING: John, 79; Martha, 79, 89
BREEDLOVE: Nathan, 118; Tirviah, 119
Brian, 142
Brichche, 45
BRICHETT: Martha, 147; William G., 147
BRICHETT Jr.: Peter, 147
BRICHETT Sr.: Peter, 147
Bricky, 188
BRIDGES: Benjamin, 79, 89
Bridget, 42, 78, 87, 125, 148
BRIGGS: Dorothy, 73; Gray, 73
Brister, 64
Bristo, 87, 97
BRISTOE: Richard, 176
Bristol, 43, 80, 83, 84, 94, 113, 151, 171
Bristor, 88, 140

BRITTELL: James, 194
BROADUS: Betsy, 103
BRODNAX: Cadwallader, 42; Frederick S., 41; Jack P., 42; Mary, 41; Robert, 42; William F., 42
BRODREAX: Meriweather, 45
BROOCKE: Cornelius C., 99; Elizabeth, 99; Frances A.E., 99; Lewis E., 99; Sally, 99
BROOKING Sr.: William, 51
BROOKS: Thomas, 173
Brown: John, 41, 172, 187; Martha, 118; Molly, 134, 136
BROWN: Adeline, 61; Alexander, 183; Benajah, 13; Benajah A., 13; Benjamin, 13, 61; Bentley, 61; Beverly, 148; Beverly A., 13; Edward, 61; Garland, 13; Henry, 89; Huldah, 61; James, 68; John, 61, 187; Mary, 13; Meletas, 13; Milly, 61; Sarah, 148; William, 61, 148
BROWN Jr.: Henry, 89; John, 79, 88
BROWNE: Benjamin, 79, 89; Enoch, 171; Henry, 79; John, 78, 79, 88; William, 79, 88
BROWNE Jr.: Henry, 79; William, 79, 89
BRUCE: Alexander, 139; Ann, 139; Armistead, 139; James, 139; Janey, 139; Lamma, 139; Lucy, 139; Woodson, 139
BRUCE Sr.: Alexander, 139
BRUMLEY: Joseph, 103; Mary C., 103
Brunello, 3

Brunswick, 12
BRUSHWOOD: Ann, 99
Brutus, 25, 27, 61
BRYANT: John, 19
Buck, 16, 56, 74, 80, 108, 109, 164; Anamia, 151; Billy, 151
Buett, 15
BUFFIN: William, 94
BULLARD: Ambrose, 23
BUNSOLL: Major Lord, 194
BURCH: John H., 116
Burg, 161
BURGE: Bradford, 44; Lucy D., 44
BURGESS: Edward, 171, 175; Gardiner, 175; Garner, 171
BURGH: Alexander, 148; Amy, 148; Frederick, 148; James, 148; Martha, 148; Mary, 148; Nath, 148; Priscilla, 148; Sarah, 148; Thomas, 148; Woodde, 148
BURKE: Lucy, 99
Burnett, 103
BURNETT: Bolling C., 40; Mary, 40
BURNS: Frankie, 109
Burrel, 145
Burrill, 148
BURROW: Gray, 39; Henry, 39; Jerrald, 39; John, 39; Martha, 39; Susannah, 39
BURROW Sr.: Philip, 39
Burton, 127
BURTON: C.C., 159; William, 187
Burwell, 26, 114, 144
BURWELL: Carter, 80; Frances, 7; Frances T., 159;

Lewis, 7, 159; Martha, 114; Nathaniel, 80, 88, 114
BURWELL Jr.: M., 88
Burwick, 7
BUSBIE: Mildred, 53
Bush, 141
BUSH: John, 79; William, 79, 88
Buster, 74
BUTLER: John, 148; Mary, 148
BUTTERWORTH: Joicy F., 39
Byas, 123
BYRD: J__, 80; John C., 89; Mary, 31; William, 31
C__on, 154
C_hriam, 57
C_ss, 83
C_ssa, 106
C_zor, 43
CABELL: Edmund W., 13; Frederick, 13; Frederick M., 13; Lewis W., 13; William, 14
Cader, 127
Caesar, 59, 113, 154, 165
CAIN: Martha, 39
Calda, 42
Caleb, 17, 87
Calib, 16
CALLEY: Martha, 147
CALLIS: Betsy, 121; William H., 121
Calvin, 14, 143
Cambridge, 106
CAMM: John, 100
CAMP: Rebecca, 89
Campbell, 17, 71; James, 186
CAMPBELL: Charles Henry, 197; Elizabeth, 197; Hugh,

104; Sarah, 104; Sarah Buchanan, 197; Thomas H., 143; William, 197
CANADY: John, 178
CANAY: Sarah, 80
Candice, 11
Cangelow, 113
CAPLAND: William Richman, 35
CARDWELL: George, 90; Thomas, 90; William, 80, 90
Carlce, 28
Carlina, 165
CARLTAN: Lewis, 105
CARLTON: Elizabeth, 100; George K., 100; William, 100
Carly, 13
Caroline, 14, 21, 39, 42, 65, 71, 74, 78, 87, 117, 126, 131, 148, 161
Carr: Jack, 157; William, 157
CARR: John, 129, 157; Joshua, 126; Lidia, 126; Martha, 126; Mary, 126; Mathew, 126; Patsy, 129; Robert, 126; Titus, 126; William, 157
Carry, 128
Carston, 24
Carter, 8, 12, 17, 55, 71, 78, 85, 95, 116, 117, 154; James, 54
CARTER: Apphire, 169; Charles, 90, 169; Dr. James, 80; Edward, 169; Elizabeth, 111; Harmar, 111; Howard, 169; James, 89; Jane W., 67; John, 169; Lucy, 103; M. George, 169; Martha, 80; Robert C., 111; S__ecy, 101; Sally, 169, 171; St L.L., 111;

212

Thomas, 191; William Champ, 169
Cary, 77, 123, 133
CARY: Charlotte L., 144; George B., 144; Henry, 191; Mary, 194; Miles, 191, 194; Rebecca, 75; Sally Taylor, 144; Thomas, 194; Willy, 194; Wilson Jefferson, 75
Cary Ann, 144
Cary Jr., 128
Cassel, 18
Catchanah, 113
Catchena, 147
Cate, 9, 18, 25, 26, 31, 32, 35, 42, 55, 56, 69, 79, 80, 81, 82, 85, 86, 87, 88, 90, 91, 97, 104, 108, 109, 113, 118, 123, 126, 130, 131, 134, 135, 149, 151, 152, 154, 166, 180, 195
Catharine, 54, 115, 179
Catherine, 26, 44, 144, 148
Cathy, 81
Catina, 117
Cato, 1, 26, 52, 79, 82, 85, 86, 89, 94, 96, 154, 155
Cats, 55, 77, 148
CATTELL: Mrs. George, 68
Caty, 26, 54, 64, 66, 70, 114, 116, 143, 159
CAWOOD: Stephe, 197
Cealey, 60
Ceazor, 9
Celia, 16, 29, 41, 45, 73, 148, 161
Celiann, 61
Certificate of Freedom, 117, 126; Aaron, 125; Abigail, 36; Benjamin Bartley, 11; Bob Green, 64; Diana Ash, 125; George Grain, 41; Hetty Ash, 125; James Harvey Atkins, 99; Lilly, 36; Louisa Johnson, 159; Moses, 189; Moses of Boon, 129; Rachel Ash, 130; Robert Bee, 159; Tabetha, 36
Cesar, 3, 9, 26, 65, 72, 79, 83, 86, 88, 89, 102, 147, 166, 188
Cess, 78
CHAMBERLAYNE: Elizabeth, 31, 134; Thomas, 67; William, 134
CHAMBERS: Daniel, 184; Willis, 11
CHAMESY: William, 194
Champion, 86, 96
CHANCEY: Elizabeth, 90; John, 80
Chancy, 65, 101, 143
CHANDLER: Ann Elizabeth, 159; Elizabeth, 163; Hugh, 24; John, 24; Leroy, 24; Norborne E., 24; Samuel T., 24; Samuel Temple, 24; Timothy, 24
CHANDLER Jr.: David, 163; John, 24
Chaney, 18
Chany, 9
Chapman, 68
CHAPMAN: Mary, 106
Charity, 8, 11, 16, 21, 26, 75, 90, 103, 158
Charles, 1, 3, 10, 12, 14, 15, 19, 21, 22, 26, 29, 35, 41, 42, 44, 45, 47, 52, 56, 60, 67, 72, 74, 78, 79, 80, 81, 82, 84, 85, 86, 87, 88, 89, 91, 93, 94, 95, 97,

101, 104, 105, 106, 113, 119, 126, 127, 129, 133, 139, 140, 141, 143, 144, 147, 149, 153, 154, 155, 157, 161, 162, 165, 167, 169, 172, 179, 181
CHARLES: Henry H., 196; Lewis, 90; Samuel, 90; Sarah, 196; William, 90
Charley, 61, 85
Charlot, 155
Charlotte, 7, 11, 17, 21, 25, 26, 39, 40, 41, 43, 60, 63, 65, 66, 68, 75, 81, 91, 93, 95, 96, 103, 107, 115, 121, 123, 128, 149, 154, 160, 189
Chashin, 42
Chaster, 47
Chenah, 46
Chener, 41
Cheny, 9
Cherry, 39, 125, 131
Cheshire, 152
Chesley, 75
Chesses, 12
Chester, 17, 63, 89
CHICK: Susan M., 195
China, 57, 72, 127, 160
Chisley, 81, 90
Chloe, 9, 22, 39, 42, 53, 68, 128, 175, 179, 180
Christian, 26
CHRISTIAN: Catherine, 100; Emeline, 119; Etheline, 100; Fanny C.C., 100, 109; George, 22; James, 100; Joham, 90; John, 22, 80, 100; John Henry, 133; Robert M., 36, 69
Christopher, 29, 64, 77, 128, 165

Chuchaluck, 125
Church Wardens, 174, 182, 183, 186
CHURCHILL: Dorothy, 51
CHUVERIUS: _rania, 52; Abott, 52; Andrew, 52; Atwood, 51, 52; Augustin, 51; Benjamin, 51, 52; Christian, 52; Ellonor, 52; Gibson, 51, 52; Holt, 51; Irania, 51; James, 52; John, 52; Joseph, 51, 52; Mary, 51
Cibby, 78
Cilla, 67
Cillar, 188
Cindy, 19, 141
Cinow, 139
Ciss, 73, 113, 151
Cissely, 11
Citta, 46
Clace, 55
Claiborne, 60, 65, 66
CLAIBORNE: Augustine, 41, 114; Cad, 42; Gracy, 41; Herbert A., 74, 161; Martha, 41; Mary, 42; Nathaniel, 42; Thomas Augustin, 42; William, 42; William Cole, 42
Clara, 26, 29, 65, 82, 83, 96, 101, 137, 158
Clarecy, 59
Claressa, 130
Clarey, 154
Clarissa, 66, 145
Clarisy, 152
CLARK: Ann, 100; Benjamin, 100; Bolling, 40; Elizabeth, 18, 100; George, 178; Henrietta Maria, 35; John,

100, 158; Johnathan, 100; Mary, 158; Matthew, 81; Richard A., 158; Sara, 18; Solomon, 158; Thomas O., 158; William H., 158
Clarke: Zack, 67
CLARKE: James, 134; William, 134
Clary, 26, 28, 56, 60, 72, 78, 91, 92, 95, 136, 149, 152, 161
Clay, 26, 144
CLAY: Rachal, 139; Thomas, 40
CLAYTON: Arthur, 75; Hester Ann, 75; James, 100; John, 75; Mary, 75; Rebecca Parke Farley, 101; Thomas, 75; Thomas Smith, 101; William, 134, 136; William Hemden, 100
Clementine, 3, 41
CLEMENTS: Elizabeth, 114; John, 114; Lavine, 114; Lucresa, 114; Mary, 114; William Martin, 114
Clitty, 139
Cloe, 14, 35, 39, 52, 78, 80, 81, 83, 86, 88, 90, 92, 94, 96, 99, 103, 125, 141, 145, 152
CLOPTON: Ned, 84
CLOUGHEN: Mary Ann W., 70; Robert, 70; W.S., 70
CLUVERIUS: Courtney, 55
COBB: Richard, 185
COBIN: Alice, 101
Cochener, 40
Cocke, 155
COCKE: Acrill, 31; Benjamin, 61; Catesby, 157; Collin, 148, 149; James B., 149; John, 61; John Catesby, 157; Littleberry, 31; Mary B., 63; Rebecca, 31; Samuel, 61; Thomas P., 149; William Ellis, 139
COCKRAN: Richard, 114, 118
Coder, 57
Coffee, 177, 183
COLE: Abraham, 194; Ann, 80; Elizabeth, 149; James, 191; Jane, 191; John, 149, 191; Josiah, 80; Martha, 191; Mary, 32, 191; Richard, 32; Roscow, 191; Sally, 43; Susannah, 43, 191, 195; William, 32, 149, 191; William Harwood, 194; William Temple, 43
Coleman, 43
COLEMAN: Ann Mourning, 14; Betsy, 14; Elizabeth, 14; George, 14; James, 14; Samuel, 14; Thomas, 23; William, 80; Wyatt, 80
Colin, 154
COLLEY: Charles, 62
COLLEY Sr.: Charles S., 62
COLLIER: John, 24, 62; Sarah, 24, 62; Thomas, 189
Collin, 148
Collins, 3
COLLINS: Harriet Byron, 100; Jeyeux, 101; Juliett, 101; Susan, 101; William, 101
Collonel, 39
COLUNAN: William, 90
Coly, 118
Combo, 69, 193
COMBS: Joseph, 179

Conday, 11
CONDON: David, 194
Congo, 131, 171
Conn, 21
CONNELL: John H., 62, 71
CONNER: Ann, 149; Nancy, 21
CONRAD: Mary Eve, 163; Peter, 163
Coo: William, 187
Cook, 118, 152; Jack, 150
Cooke, 55, 57
Coon, 80
Cooper, 72; Jack, 153; Maria, 143
COOPER: Elizabeth, 52; John, 75, 80; Martha, 90
CORBIN: Gawin L., 76; William, 178
Cordilia, 104
CORES: Mary Ann, 75
Cornelius, 118, 141, 152
Cornwall: Margaret, 182
COSBY: Miss, 133
Cosser, 41
COTTON: Elizabeth, 129
COTTRILL: Martha A., 11; Richard, 11; William, 11
Courtney, 121
COURTNEY: Ann, 99
Cove: William, 182
COVINGTON: Charles, 129; Sarah, 101; Walter G., 102; William, 101
COWAN: Henry, 80, 90; John, 90
COWLES: Ann, 90; Edmond, 90; Edmund, 80; Henry, 90; John, 80, 90; Josia, 90;

Philip, 75; Sarah, 80, 89; Thomas, 75, 80, 90
COWLES Jr.: Edmond, 90
COWLING: Ann L., 126; Samuel, 126
COX: Benjamin, 14; Eliza S., 14; Elizabeth, 14; George, 14, 52; George H., 14; Harriet K., 14; Josiah A., 14; Kejiah C., 14; Mary Ann, 66; Mary G., 40; Matthew, 14; Patrick, 14; Polly, 66; William, 40
COY: Murdy M., 176
CRABB: Elizabeth, 199
CRAFFORD: John, 191; Patsy Cany, 191
Crandon, 21
CRANLEY: Samuel, 80
Crann: Peter, 182
CRAWFORD: Jennet, 8
CRAWFORD Jr.: Samuel, 8
Crawley, 142
CRAWLEY: Joseph, 80, 90
Creary, 144
CRENSHAW: Allain, 139; Charles, 24, 25; Frances, 24, 62; John, 24, 62; Mary, 139; Nathanial, 24; Richard, 25
Cressy, 44, 94
Cresy, 41
Cretix, 155
Cretty, 116
Crisia, 53
Critt, 12
Critty, 155
CROCKFORD: John, 101
CROFT: Daniel, 5
Cromwell, 86, 96

CROSS: Benjamin, 126; Hardy, 126; Jane, 35; John, 35; Margaret, 126; Martha N., 126; William, 139; William H., 126
CROWDER: Polly, 43; Simon, 43
CRUMP: Charles A., 139; George P., 135; John P., 40; Mary, 134; Mildred, 134; Robinette, 135
Crusoe, 89
Cue, 78
Cuffey, 199
Cuffy, 1, 73, 103
Cug, 118
Cumbo, 80
CUNNINGHAM: Mary M., 52; Nathaniel, 52; William, *181*
CUNY: John M., 5
Cupid, 10, 52, 54, 55, 68, 83, 86, 87, 93, 96, 97, 181
Cupit, 113
CURD: Elizabeth W., 14
CURLE: Bennett, 80, 90; David, 75, 129; Lockey, 192
CURTIS: Christopher, 191; Daniel, 191; Edmond, 191; Nancy, 191; Nancy Drewey, 191; Rev. Thomas, 191; Robert Gray, 191; Samuel Gray, 191; Thomas Crandol, 191; William Henry, 191
CUSHENBURY: Polly, 139
Custer, 115
Cusy, 87
CUTLER: William, 40
CUTTING: Sally Carter, 171
Cutty, 85, 90, 95
Cuz, 82, 92

Cuzzy, 66
Cynthia, 26
Cyrus, 26, 41, 78, 84, 113, 114, 117, 127, 159, 161
Cyrus Jr., 130
Czbeo, 32
Dabben, 86
Dabney, 14
DABNEY: B.F., 118; Thomas L., 135
Daffney, 21
Dafney, 14, 148
Dahhne, 75
Dal, 31
Dallas, 128
Damus, 93
Danbar, 86
Dandridge, 63
DANDRIDGE: Nancy, 67
DANGERFIELD: Henry W., 119
Daniel, 10, 13, 14, 17, 18, 21, 26, 27, 32, 38, 40, 41, 42, 43, 46, 61, 62, 65, 71, 72, 78, 79, 80, 83, 84, 85, 87, 88, 89, 91, 93, 94, 95, 96, 97, 103, 113, 114, 117, 119, 131, 134, 141, 142, 144, 147, 148, 149, 161, 165, 166, 167, 181, 183, 186, 188, 196, 199
DANIEL: Daniel, 175; Peter, 179
Daphine, 19, 26, 67
Daphne, 66, 81, 82, 86, 91, 92, 96, 158
Daphney, 24, 26, 28, 84, 94
Daphnie, 85
Darby, 51, 52
Darcus, 35, 67, 155
Darky, 165

Darl__, 80
DARRACOTT: William, 62
Dasha, 85
DAUGHTNEY: Cheary, 127; Susan, 127
DAUGHTNEY: Patrick H., 126
DAUGHTREY: Barnes, 127
Daughtry, 126
Dave, 92
DAVENPORT: Ann, 14; David, 25; Osburn, 14; Thomas, 14
Daves: Randall, 174
Davey, 148, 155
David, 10, 14, 18, 22, 25, 26, 39, 41, 43, 53, 62, 64, 65, 66, 70, 76, 79, 80, 81, 82, 85, 86, 88, 89, 90, 91, 92, 94, 95, 119, 125, 134, 141, 145, 148, 149, 152, 197
DAVIDSON: Alexander, 33
Davie, 201
DAVIES: Nancy, 163; Robert, 163
DAVIS: Elizabeth, 62, 139, 140; Esther, 14; Henry, 62; Jacob, 140; John, 81, 90; Lewis, 62; Matthew, 139, 140; Moses, 134; Rhoda, 62; Robert, 15; Staige, 107; Stephen, 140; Thomas, 14, 139, 140; Thomas E., 136; William, 14, 186
Davy, 14, 17, 22, 28, 38, 68, 71, 75, 79, 81, 82, 83, 87, 89, 93, 103, 113, 114, 133, 134, 135, 136, 140, 154, 155, 177
Dawson, 103
Day, 135
Dean, 78

DEANING: Henry, 49
Deck, 127
Dedan, 189
Dedo, 114
Deds, 148
DEJAMATTE: Bowler, 140; John, 140; Judith W., 140; Martha W., 140; Rachel, 140; Reuben H., 140
Del, 3
DELACROUX: Peter, 81, 90
DELANEY: Nancy, 37
Delce, 73
Delcie, 101
Delia, 77, 133, 141, 143, 153
Deliah, 154
Delila, 18
Delilah, 109
Dell, 26
DELMORE: John, 62; Mary, 62
Delph, 113, 114, 166
Delpha, 106
Delphia, 38, 63, 65, 68, 77, 106, 115, 142
Delphy, 19, 24, 59, 119, 148
Delsey, 1, 40, 44, 47, 97
Delsy, 89
Dembo, 188
DEMOVALL: Sampson, 185
Denby, 82
Dennis, 14, 18, 126, 147, 171
DENNIS: William, 81, 90
DENT: Elizabeth, 171; George, 171; Judith A., 171
DERMONT: Michael, 157
Diana, 86, 96, 125, 141
Dianer, 158, 193
Dice, 26
Dicey, 92

Dick, 10, 14, 18, 21, 25, 26, 27, 31, 32, 37, 39, 41, 42, 45, 54, 55, 56, 64, 68, 69, 70, 78, 79, 80, 81, 82, 84, 85, 87, 88, 89, 90, 91, 92, 94, 95, 97, 104, 114, 127, 128, 133, 134, 139, 140, 141, 144, 147, 148, 162, 165, 181, 184, 187, 188, 196, 197
DICKERSON: Davie, 27; Samuel, 27; Thomas, 64, 70
DICKINSON: Asa D., 140; Henry, 127; Jacob, 127; James, 129; Joanna, 194; John, 129; Jonathan, 194; Martha, 129; Mary, 127; Mary A., 140; R.H., 106; Thomas, 140; William, 127; William P., 140
Dicky, 82
Dicy, 14, 19, 63, 77, 141
DIDLAKE, 107; Mary, 107; Robert D., 99
Dido, 75
DIE: William, 187
DIGGES: Isaac, 108; Sarah, 192
Dilce, 70
Diley, 46
Dillard, 78
DILLARD: Eliza, 63; Josiah, 63; Lucy, 63; Margate, 63; Mearey, 63; Stephen, 63; Stephen H., 63; Thomas, 63; William, 108
Dilley, 64
Dillo, 9
Dillon: Ann, 186
Dilsey, 140
Dilsy, 154

Dimbo, 94
Dina, 8, 128, 165
Dinah, 9, 12, 17, 22, 26, 39, 42, 43, 51, 56, 61, 63, 78, 80, 81, 83, 85, 86, 87, 88, 89, 90, 92, 93, 95, 96, 97, 109, 117, 127, 129, 143, 144, 147, 148, 172, 175, 188
Dine_, 44
Diner, 166
Dingo, 116
DINPHEY: Sally, 21
Disey, 90
DIX: Mary, 105
Dixon, 75, 79, 89, 104; Ned, 77
DIXON: Mary, 5
Dizey, 87
DO__LL: Mary, 149
DOBBINS: Charles, 101
DOBSON: Ann Frances, 52; John, 52; Joseph, 52; Martha Ann, 52; Rebecca, 52; Susan, 52
Docia, 15
Doctor, 42, 55, 78, 85, 87, 94, 133, 154
DODD: William, 81, 90
DODMAN: John, 195
DODSON: Joshua, 188
Dole, 46
Doll, 25, 39, 46, 64, 68, 70, 79, 84, 85, 86, 87, 89, 90, 94, 95, 96, 97, 129, 139, 148, 151
Dolly, 25, 53, 57, 67, 113, 143, 145, 149, 151, 187
DONIPHAN: Matt, 185
Dorcas, 77, 80, 90
Dorcus, 18, 158
Dorinda, 115, 179
DORLON: John, 125

Dosha, 83, 84, 95
Doshe, 93
Dosie, 61
DOWCHER: John, 194
DOWNE: John, 25; Lucy, 25; Mildred, 25; Robert, 25
DOWNER: William, 25
DOZWELL: Mary Elizabeth Poythrip, 149; Peter Epes, 149
DRAKE: Francis, 88
Drew, 128
DROINGOOLE: Fanny, 52
DRUMMOND: John, 81, 90
Duas: Mary, 183
Dublin, 85, 95, 188
Dudly, 95
Duffin, 82, 92
DUGAR: Reuben, 114
DUKE: Betty, 64
Dulcey, 155
DUMPHIN: Ann, 106
Dumphrey, 44
Dunbar, 96
DUNBAR: John, 90
Duncan, 164
DUNCAN: Charles, 147; Gabriel, 14; Joseph, 14
DUNCLE: John, 163; Margaret, 163; Mary, 163
DUNFORD: Wills, 81, 90
DUNN: Sally, 17; Susan B., 52; Washington V., 52
DUPUY: Mary, 140
DURFEY: Goodrich, 90; Samuel, 81, 90
DURFEY Jr.: Samuel, 90
DuVAL: Robert, 71
DYE: William, 178

DYSON: Francis, 140; H.I., 140
EA_LEY: Martha Susan, 126
EADES: Joseph, 15
EARL: Samuel, 178
Early: Honour, 174
EARNEST: William, 96
Easter, 10, 31, 39, 41, 45, 53, 56, 65, 80, 90, 92, 94, 96, 100, 139, 155
Easther, 104
EATON: John, 184
Eatt__, 70
Eave, 80
Eday, 37
Eddy, 77
Ede, 26
Edey, 133
Edgar, 26, 40
Edie, 28
Edith, 36, 69, 126
Edloe, 77
EDLOE: Carter H., 149
Edmond, 14, 56, 70, 80, 90, 93, 94, 95
EDMONDSON: Elizabeth, 35; Robert, 197
EDMONSON: William, 109
Edmund, 24, 26, 28, 46, 66, 68, 70, 78, 80, 82, 83, 88, 90, 91, 92, 93, 128, 141, 152, 154
Edward, 21, 64, 65, 117, 141, 142, 147, 149
EDWARDS: Charles H., 121; Charles S., 119; Frances, 55; Mary Susan, 103; Mary T., 121; Susanna, 10; Thomas, 121; William Henry, 55
Edwin, 16, 66

Edy, 16, 71, 78, 79, 80, 83, 84, 86, 87, 88, 90, 91, 93, 94, 96
Effy, 95
EGGLESTON: Fanny, 201; Frances, 81, 91; Richard, 91
EGGLESTON Sr.: Richard, 81
Elam, 161
Eldridge, 15
Eleanor, 24, 26, 29
Eleck, 45
Elenor, 123
Elick, 17, 56
Elijah, 13, 61, 80, 140
Elik, 41
Elisha, 44, 71
Eliza, 3, 12, 14, 17, 20, 24, 26, 42, 65, 66, 74, 102, 115, 121, 123, 136, 141, 143, 144, 145, 152, 158, 161
Eliza Jane, 171
Elizabeth, 24, 40, 65, 82, 119, 134, 174, 186
Elizajane, 141
Ell_, 65
Ella, 143
Ellen, 43, 115, 157
Ellick, 10, 39
ELLINGTON: Ridley, 139
Elliott, 26; Jane, 186
ELLIOTT: Martha, 9
ELLIS: Polly S., 39
Ellison, 119
ELLITE: Frances W., 67
Elly, 133
ELLYSON: John, 134, 135
ELMORE: Elizabeth, 139; Rebecca, 140; William Watkins, 139
Elnora, 100, 143
Else, 51, 52, 87, 92

ELSEY: John, 171; Thomas, 171
Elvey, 136
Elvia, 13
Elvira, 19
Elvy, 77
ELZEY: Jane, 171; John, 171; Lewis, 171; Thomas, 171
Emancipated, 75, 76, 150; Aaron, 125, 136; Abbey, 75; Abner, 157; Aggy, 111, 137; Alexander, 78, 88; Alley, 61, 136; Amey, 136; Amy, 134; Ann, 130; Archer, 17, 161; Archy, 112; Armistead, 142; Armstead, 66; Avery, 136; Ballock, 27; Barbara, 164; Bartlett, 111; Bauston, 166; Beck, 39; Benjamin, 165, 166; Betsy, 42, 161; Betty, 39, 61, 133; Bill, 169; Bob, 39, 133; Branch, 142; Calda, 42; Carlina, 165; Cate, 134, 151, 166; Cats, 77; Celia, 161; Charles Quash, 169; Charlotte, 75; Chester, 17; Chloe, 39; Christopher, 77, 128; Clara, 137; Clary, 136; Daniel, 27, 61, 134, 166; Davy, 136; Delph, 166; Dick, 27, 56; Dinah, 39; Dixon, 75; Doctor Sawney, 20; Edey, 133; Eliza, 17, 143; Elizabeth, 134; Elnora Boler, 143; Elvy, 77; Emily, 42; Essex, 73, 161; Esther, 133; Fabries, 130; Fanny, 111, 133, 142; Frank, 61, 134; Gabe, 137; Gary, 133; George, 143, 153, 164, 167;

George Boler, 143; Gilbert, 133; Gilly, 133; Grace, 27; Granason, 165; Gray, 17; Hannah, 17, 75; Henny Harris, 158; Henrietta, 42; Henry, 142; Hetty, 73, 161; Isaac, 7, 17, 66, 164; Isham, 136; Jack, 61, 128; Jack White, 31; Jacob, 78; Jame, 134; James, 111, 130, 142; Jane, 39, 137; Jeffrey, 93; Jemima, 134; Jerry, 11, 39, 137; Jesse, 75; Jim, 128, 137; Joanna, 17; Joba, 75; Joe, 49, 76; John, 66, 111, 133, 161; Johnny, 73, 161; Juba, 73, 161; Judy, 39; Julian, 165; Jupiter, 73, 161; Kate, 5, 151; Lavin, 137; Lavinia, 200; Liddy, 164; London, 66; Lotty, 61; Louisa, 42, 142; Lucy, 42, 70, 111, 134, 153; Lucy Ann, 153; Maria, 17, 128; Martha, 42, 136; Mary, 134, 143; Matilda, 111; Micall, 61; Milia, 134; Millicent, 130; Milly, 164, 165; Miranda, 42; Moll, 155; Moses, 39, 164; Mouring, 66; Nancy, 39, 73, 133, 137, 143, 161; Nany, 128; Nat, 151; Ned, 39, 61, 133; Nell, 133; Nelson, 18, 56; Orange, 127; Pamela, 17; Patience, 61; Patty, 61, 136, 164; Paulina, 17; Pers, 75; Peter, 133, 134; Philip, 75; Philis, 17, 39; Phill, 169; Phillip, 61; Polly, 159; Queen, 73, 161; Rachel, 165; Randolph, 148; Richard, 143; Riger, 136; Robert, 134, 153; Robin, 33, 42, 130, 165; Roper, 134; Sally, 75, 133, 200; Sam, 73, 77, 133, 137; Samuel, 130, 166; Sarah, 61, 133, 134, 135, 166; Sela, 166; Seller, 27; Seth, 169; Shadrack, 59; Stephen, 86; Stepney, 133, 169; Suky, 17; Tabb, 39, 61; Taner, 134; Tom, 39; Tom Thandy, 201; Tone, 17; Venus, 136; Violet, 8; Warwick, 73; Will, 33; William, 61, 111, 134, 153; Willis, 130; Wilson, 137; Winney, 39

Emanuel, 18, 45, 52, 111

EMBRY: Elizabeth, 9; Ermin, 9; Henry, 9; Martha, 9; Mary, 9; Sarah, 9; William, 9

Emeline, 60, 65

Emily, 16, 19, 42, 65, 66, 102, 142

Emma, 115

Emmanuel, 26

Enos, 28, 145

Eoney, 39

EPES: Amey, 40; Archibald, 149; Catharine, 145; Edmund, 154; Francis, 140, 149; Isham, 40; John, 145; John S., 148, 149; Martha, 149; Mary, 147, 150; Peter, 149; Rachel, 145; Richard, 149; Sarah, 149; Sarah G., 140; Susanna, 149; Thomas R., 145; Travis H., 143; William, 40, 149, 150; William Mo_ion, 149

Ephrain, 41, 152

EPPES: Ann G., 15; Archibald, 150; Christian, 150; Daniel, 150; Eliza W., 15; Elizabeth, 41, 150; Frances, 150; Francis, 40, 150; John, 15; Martha B., 15; Polly, 150; Richard, 150; Robertson, 150; Thomas, 150; William, 40; Willie J., 15
Esau, 24
Eseau, 149
Essea, 25
Essex, 73, 78, 131, 141, 161, 179
Ester, 125, 158
Esther, 15, 21, 25, 26, 29, 36, 37, 42, 56, 57, 79, 80, 83, 84, 85, 86, 88, 94, 101, 103, 106, 113, 119, 133, 150, 154, 188
Ethalinda, 66
ETHERINGTON: William, 177
Etta, 102
EUBANK: Ellen, 106; Maud Henden, 100; Richard, 114, 115; William, 114
EUBANK Jr.: Thomas, 63
EVANS: Rebecca, 189; William, 189
Eve, 90
Evelina, 18, 102
EVENS: Charles R., 101; Mary E., 101
Everand, 162
Evie, 147
EWELL: James B., 157
Ezekiel, 26
F_ak, 90
Fabries, 130
FAIR: Benjamin, 81; Turner H., 81

Fallmore, 52
Fan, 62, 64, 70
Fann, 53
Fanna, 63
Fannie, 128
Fanny, 10, 11, 13, 16, 21, 24, 26, 39, 41, 42, 43, 44, 45, 52, 54, 56, 57, 59, 60, 61, 63, 64, 65, 66, 72, 73, 77, 78, 79, 80, 81, 82, 83, 84, 85, 86, 87, 88, 89, 91, 92, 93, 94, 95, 96, 97, 101, 106, 111, 113, 114, 116, 118, 133, 135, 141, 142, 144, 145, 147, 149, 151, 152, 154, 157, 165, 171, 187, 192, 196
FARINHOLL: Robert, 101
FARMER: Samuel Madison, 72, 160
FARRELL: Eliza, 70
Farthing, 9
FARTHING, 81; Ann, 81, 91; Edward, 91; John, 79, 81; Milly, 91; Richard, 81, 91; William, 81, 91
FAULKNER: Mary, 101
FAUNT: Samuel G., 104
FAUNTLEROY: Ann Willis, 119; Moore G., 101
Fayette, 24
FEAR: Benjamin, 91
Feby, 85
Federick, 88
Feel, 106
Felicia, 158
Fenda, 31
FENELL: Susannah, 28
FENN: Daniel B., 150; Priscilla, 150; Susan E., 152; Virginia B., 152
Fenton, 42, 61

FENTON: John, 91
Fergerson: Billy, 111
FERGUSON: David H., 15; Dougald, 15; Elira Susan, 15
Fester, 130
Fidler, 113
FIELD: Ann, 107; George, 37; Henry, 37; Henry William, 37; James, 150; John, 37; Joseph, 37; Molly, 37; Sarah, 37; Stephen, 107; Theophilius, 150; Thomas, 37, 150
FIELDS: Ann, 107
FIGG: Benjamin, 115; Mary W., 115; Robert, 115; Sarah Frances, 115
Fill, 61
Fill_o, 11
Fillis, 45, 114, 145
Finton, 123
FISHER: George, 44
FITZGERALD: Francis, 141
FITZHUGH: Camp, 81, 91; Henry, 182; John, 182; Thomas, 181
FLEET: Christopher, 101
Fleming, 19, 66, 133
FLEMING: Elizabeth, 63; William, 63
Fleming Jr., 66
Flemming, 83
FLESCHWAR: Elizabeth, 34; Stephen, 34
FLETCHER: Thomas, 178
FLOOD: Eliza Bolling, 3; J.W., 3
Flora, 12, 37, 46, 84, 85, 95, 187, 188
FLYNN: Owen R., 129

FOLEY Sr.: John, 182
FONTAINE: Walter S., 16
FOOTE: Richard, 176
FORD: Addison, 13; Ann, 140; Joseph, 155; Mary, 13; Milton, 140; Samuel, 72, 140; Waller, 140; Zachary, 140
Forest, 134
Fortune, 10, 29, 131
FOSTER: George, 25; James, 25; Patty, 25; Thomas, 119; William, 25
Foulk: Henry, 49
Fountain, 18, 26
FOUSHEE: John, 178, 183
FOWKE: Capt. Gerard, 172; Chandler, 173; Gerard, 182, 183, 187
FOWLKES: Edward B., 141; Hiram, 141; Kennen, 141; Kenner, 141; Nancy B., 141; Opie, 141; Pamelia, 141; Rafe, 141; Ranson, 141; Sally, 141; Samuel H., 141; William, 141; William A., 141; William C., 141
Fox: Billy, 19
FOX: Charles, 63; Cornelus, 43; Edwin, 63; Elizabeth W., 63; James, 63; Lewis, 63; Nathaniel, 63; Richard, 63; Susan, 63
Fran, 17, 62
Frances, 19, 78, 87, 141, 148, 186
Francis, 16, 63, 116, 151, 180, 182
Frank, 1, 9, 10, 14, 17, 18, 19, 21, 25, 26, 27, 28, 31, 32, 37,

39, 42, 43, 46, 47, 52, 53, 55, 61, 62, 63, 65, 67, 68, 71, 73, 75, 78, 81, 83, 85, 86, 87, 88, 89, 91, 92, 93, 95, 96, 97, 101, 104, 109, 113, 114, 115, 116, 123, 127, 134, 141, 147, 148, 150, 152, 154, 158, 165, 172, 176, 180, 188, 196, 199
Franklin, 128
FRANKLIN: Betsy, 14, 15; David B., 65; Esther, 15; Frances I., 65
Franky, 18, 41, 54, 57, 117
FRASER: Alexander, 41
Frazier: Isbell, 184; Mary, 185
Fred, 147
Frederick, 3, 14, 26, 36, 54, 77, 86, 96, 114, 116, 155, 199
Fredrick, 15, 80, 149
Free Person of Color: Betsy Scott, 20; Daniel P. Vanderwall, 162; Mahala, 65; Maria Cooper, 143; Matilda, 152; Solomon McClure, 129
Freeman, 41, 139, 140
FREEMAN: Derry, 7; James, 81, 91
FRENCH: E.H., 171; John, 127, 171, 183
FRIEND: Archibald E., 151; Charles, 151; John G., 151; Noth, 151
FROMAN: Elijah, 89, 91
Fuller, 75, 113
FULLER: Machum, 55
FULTON: Elizabeth, 163; James, 163; Martha, 163; Thomas, 163

FUQUA: Aaron, 15; Amile, 15; Gracy, 14; Joseph, 15; Moses, 15; Samuel, 15
Furguson: Duncan, 164
G_cy, 86
Gabby, 72
Gabe, 79, 89, 137
Gabey, 81, 84, 94
Gabrelly, 114
Gabriel, 21, 26, 51, 64, 70, 78, 109, 162, 166
Gabriella, 114, 116, 118
Gaby, 42, 73, 78, 80, 85, 86, 89, 90, 94, 96, 191
GADBERRY: John, 81, 91
GADDEN: Edmund, 82, 91; John, 82, 91
GADDY: William, 82, 91
GAGNO: Frances, 63
GAINES: Richard, 102
GALT: Dr. John M., 81; John M., 91
Gambia, 154
GANARD: Elisabeth, 172
Gandfry, 26
Gandy, 86, 96
GANNAWAY: Theoderick C., 15
GARDNER: Anthony, 102; Dr., 109; Elizabeth, 61; James, 102; John, 102, 107, 108; Mary, 108; Miles H., 61; Reuben, 63; Thomas, 63; William, 102
Garland, 61, 65
GARLICK: Mary, 100; Mary C., 115; Mildred C., 115
GARNETT: Margaret, 104
GARRARD: William, 185
Garrett, 86

GARRETT: Edward, 102; Elizabeth, 28; Richard, 102; Robert L., 102
Garrick, 36, 69
Garrison, 72, 160
Garthwright, 86
Gary, 43, 69, 82, 133
GATES: Allen, 11; Elizabeth, 11; Horatio, 70
GATHRIGHT: Joel, 96
Gay, 80
GAYLE: Susanna, 121
Gayney, 113
GEDDY: Francis, 75; Richard, 91
GEE: Henry, 150; James S., 150; Winfield, 150
GEERS: Robert, 140; Thomas, 140
General, 21
Geoffrey, 82, 179
George, 1, 8, 11, 12, 15, 16, 19, 20, 21, 23, 24, 25, 26, 27, 29, 32, 33, 35, 37, 38, 41, 45, 46, 47, 52, 53, 55, 56, 63, 65, 68, 69, 71, 77, 78, 79, 80, 82, 83, 84, 85, 86, 87, 88, 89, 90, 92, 93, 94, 95, 96, 100, 101, 102, 104, 111, 113, 114, 115, 116, 119, 123, 130, 143, 144, 148, 149, 153, 154, 155, 158, 159, 162, 163, 164, 167, 171, 175, 183, 188, 196, 199; Christian, 26
GEORGE: Agnes, 29; Anner, 25; Byrd, 25; Catharine, 29; Hamilton U.S., 95; John, 23, 25, 27, 30, 129; Louisa Catharine Wilson, 29; R., 25;
Reuben, 23, 25, 29; Samuel, 81, 91; William, 25, 102, 176
GERRARD: William, 184, 185
Gerrat, 172
GERRY: Anne, 47
GHOLSON: Nancy, 144
GIBBS: Ralph, 127; Thomas, 32
Gibson, 21
Gideon, 26, 38
Gift, 27
Gilbert, 19, 25, 26, 84, 86, 94, 104, 123, 127, 133, 145, 158
Giles, 19, 86, 155, 166
Gill__, 90
GILLIAM: Elisabeth, 154; Jane, 150; John, 151; Reuben, 141; Reuben M., 151; Robert, 154; Thomas Griffin Peachey, 151; Walter Boyd, 151; William, 151
GILLIAM Sr.: John, 150
GILLIAT: William, 74, 161
Gilly, 119, 133
Ginney, 19
Ginny, 42, 115, 154
GIPSON: Laban, 16
Gla_eo, 113
GLAREBROOK: James, 91
Glasgow, 36, 39, 181
Glory, 116
Gloucester, 53, 113
GLOVER: Benjamin Clapton, 11
God__cy, 82
Godby, 188
Godfrey, 78, 88, 91, 105
GODWIN: Sally K., 131; Susannah, 192
GOFF: Horatio, 3

GOLDSBY: Peter, 19
GON_ER: Richard, 33
GOODALL: John, 91; John, 81; William, 91
GOODALL Jr.: John, 91
GOODE: Robert, 160; Robert R., 160
GOODELL Sr.: John, 82; Turner, 82
GOODMAN: Barnes, 127; James, 127; James B., 127; Priscilla, 127; Samuel, 63
GOODWIN: Robert, 64
GORDON: Alexander, 153; Archibald Turner, 16; Eliza L., 7; James A., 7; Mary, 153; Samuel, 73; Thomas, 153
Grace, 9, 21, 27, 42, 52, 62, 80, 82, 83, 85, 89, 92, 93, 95, 113, 119, 127, 141, 145, 150, 174, 188
GRADY: Patrick, 186
GRAHAM: Dr. William, 157; Elizabeth, 157; Jean, 157; Jenny, 157; John, 157; Walls, 157; Walter, 157
Grain: George, 41
GRAMMAR Jr.: Rev John, 45
GRAMMON: Emily D., 195
Granason, 165
Granderson, 72, 160
GRANEMER: Rebecca, 154
GRANTHAM: Elizabeth, 152
GRAVES: Benjamin, 23, 27; Beverly, 23; Edward, 37; Frances, 23; John, 82, 91; John G., 27; Richard, 96; Sarah, 37; Travis, 27; William, 35

GRAVIS: Benjamin, 23; Francis, 23; John G., 23
Gray, 17, 184; Lucy, 73
GRAY: Gilbert W., 130; Nathaniel, 127; William, 134
Green, 39
GREEN: Alexander, 91; Annaliza, 44; Bob, 64; Elizabeth, 31; Henry G., 44; Jane L., 65; Ohray, 150; Philmer, 82, 91; Thomas, 82; William B., 69
Greg, 62
GREGG: Jane, 171; John, 179
Gregory, 55
GREGORY: Samuel, 16
GRESHAM: Elizabeth, 41; Samuel, 102; Susannah, 102
GRIFFEN: Samuel, 81
Griffin: Fanny, 151
GRIFFIN: Elizabeth, 159; John, 159; Richard, 159; Samuel, 92, 159; Tabitha, 159
GRIGSBY: Moses, 177, 178
GROTMAN: Samuel, 33
GRUBBS: Peter W., 65; Rebecca A., 65
GUBB: Nancy, 52
GUENAUT: Stephen, 16
Guley, 111
Gun: Day, 135
GUNN: Ann E., 142; Burwell, 142; Elisha G., 142; James, 71; James W., 142; John, 71; Lucy, 71; Roth C., 142; Thomas, 91; Thomas J., 142; William B., 142
GURLEY: John W., 150
Guy, 83, 88, 91, 93, 96, 195

GUY: Mary P., 145; Thomas, 27; Warren W., 145
GWATHMEY: John, 115; Major Joseph, 115; Martha, 115; Mary, 115, 116; Susanna, 115
H__t__t, 70
H_RY: Samuel H., 109
HACKELD: Susannah, 28
Hagan, 67
Hagar, 80, 89, 108, 109, 134
Hainy, 165
Hal, 18
HALES: Richard, 82, 92
Hall, 41, 43, 139, 151
HALL: Beverly, 52; Henry, 52; James, 34, 52; John, 53; Nathan, 52, 55; Sarah, 52, 53, 55
HALLEN: Elizabeth, 82; George, 82
HAMILTON: John, 173, 174, 175
Hamlin, 88
HAMLIN: George Willoughby, 41; John, 41; John Francis, 41; Stephen Henry, 41; Thomas Browne, 41
Hampshire, 86, 96, 180
Hampton, 73, 86, 96, 108, 109
HAMPTON: Thomas, 186
Hancock, 105
Handen, 75
HANDLEY: Martha, 63
Handy, 102
Haney, 68
HANKIN: Archer, 82, 92; Charles, 82; John, 82, 92; Robert, 82, 92; Seth, 82; William, 82, 92

HANKIN Jr.: William, 92
Hannah, 1, 8, 9, 11, 15, 16, 17, 19, 21, 25, 26, 27, 29, 33, 35, 36, 37, 42, 43, 44, 45, 47, 52, 53, 56, 57, 68, 69, 71, 75, 77, 78, 79, 80, 81, 82, 83, 84, 85, 86, 88, 89, 90, 91, 92, 93, 94, 95, 96, 101, 102, 103, 105, 106, 111, 113, 116, 117, 125, 129, 136, 141, 143, 148, 150, 151, 153, 154, 157, 158, 164, 165, 166, 172, 181, 183, 188, 189, 191, 193, 194, 195, 196, 197
Hanner, 118, 141, 148, 192
Hannibal, 46, 154
Hannibal Jr., 153
Hanover, 117
HANSBERGER: Henry, 171; Louise F., 171; William F., 171
HANSBERGER, Jr.: L., 171
HANSBROUGH: James, 175
Hany, 57
HARDAWAY: Daniel H., 142; John, 41
Hardenia, 60
Harding: Lymon, 194
HARDING: George, 184
HARDWICK: Solomon, 183
HARDWOOD: Archibald, 104; Robert M., 193; Thomas, 104
Hardy, 39, 71, 141
HARDYMAN: Elizabeth, 35; Francis, 35; Mary, 35
HARG: Elizabeth W., 29
Harlow, 171
HARMAN: Hen_y, 34
HARNESBERGER: Jacob, 163

HARPER: Mary Anne Frances, 40
Harriet, 15, 39, 41, 55, 63, 101, 103, 117, 119, 123, 128, 133, 141, 142, 149, 151
Harriett, 65, 114, 149, 152
Harris: Nathaniel, 158
HARRIS: Ann, 32; Edward, 82, 93; Frances, 14; Francis, 123; John, 78; Mary, 62; Mrs., 123; Robert, 14; William P., 97
Harrison, 41, 93, 99, 114, 191
HARRISON: Ann, 35; Anna Martha, 151; Benjamin, 16, 35; Carter B., 35, 151; Carter Basil, 151; Carter Henry, 35; Dolly P.G.B., 43; Elizabeth P., 153; George E., 151; Grace, 164; Henry, 35; Isabella H., 151; Jesse, 164; John, 164; John Henry, 151; Martha, 13; Molly, 111; Nathaniel, 161, 162, 175, 180; Nicholas, 34; Polly, 16; Randolph, 16; Richardson, 111; Robert, 35; Thomas, 32, 164; William Allen, 151; William H., 35
Harry, 9, 18, 19, 20, 21, 24, 25, 26, 36, 38, 42, 43, 44, 47, 53, 55, 57, 64, 66, 68, 70, 78, 79, 80, 81, 82, 83, 85, 86, 87, 88, 89, 90, 91, 92, 93, 95, 96, 97, 101, 104, 109, 113, 114, 115, 117, 118, 119, 126, 127, 128, 141, 143, 145, 148, 151, 153, 154, 155, 157, 163, 166, 172, 173, 177, 179, 185, 188, 192, 194

HART: Elizabeth, 107; Silas, 164; William, 82, 92
Hartwell, 41
HARTWELL: John, 127; Richard, 9
Harvey, 199; Daniel, 186
HARVIE: John, 71; Margaret, 71
HARWOOD: Barsheba, 61; Capt. Thomas, 193; Humphrey, 92; Lucy E., 53; Tabetha, 154; Thomas, 92; Thomas S., 53; William, 82, 192
HASLETT: Jethro, 128; Sophia Ann, 128
HATTON: Elizabeth, 92
HAUKINS: Charles, 92; Nathaniel, 92
HAWES: Richard.
HAWKES: Alexander H., 142; George A., 142; Philip, 142; Reuben, 142
Hawood, 78, 88
HAWOOD: William, 194
HAY: Edward, 116; James, 111; James H., 116; John H., 116; Martha, 116; Nancy, 114, 116, 118; Thomas, 194
HAYES: Nancy, 114
HAYNES: Elizabeth, 126; Jane, 191
HAZELWOOD: Richardson, 82
HAZLEWOOD: John, 92; Stephen, 92
HEATH: James, 34; Patsey, 152
Hector, 43, 78, 87

Hedge: Frank, 26; Ned, 26; Phill, 26
HEFFINGTON: Brumage, 127
Helen, 145, 158
HEMING: Bristo, 92
HENDERSON: Alexander, 158; David, 128; James, 201; Jane, 201
HENDRICK: Ann, 16; John, 16
Henley, 82
HENLEY: Elizabeth, 92; Leonard, 75, 82, 92; William, 85, 92
Henny, 118, 158
HENNY: Andrew, 186; James, 186
Henricka, 19
Henrietta, 42, 51, 52
Henry, 8, 11, 13, 15, 16, 18, 19, 20, 21, 24, 25, 26, 35, 41, 44, 47, 49, 54, 55, 61, 64, 65, 67, 72, 76, 78, 81, 99, 100, 102, 106, 115, 118, 130, 133, 141, 142, 143, 152, 155, 160, 161, 165, 172, 182
Henry Baugh, 150
Henry Wilson, 142
Herbert, 86
Herculas, 155
HERDMAN: John, 164
HERNDON: Edward, 176; Mary, 29
Hero, 28
Hester, 88, 95
HETH: William, 71
Hetty, 73, 125, 161
HEWIT: Dorothy Harwood, 192
HEWLETT: Austin, 136
HIBBLE: Ann, 53; Lucy F., 53

Hick, 36
HICKMAN: John W., 75
HICKS: Robert, 148
HIGASON: Hellen, 67
HIGHTOWER: Nancy, 140
HILL: Elizabeth, 63; James, 64; Jinny, 63; Juda, 63; Kezia, 63; Mary, 63; Mary Ann, 63; Michael, 151; Newton, 64; Robert, 16; Sarah, 63; Walker, 64; William, 36, 38, 64; William E., 69
HILL Sr.: James, 64; Mary, 64
HILLIARD: Armistead, 136; Benjamin, 68; Catey Ray, 68; Richard, 136; Sally, 136
HILLYARD: Joseph, 116
Hiram, 17
Hit, 89, 153
HIX: Daniel, 82; Joseph, 82
HOBDAY: Margery, 53
HODNELL: Ayres, 16; Philip, 16
HODNETT: Ayres, 16; Philip, 16
HOG: Elizabeth, 164; James, 164; Peter, 164
Hogin, 141
HOLLAND: John, 184; Samuel H., 131
Hollford: Ann, 34
Holliday, 25
Hollon, 39
HOLLOWAY: Thomas, 128
HOLMES: Basil, 79; Thomas, 195
Homer, 85
Homes: Caty, 66
Honour, 174

HOOE: Ann, 158; Ann Frances, 158; Anne, 172; Bernard, 158; John, 158, 172, 175; Mary, 172; Susanna Fowke, 158; William, 158
HOOE Jr.: Henson, 180; John, 176
HOOKER: William, 194
HOOMES: Armistead, 26; John, 26; John Waller, 26; Judith, 26; Richard, 26; William, 26
HOOVER: John, 165
Hope, 123
HOPKINS: Charles, 64; David, 64; Elizabeth, 64; Frances, 64; John, 64; Mary, 64; Peter, 64; Sarah, 64; Susannah, 64; William, 64, 95
HORD: Patty, 29
Hornsby, 89
HORNSBY: Joseph, 82, 92
HORSBURGH: Innus K., 201
HORSLEY: John, 17
HORTH: John, 79
HORTON: John, 184; S__dele, 178; William, 184
Hosa, 119
HOSKINS: William, 102
HOSLEY: Mildred M., 13
HOTTEL: Henry, 165; Joseph, 165
Housday, 27
HOWARD: James, 33; Sarah, 67
HOWERTON: Ann W., 102; Ellen V., 103; Robert, 102; Sara, 102
Howett, 90

HOWLE: Edmund, 136; Mary, 136
HU_H: Burnett, 16; Frances, 16
HUBARD: Sarah, 15
Hubbard, 26
Hubert, 97
HUDGEN: Sarah, 106
HUDGINS: Walter G., 121
HUDSON: Juby, 41; Penelope, 41; Prudence, 139; Tuttle, 41; William, 41
Hugh, 181
HUGHES: John, 192; Margaret, 192
HUGHES: Martha, 82, 92; Mary Richardson, 68; Sarah, 101; Stephen, 134
HUGHS: John, 177
Huks: Adam, 42
Huldah, 67
HULLARD: Elizabeth, 74
Humphrey, 80, 83, 89, 93, 101, 102, 116
HUNLEY: Rose, 53; Wilkinson, 53
HUNNICUTT: Lemuel, 152; Sarah, 152
Hunt: Harry, 153
HUNT: John, 73; William, 32
Huny, 144
Hurcules, 16
HUTCHESON: Ann Foster, 103
I_ONROE: Thomas, 181
Ian, 89
ill, 11
Imy, 16
Indian Sue, 40
Indio, 172
INGLISH: John, 185

INTOSH: Richard W., 192
Ira, 171
IRBY: Douglas, 40; Elizabeth, 145; William, 145
Iris, 42, 155
IRONMONGER: Elizabeth, 24, 62
IRVING: Charles, 16, 17
Isaac, 7, 10, 14, 15, 17, 18, 26, 31, 35, 36, 38, 40, 53, 56, 59, 65, 66, 67, 79, 80, 83, 84, 88, 89, 90, 93, 94, 97, 104, 114, 119, 123, 127, 136, 143, 144, 155, 164, 165, 197
Isabel, 94, 144
Isabell, 26, 131, 184, 185
Isabella, 46, 56, 106, 117, 140
Isabelle, 41
Isaiah, 126
Isbel, 42
Isbell, 42, 56, 87, 184
ISBELL: Daniel, 23, 27; James, 23, 27; Mary, 23; Nancy, 23, 27
Isham, 11, 40, 45, 60, 83, 93, 136, 139, 145, 149, 150, 152
Israel, 7, 35, 43, 77
Issac, 15, 65, 153
Iverson, 65, 103
Ives, 72, 161
Iycer: Elizabeth, 174
Izbel, 145
J_done, 133
Jack, 8, 10, 12, 14, 16, 17, 20, 26, 27, 31, 32, 34, 36, 39, 40, 42, 43, 45, 46, 51, 56, 57, 61, 65, 67, 71, 72, 76, 78, 79, 80, 82, 83, 84, 85, 86, 87, 88, 89, 90, 91, 92, 93, 94, 95, 96, 97, 99, 104, 113, 116, 119, 123,
125, 128, 129, 131, 133, 135, 139, 141, 147, 148, 151, 152, 153, 154, 157, 158, 161, 164, 171, 175, 176, 183, 188, 191, 194, 197, 199
Jackson, 54, 82, 102, 126, 162; Grace, 174; Hannah, 83; Patty, 151
JACKSON: Charles, 25; Edwin B., 142; Jane, 142; John L., 142; Lucy Jane, 142; Richard Worth, 142; Thomas, 142; Thomas L., 142; Ty__ B., 142; Virginia Mir__, 142; William H., 142
Jacob, 9, 10, 18, 19, 21, 26, 31, 36, 38, 39, 41, 44, 62, 65, 66, 71, 78, 83, 85, 87, 88, 93, 94, 95, 113, 116, 130, 148, 155, 158, 172, 187, 197
Jainett, 116
Jaky, 128
Jambo, 69
James, 1, 10, 12, 13, 18, 21, 25, 26, 36, 37, 38, 39, 41, 42, 43, 44, 53, 54, 59, 61, 62, 65, 67, 68, 74, 76, 78, 79, 80, 81, 82, 83, 84, 85, 86, 87, 88, 89, 90, 92, 93, 94, 95, 96, 97, 101, 102, 103, 104, 106, 107, 108, 111, 114, 115, 116, 123, 125, 127, 130, 134, 142, 143, 145, 148, 149, 151, 155, 158, 161, 164, 165, 171, 172, 175, 176, 181, 186, 188, 192
JAMES: Frances R., 24; George, 173; John, 83, 93; Joseph J., 24; William, 83, 93
James Jr., 128
James Sr., 128

James,, 36, 41
Jamey, 153, 196
Jamima, 7, 158, 182
JAMISON: Hizabeth, 148
Jammey, 196
Jammy, 1, 10, 74, 82, 86
Jamy, 85, 94, 145
Jancy, 96, 152
Jane, 1, 3, 14, 19, 26, 29, 31, 33, 39, 40, 42, 44, 47, 66, 83, 85, 89, 96, 100, 102, 118, 123, 134, 137, 141, 142, 147, 148, 158, 167, 172, 175, 182, 186, 187, 188
Janeel, 61
Janer, 78
Janet, 24, 69, 104
Janey, 26
Janny, 73, 86, 95, 119, 164
Jany, 42
JARRETT: Elizabeth, 22
Jary, 78
Jasper, 26
Jean, 34, 45, 64, 197
Jeanie, 109
Jeanings, 141
Jeanne, 45
Jeanny, 147
JEFFERICE: George, 180
Jefferson, 116; Joseph, 186
Jeffery, 19, 42, 80
Jeffrey, 18, 93, 131, 134, 154
JEFFRICE: Alexander, 176; James, 181
JEFFRIES: Elizabeth Meriah, 101; James M., 105
Jeffry, 148
Jem, 28
Jemima, 77, 134
Jeminy, 42, 133

Jemmy, 91, 117
JENKE: Gerrard, 173
JENKINS: Elizabeth, 128; Exum, 128; John B., 128; Leora B., 128
Jenney, 113, 188
Jennie, 130
JENNINGS: Barbara, 65; Betty, 65; Henry Archer, 143; James R., 143; John Garland, 64; Joseph, 143; Mary, 64, 65; Robert, 64, 65; Robert P., 143; Rotert H., 143; Sara, 65; William M., 143
Jenny, 8, 9, 21, 28, 36, 40, 43, 44, 45, 46, 53, 54, 61, 63, 64, 66, 75, 78, 79, 80, 81, 82, 83, 85, 86, 88, 89, 90, 91, 92, 93, 94, 96, 101, 104, 113, 116, 117, 118, 119, 126, 133, 134, 139, 140, 144, 147, 148, 150, 153, 154, 155, 173, 176
Jered, 171
Jeremiah, 14
Jeremy, 39, 53
JERMAN: Mary Ann, 13; Miletas, 13; Sarah T., 13
Jerre, 199
Jerry, 11, 13, 19, 20, 21, 24, 28, 29, 36, 39, 56, 60, 64, 75, 78, 80, 86, 87, 88, 91, 102, 104, 114, 115, 118, 128, 137, 141, 172, 188
Jesse, 1, 14, 15, 18, 21, 24, 26, 42, 53, 68, 75, 80, 82, 90, 101, 139, 140, 141, 145, 158
Jessy, 80
JETER: Albert A., 143; Susan C.I., 143
Jew, 34, 199

Jiles, 79, 96
Jilina, 74, 161
Jim, 7, 8, 11, 14, 18, 21, 41, 45, 55, 81, 90, 94, 101, 115, 121, 126, 128, 129, 137, 139, 141, 148, 149, 152, 154, 155, 157, 159, 162, 166, 189
Jimbo, 113
Jime, 105
Jimmy, 64, 88, 89, 94
Jimy, 55
Jinnetta, 18
Jinney, 18, 116, 123
Jinny, 14, 21, 39, 60, 79, 89, 94, 95, 104, 119, 194
Jinty, 114
Jo, 62
Joan, 71, 87, 97, 165
Joane, 199
Joanna, 17, 144, 173
Job, 11, 199
Joba, 75
Joe, 12, 16, 17, 18, 21, 24, 26, 29, 35, 42, 45, 49, 55, 62, 63, 65, 66, 67, 68, 70, 76, 78, 79, 80, 81, 82, 83, 84, 85, 86, 87, 88, 89, 91, 92, 93, 94, 95, 96, 97, 102, 106, 107, 114, 115, 118, 119, 130, 141, 142, 145, 148, 151, 153, 158, 166, 182, 183, 184,187, 191, 197
Joe Jr., 128
Joe Sr., 128
Joel, 154
Joham, 89, 92
Johann, 17
Johanthan, 36
John, 3, 8, 11, 14, 15, 17, 18, 21, 24, 25, 26, 29, 31, 34, 35, 36, 39, 41, 42, 43, 44, 45, 46, 47, 54, 55, 61, 65, 66, 67, 68, 71, 72, 73, 78, 80, 81, 82, 83, 85, 86, 87, 88, 89, 90, 92, 93, 94, 95, 96, 100, 101, 102, 104, 105, 111, 113, 114, 118, 119, 121, 123, 128, 133, 139, 142, 147, 151, 153, 155, 158, 159, 160, 161, 166, 172, 174, 176, 177, 178, 179, 183, 186, 187, 188, 192, 197
John Turner, 126
Johney, 93
Johnny, 35, 36, 73, 86, 93, 96, 115, 154, 161
Johnson, 78, 87; Julia, 143; Louisa, 159; Martha Ann, 143
JOHNSON: Augusta Ann, 59; Catharine, 83, 92; Francisca Turnover, 59; John H., 17; Milly, 17; Peyton, 17; Richard, 17; Robert, 27; Solomon, 128; Susanna A., 59; Thomas, 186; William, 177
Joice, 26, 114, 116, 118
Jonas, 43
Jones, 15, 41; Eliza, 144; James, 17; Maria, 65; Tom, 26
JONES: Albert Timms, 65; Ann, 41; Augustine C., 41; Barbara A., 83, 93; Capt. Scervant, 192; Caroline F.W., 19; Catherine, 143; Christopher T., 42; Daniel, 83, 92; David C., 21; Edmond, 121; Edward, 17, 83; Edward Wiley, 18; Eleanor, 143; Elizabeth, 17,

18, 143; Elizabeth Chamberlain, 144; James, 17, 83, 123, 143; James S., 18; Joel, 65; John, 152, 192; John A., 196; Jonas, 17, 18; Joseph Addison, 143; Josias, 17; Judith W., 144; Kennen, 44; Lucy, 152; Martha, 18; Mary, 17, 42, 53; Mary Ann, 42; Mildred, 44; Nancy, 17; Peter, 42, 144, 152; Polly, 17; Powhatan, 17; Samuel, 17; Sarah, 152; Sarah F., 143; Scervant, 192; Sophia E., 67; Spotswood, 17; Thomas, 17; Thomas S., 18; Walter F., 53; Washington, 65; William, 18, 178; William A., 18
JONES Jr: Abraham, 152
JONES Sr.: William, 192
Joney, 152
Jonney, 45
Jonny, 61
JOPLING: Alsey, 11; Jesse, 11
Jordan, 143
JORDAN: Ann, 128; Elizabeth, 145; Jeremiah, 27; Josiah M., 152; Rebecca B., 152; Samuel, 14, 135; Samuel P., 152; Thomas, 145
Jorden, 127
Joseph, 64, 114, 123, 128, 141, 171, 172, 176, 182, 186, 187, 199
Josey, 141
Joshua, 21, 40, 41, 80, 147, 163, 197
Josiah, 82
Juba, 14, 21, 73, 86, 161
Juboy, 90

Jubu, 13
Juda, 20, 69, 180, 183
Judah, 21, 62, 103, 127, 145, 154, 155
Jude, 19, 20, 27, 37, 38, 45, 62, 83, 93, 118, 165, 166, 172
Judea, 14
Judes, 61
Judith, 10, 17, 36, 42, 45, 56, 65, 101, 103, 163, 174
Judy, 9, 17, 18, 21, 22, 24, 25, 36, 39, 43, 46, 53, 54, 57, 63, 68, 77, 78, 79, 80, 81, 82, 83, 85, 86, 87, 88, 89, 90, 91, 92, 93, 94, 95, 96, 97, 102, 104, 105, 106, 116, 117, 147, 148, 150, 153, 175, 193
Jugg, 184
Juggy, 66
Juley, 41
Julia, 26, 70, 77, 125, 142, 145
Julian, 141, 165
Julianna, 66, 142
Juliet, 115, 157
Julius, 79, 83, 85, 89, 93, 95, 115, 192
Jumfred, 40
June, 38, 46, 102
Junior, 87
Junn, 131
Juno, 20, 24, 27, 53, 175
Jupiter, 45, 73, 81, 87, 113, 161
Jusanna, 174
Justin, 78
K__TON: Martha E., 141
Kadas, 126
Kate, 5, 11, 16, 26, 51, 52, 67, 90, 93, 94, 96, 97, 126, 140, 151, 155, 162, 173, 188
Kato, 83, 93

Katy, 15, 26, 28
KEEBLE: Walter, 53
KEELING: Charlotte, 128; John W., 128
KEELING Sr.: Jacob, 128
KEENE: Matthew, 172
KEININGHAM: Esther W., 52
Kendal, 15, 73, 116
KENDALL: William, 179
KENNEDY: Charles, 65
Kenny, 45
KENNY: James, 176
Kenzie, 118
KERBY: John, 83, 93
KERR: Francis, 103; George, 103; Sarah, 107; William, 103
Keshia, 20
Kesiah, 154
KETCHION: Edwin, 103; Lucy, 103; Thomas, 103
KEY: Henrietta, 112
Kezia, 21, 79, 83, 93
Keziah, 123
Keziah, 21, 26, 60
Keziah, 140
Keziah, 141
Kiah, 18
KIDD: Elizabeth, 18; Moses, 18
KIDLEY: Ann, 134
KILBY: John R., 128, 129, 130; Martha, 128; Thomas J., 131
King, 84, 94, 97
KING: Anne, 31; James, 197; Mary, 165, 197; Philip, 31; Sarah, 197; William, 165, 176, 197
KING Sr.: John, 165
KIRKLAND: Billy, 46
Kisiah, 18, 154

Kit, 86, 93, 96, 102, 109, 115
Kitt, 40, 51, 52, 79, 103, 158
Kitty, 18, 19, 26, 57, 62, 85, 90, 94, 95, 101, 104, 109, 123, 166
Kizey, 44
Kizzy, 46, 68, 148
KNEWSTEP: Ann, 83, 93
KNIGHT: Elizabeth G., 140; John H., 144
KOON: Matthew, 172
KRING: Catherine, 165
KRING Sr.: John, 165
KYLE: Sarah, 7; William, 7
LABAT: Mr., 43
Labia, 141
Lace, 84
LACKLAND: Elizabeth, 18; John, 18; Lillian, 18; M.C., 71, 159; Mary, 18; Rachel, 18; Sarah, 18; Zadock, 18, 20
LAMBERT: Sterling, 144
LAMKIN: Jane, 144
LANCASTER: Nathaniel, 14
Lancastor, 90
Lander, 90
Landis, 61
LANDRUM: Lydda, 20
LANDUM: Sarah, 34; Thomas, 33
Lane: Joseph, 175
LANE: Perry Thomas, 32
LANG: George, 192; Mary, 192
LANGBY: George, 192
LANGHORNE: Ann, 192; Elizabeth, 192; John, 192; Martha Cary, 192; Maurice, 192; William, 192
LANGLEY: Elizabeth, 73; Robert, 73

LANGORN: Maurice M., 13
LANGSTINE: Isaac, 128; Lucretia J., 128
LANGSTON: John, 127; Nancy, 127
LANISS: Richard, 68
LANKFORD: Ann A., 160; Dorcas, 160
LANSON: Thomas, 82
Larry, 78
Lat, 79
LAUGHLIN: Mrs., 26
Laura, 19, 118
Lavin, 137
Lavinia, 3, 26, 101, 102, 117, 160, 200
Lawrence, 105
LAWRENCE: Elizabeth, 129; John, 129; Jonas, 129; Joseph J., 129; Lemuel, 129; Michael, 129; Phoebe, 129
LAWSON: Lawson, 93
Leah, 101
Leander, 149
LEAR: John, 129
LEATH: Eppes, 152; Lewis, 72, 160; Mary Ann, 152; Stephen, 152; Truman Eppes, 152
LEATHERER: Margaret, 37; Paul, 37
LEAVIT: Catharine Lucretia, 54; Edmund, 53; Elizabeth, 53; John W., 54; Lucy Ellen, 54; Rebecca Allen, 54; Thomas, 53; William A., 54; William F., 54; Wyndham Hackney, 54
Ledia, 81, 113

LEE: Abigail, 129; Hancock, 199; Henry, 199; John, 158, 199; Mary E., 158; Matthew A., 158; Nathan, 152; Pleasant, 152; Richard, 199; William, 83, 93; William L., 83, 93; William Ludwell, 76
LEE Jr.: John, 199
LEED: Martha Harrison, 13
Leeda, 154
LEIGH: Ferdinando, 42; Jane B., 54; John, 54; Maria L., 54; William, 42
Leland, 106
LELAND: Francis G., 38
Lena, 133
Lender, 96, 103
Lenny, 43, 172
Leonard, 8, 66, 173
Lester, 93, 153
LESTER: Richard, 84; Timothy, 83
Lett, 27, 45, 53, 84, 94, 106, 114
Lette__, 88
Lettice, 192
Lettse, 79
Letty, 26, 53, 54, 74, 83, 85, 86, 87, 93, 95, 96, 105, 119, 141, 145, 148, 149, 161
LEVELL: Edward, 27; Elizabeth, 27
Leville, 21
Levina, 117
Levinia, 61
Lewey, 93, 97, 109
Lewis, 7, 13, 14, 26, 39, 40, 42, 43, 45, 54, 59, 66, 68, 78, 79, 80, 81, 83, 84, 87, 88, 89, 93, 95, 99, 102, 103, 104, 109,

116, 118, 128, 131, 141, 144, 145, 146, 152, 158, 159, 184, 191; Sarah, 135
LEWIS: Addison, 54; Andrew, 7; Edward, 93; John, 54, 65, 83, 93; John L., 70; Rebecca, 54; Robert, 64, 70; Sara C., 54; Thomas, 165; Warner, 54; William, 19; William I., 83, 93
Lewy, 80
Lia_, 201
Lib, 94
Libby, 67
Lidda, 31, 66
Liddy, 13, 35, 61, 145, 164, 197
Lidwell, 65
Lidya, 85, 166
LIGHTFOOT: Edward, 80; Jacquelin, 93; Nicholas, 94; William, 83, 93
LIGHTFORD: Edward, 88
LIGIN: Elizabeth, 18; Joseph E., 18
Lilly, 36, 40, 147, 155
Lily, 7, 150
Limbrick, 181
Limehouse, 145
Linda, 143
Lindia, 26
Lindsay, 93
Lindsey, 21
LINSEY: Jesse, 83, 93; Jestina, 83, 93; Sandy, 83
LIPSCOMB: Conway O., 116; John, 116; John H., 117; Madison, 116; Nancy P., 116; William B., 117
LIPSCOMBE: Mary B., 65; Nathaniel C., 65

Littis, 44, 47
Littlepage: Lucy Ann, 117
LITTLEPAGE: Edmund, 117
Littleton, 86
Lively, 55
LIVESAY: Elizabeth, 154
Livy, 154
Lizer, 24
LIZER: George, 114
Lizza, 3
Lizzy, 42, 46, 77, 128, 148, 158
Lockey, 133
Loland, 60
Lolly, 158
London, 60, 66, 99, 114, 123, 152, 163, 177, 180, 183, 199
Long: Billy, 26
LONG: Henry, 165; John, 164; Mary, 28; William, 84, 94
Lorain, 115
Lott, 133
LOTT: John Gane, 33
Lotty, 61
Louis, 46
Louisa, 14, 18, 41, 42, 55, 66, 71, 77, 105, 115, 118, 133, 136, 140, 141, 142
Louise, 3
Louisiana, 17
LOVE: Maria, 40; Theoderic, 40
LOVELL: Elizabeth, 53
Lovlip, 123
Lowry: Ann, 186
Lu__az, 11
Lu__ordy, 94
Lucas: Sarah, 173
LUCAS: John, 193; Robert, 193; Tom, 193
Luce, 40, 76, 113

Lucendy, 56
Lucien, 171
Lucinda, 16, 41, 115, 117, 125, 171, 192
Lucius, 84, 94
Luckinny, 9
Lucky, 102
Lucy, 1, 8, 10, 11, 15, 16, 18, 19, 21, 24, 26, 29, 36, 38, 40, 42, 43, 45, 53, 55, 56, 57, 61, 63, 65, 67, 68, 70, 71, 73, 76, 77, 78, 79, 80, 81, 82, 83, 84, 85, 86, 87, 88, 89, 90, 93, 95, 96, 97, 100, 101, 102, 104, 111, 113, 114, 115, 116, 118, 119, 121, 123, 128, 130, 133, 134, 140, 141, 142, 144, 145, 148, 151, 152, 153, 154, 157, 158, 161, 163, 164, 166, 171, 173, 175, 176, 180, 181, 187, 188, 191, 192
LUCY: William, 34
Lucy Ann, 153
Luddy, 68
Luend, 158
Luis, 145
Luke, 78, 86, 87, 128, 131
LUMSDEN: David, 152
Lunsford: Judith, 174
Lutty, 96
Lyda, 40, 44, 47
Lydda, 19, 40, 166
Lyddia, 83, 91, 92, 93, 96, 97
Lyddie, 60
Lyddy, 83
Lydia, 78, 80, 83, 86, 87, 93, 94, 102, 104, 130, 157, 172, 188
Lye, 26
Lyida, 79

Lymon, 194
LYNE: William, 103
Lyon, 93
LYON: Humbeson, 197
M___ier, 145
MA__: Mary B., 142
Ma__va, 152
MA_D_: Capt. James, 52
MACHANDREE: John, 84, 93
MACHEN: Mary, 121
MACHEY: John, 129; Martha, 129
Machlen, 79
Machlin, 84, 94
Mack, 26, 79, 89, 91
MACKALL: Frances Holland, 165; John, 165; John James, 165
Mackey, 90, 94
Macon, 26
MACON: Edmund, 135; Elizabeth, 117, 135; Gideon, 135; Henry, 108; Rebecca, 135; Rebecca Walker, 135; Sarah, 135; William, 108; William H., 135
Macrae: Daniel, 157
MACTYRE: John, 84, 93
MADDISON: James, 94; Rev. Bishop, 84
MADDUX: John, 141
Maddy, 173
Madison, 14
MADISON: Agatha, 8; John, 8
Madon, 40
Maggy, 11
Mahala, 65, 106
MAHONE: Major, 84, 93; Major Willis, 77; William, 84
Major, 102

Malbrough, 114
Malcom, 113
Malinda, 115
Mall, 147, 199
MALLICOTE: Eliza Ann, 193; Frances, 193; George, 193; John, 193; Maria D., 193; Mary, 193; Thomas, 193
MALLORY: Milly, 62
Manah, 154
Manda, 141
Mandey, 127
Mankey, 147
MANLOVE: Christopher, 42
Manmouth, 151
MANN: Robert, 103; Susan D., 103; Thomas, 103, 106; William, 8
MANNING: Samuel, 91
Manny, 55, 85
MANQUIN: James, 39
Manser, 41
Manuel, 42, 66, 113, 141
Marcus, 47, 95
Mardin, 186
Mardy, 151
Marg, 96
Margaret, 19, 96, 118, 159, 167, 173, 177, 182, 183
Margery, 9
Margy, 56
Maria, 12, 14, 16, 17, 19, 26, 54, 55, 60, 65, 66, 68, 71, 76, 96, 102, 104, 105, 106, 115, 119, 123, 128, 130, 142, 143, 147, 148, 149, 154, 158, 187
Maria Ann, 101
Maria Jane, 19
Maria Louisa, 133

Mariah, 14, 17, 21, 45, 69, 86, 102, 141, 150
Marinda, 88
Mark, 83, 92
MARKS: Edmund, 152; Edward, 152; Elizabeth P., 153; John H., 152; Richard, 153; Richard E., 153
Marmion, 102
Mars, 85, 94
Marsha, 21, 149
MARSHALL: Lucy, 106; Richard S., 144; Thomas Griffin, 72; William, 72, 160
Martha, 3, 12, 20, 24, 35, 42, 47, 54, 56, 57, 65, 66, 67, 74, 76, 85, 99, 102, 104, 105, 106, 111, 115, 118, 123, 133, 136, 141, 151, 154, 161
Martha Ann, 142
Martha Jane, 14
Marthew, 63
Marthey, 127
Martin, 19, 37, 66, 67, 84, 95, 115, 144; Lewis, 144; Patty, 143
MARTIN: Ann, 106; Elizabeth, 84, 94; Elizabeth B., 3; John Buckler, 117; Julia Harriet Thomasa, 117; Louisa, 150; Thomas B., 117; Thomas Brumby, 117; William, 39; William F.B., 150
MARX: Joseph, 72, 160; Richa, 72, 160
Mary, 8, 11, 12, 13, 14, 15, 21, 24, 26, 38, 40, 41, 44, 56, 60, 61, 63, 65, 66, 67, 68, 69, 74, 77, 79, 80, 81, 83, 89, 90, 91, 92, 93, 99, 101, 102, 104,

106, 109, 113, 116, 126, 134,
   136, 140, 141, 143, 144, 145,
   150, 161, 165, 166, 172, 173,
   182, 183, 184,185, 191, 197
Mary Anne, 157
Mary Ellen, 118
Mary Grace, 177
Mary Jane, 135
Mary Louisa, 24
Maryan, 68
Maryann, 188
Mason, 9, 39, 40, 152
MASON: Ann, 173, 181, 182;
   Crocha, 27; George, 173;
   James, 8, 9; John, 27; Sarah,
   173
Massey, 158
MASSEY: Margaret
   Crittendson, 80; Thomas, 173
Mat, 39, 68
Mathew, 173
Matilda, 17, 21, 24, 42, 54, 60,
   67, 76, 102, 111, 118, 123,
   128, 130, 141, 144, 152, 158
Matt, 32, 33, 62, 64, 80, 82, 84,
   93, 103, 114, 118, 148, 151,
   153, 172, 188
Matthew, 113
MATTHEW: Henry P., 158;
   Jane Mtilda, 158
MATTHEWS: Mary, 68
MATTHEWS Jr.: William, 181
Maud, 100
MAUPIN: Gabriel, 84, 94
Maurice, 12
MAUZY: John, 180
Max, 128
MAXWELL: James, 178
MAYHEW: Lucy M., 41
MAYOR: Jane, 51

McABOY: Elizabeth, 177
McALISTER: Andrew, 129
McASHAN: Elizabeth, 18;
   Nehemiah, 18
McCANDLISH: Rebecca, 201;
   Robert, 201
McCLANAHAN: Sarah, 8;
   William, 8
McClure: Solomon, 129
McCLURE: Elizabeth, 8;
   Malcolm, 8
McCollister: Agnes, 187
McCUNE: John, 5, 166
McGEE: Mary Etta, 65
McGEORGE: Elizabeth, 117;
   John F., 117; John Franklin,
   117; Mary Ann, 117;
   William, 117; Wily R., 117
McGILL: John D., 105
McKanzie, 116
McKAY: Addison, 42; Donald,
   42
McKenzie, 114
McKINNEY: Charles D., 18
McKINZIE: Thomas, 166
McLAURINE: Paulina
   America, 65
McMURDO: Charles J., 44
Me_ain, 27
MEADE: Andrew, 129; John
   E., 154
MEARITT: Mary, 9
MEDICOTT: Samuel R., 54
MEFFORD: Gasper, 166
Meles, 141
Melinda, 61, 81, 90
Mendy, 128
MENETREE: Ann, 84, 93;
   Joham, 84, 93
Mercer, 26

241

MERCER: John, 172, 179, 181
Mercia, 114
MEREDITH: Albert F., 135;
   Mary A.E., 135; Mary F.,
   135; Samuel, 135
Meriah, 25
Meridith, 79, 89
Merit, 47
Mica, 15
Micael, 136
Micall, 61
Michael, 53, 80, 83, 86, 87, 88,
   96, 134, 178
Michel, 194
MICHELB__Y: Mary, 106
Mick, 93
MICKELBOURROUGH:
   Henry, 102
Mickey, 21
Micky, 21
MIDDLETON: Sarah, 140
Mike, 89
Mildred, 66, 135
Miles, 65, 125, 144, 162; James
   M., 128
MILES: John W., 129
Milia, 134
Milla, 10
Mille, 149
MILLER: Anderson B., 144;
   Sally, 68; Samuel, 166
Milley, 38, 155
Millia, 95
Millicent, 130
Mills: Jamima, 182
MILLS: Betsey Waide, 68;
   John, 144; John N., 68;
   Matthew, 27; Thomson, 27;
   William, 174, 182

Milly, 7, 8, 13, 15, 16, 19, 20,
   21, 23, 26, 27, 29, 36, 37, 40,
   42, 43, 46, 57, 60, 62, 65, 67,
   68, 74, 78, 79, 80, 81, 82, 83,
   84, 85, 86, 87, 89, 91, 92, 93,
   94, 96, 97, 100, 103, 104,
   109, 113, 115, 139, 140, 145,
   152, 155, 164, 165, 172, 184,
   196, 197, 199
Milton, 140
Mima, 76, 123, 144
Mime, 26, 27
Mina, 32, 44
Minah, 145
Miner, 21, 80, 141
MINER: Sarah A., 54; Thomas,
   54
Minerva, 19, 60, 68, 142, 152
MINGE: Capt. David, 31; Mary
   Anna, 154
Mingo, 9, 34, 69, 78, 87, 97,
   129, 148, 151, 153, 158
Mingoe, 145
Minney, 53
Minon, 41
Minor, 62, 66, 84, 94, 149
Mira, 103, 128
Miranda, 42, 143, 184
Mirti__, 196
MITCHIE: Elizabeth, 69
MITTO: Martha P., 148
Moch, 19
Mol, 61
Molbourgh, 113
Moll, 1, 9, 12, 36, 43, 62, 73,
   78, 80, 81, 82, 84, 87, 89, 90,
   91, 92, 94, 95, 103, 106, 113,
   116, 129, 150, 152, 153, 155,
   176, 188, 189, 191, 194, 196
Mollie, 61

Molly, 11, 12, 23, 24, 26, 35, 47, 55, 56, 59, 64, 68, 70, 71, 77, 78, 79, 80, 81, 82, 85, 87, 88, 89, 91, 92, 94, 119, 134, 136, 139, 141, 144, 145, 147, 148, 155, 199
Molly Bigham, 12
MONDAY: John, 79
Mondica, 141
Money, 13
MONNON: Derrik, 187
Monroe, 13, 129
Montriville, 54
Monts, 38
MOODY: Thomas, 153
MOON: Arthur H., 19; Elizabeth, 19; James D., 19; Jane, 19; Jane M., 19; Littleberry, 19; Mary H., 19; Samuel O., 19; Sarah I., 19
Moore, 68, 103
MOORE: Ann, 118; Augustine, 117, 192; Elizabeth, 117, 153; Horatio, 153; Mary, 129; Richard, 78
MOORS: Sally P., 20
MOORY: Phillip, 195
MORDIGS: Lucy, 140
More, 131
MORECOCK: William B., 136
Morning, 80, 140
Morocco, 76
MORRIS: Henry, 9; Joshua, 84, 94
MORRISON: Francis G., 160
MOSBY: Elizabeth, 52; Virginia, 13
MOSELEY: Alexander, 14; Philip Terpin, 66; Robert, 66; Sarah, 66; William, 66

MOSELY: Robert P., 15; Sally, 14, 15
Moses, 10, 12, 13, 17, 19, 26, 35, 38, 39, 41, 43, 46, 52, 53, 59, 60, 61, 62, 63, 64, 78, 80, 81, 84, 87, 91, 94, 97, 114, 119, 130, 134, 136, 145, 147, 148, 151, 155, 158, 164, 166, 173, 189
MOSS: Elizabeth, 123; Joshua, 123; Sylvester, 178
MOTLEY: Edwin, 103
Mott, 33
Mottley, 52
MOUNTJOY: Alvin, 172; Edmund, 172; Edward, 172; Mary, 172; William, 172, 173
Mouring, 66
Mourning, 11, 36, 56, 87, 96, 116, 128
MUCKLEBURROUGH: Robert, 27
MUIR: Caroline, 43; Douglas, 43; Francis, 43; Gustavus Adolphus, 43; Marianne, 43
MUIRE: Absalum, 104
MULTON: Sarah, 84
Munday, 89
MUNFORD: Robert, 35, 153
Murray, 136
MURRAY: Ann, 153; Anne, 153; Anne Bolling, 153; Anthony, 19, 172; Elizabeth, 153; James, 153; John, 153; Margaret, 153; Richard, 19; Susanna, 153; Thomas, 153; William, 153
Murrear, 9
Mya, 79

MYERS: Catharine, 72, 160;
   Harriet, 72, 160; Julia, 72,
   160; Moses M., 72, 160
Nace, 102
NAILOR: Elizabeth, 65
Nalanline, 180
Nan, 11, 14, 22, 26, 27, 28, 46,
   53, 62, 65, 78, 80, 85, 88, 93,
   94, 95, 96, 97, 106, 125, 127,
   129, 147, 153, 154, 155, 158,
   165, 171, 173, 188
Nancy, 8, 12, 13, 15, 16, 19, 21,
   26, 36, 37, 39, 40, 41, 42, 43,
   44, 54, 56, 57, 60, 61, 64, 65,
   67, 68, 69, 70, 73, 77, 78, 81,
   82, 83, 84, 85, 87, 93, 94, 96,
   103, 104, 127, 128, 129, 133,
   135, 136, 137, 139, 140, 141,
   143, 144, 145, 148, 151, 152,
   155, 157,161, 162
Nane, 18
Nanney, 14
Nanny, 13, 16, 24, 31, 41, 42,
   45, 57, 78, 79, 80, 81, 82, 83,
   84, 86, 87, 88, 89, 92, 93, 94,
   95, 96, 97, 99, 104, 106, 117,
   127, 129, 141, 145, 148, 154,
   192, 196
Nany, 128
Napoleon, 102
Napper, 74
Narmo, 199
Narsetta, 123
Nat, 12, 64, 72, 80, 85, 86, 94,
   96, 115, 128, 147, 148, 151
Nate, 97
Nathan, 101, 130, 141, 144
Natt, 26, 41
Neale: Joseph, 182
NEALE: Ann, 119

Ned, 9, 10, 12, 15, 21, 22, 26,
   31, 34, 35, 39, 40, 43, 45, 46,
   51, 60, 61, 62, 64, 65, 68, 72,
   73, 78, 79, 80, 81, 82, 83, 84,
   86, 87, 88, 89, 90, 92, 93, 94,
   95, 96, 97, 103, 108, 109,
   118, 125, 127, 128, 133, 141,
   144, 145, 151, 154, 158, 160,
   180, 188
Nee_, 43
Neive, 12
Nelifer, 12
Nell, 42, 54, 67, 113, 133, 155,
   173, 175, 197
Nella, 12
Nelle, 26
Nelly, 8, 9, 12, 14, 17, 25, 26,
   39, 54, 71, 80, 86, 96, 114,
   115, 131, 141, 165
Nelson, 18, 19, 21, 26, 37, 41,
   56, 61, 65, 66, 67, 68, 89,
   102, 104, 113, 117, 128, 141,
   158
NELSON: Elizabeth Wythe, 77;
   F., 100; Mary S., 135
Nelus, 14
Neptune, 21, 117
Nero, 26, 84, 94, 127
Netty, 128
NEW: Elizabeth Ann, 42
NEWELL: Martha, 154
Newsom, 131
Newton, 199
NEWTON: Betty, 29; Garret,
   199; John, 199
Nice, 173
NICHOLAS: Dolly P., 43;
   John, 19, 166; Robert Carter,
   43

NICHOLS: Anna, 104; Hannah, 104; John, 104; Mary, 104
Nick, 153
Nilsy, 153
Nimby, 1
Nimey, 60
Noar, 127
Noar Sr., 127
Nobby: Peter, 130
NOEL: Frances, 106
Noon, 154
Nora, 100
Norman, 106
NORMAN: Thomas, 176
NORRIS: John, 180
NORTH: Bolling C., 40; Elizabeth, 40; John, 79
NORTHINGTON: Polly H., 123
Norton, 26
NORVELL: William, 76
Nottingham, 81, 91
NOVELL: William, 94
November, 127
NUCKOLS: William, 66
NUEMAR: Vincent D., 87
Numa, 69
Nut, 96
Nutty, 86
O BRION: John, 123
O. Harry, 65
O'LOCHLON: Catherine, 158; Cornelius, 158
Obadiah, 14, 118
OBAIN: Darby, 187
Obe, 99
Obey, 78, 88, 92, 95
OCAIN: Dar by, 182; Darby, 179
Octavia, 115

Olive, 108, 109, 142, 149
Oliver, 24, 55, 115, 128, 154; James, 143; Maria, 65; Rachel, 65
OLIVER: Ann, 143; Ann A., 66; Anne, 140; Iman, 143; John, 25, 123, 140; Joseph, 143; Lucy, 25; Martha, 104, 143; Micajah, 143; Molly, 143; Nancy, 60; Richard, 143; Rutha Ann, 104; William, 104
OLIVIER: Mary A., 54; Warner, 54
Orange, 127
Orphus, 173
Orson, 174
Orville, 54
OSBORN: Elias, 34
Osborne, 123; Jane, 175
Osco, 128
Osman, 75
Osmond, 116
Osmyn, 75
Otey, 85, 95
Otoway, 77
Ourney, 115
OVERALL: Catherine, 187; Nathaniel, 176
OVERBY: Nicolas, 33
Overton, 67
OVERTON: Maria, 70; Mary, 140; Samuel, 66, 72, 160; Thomas P., 72, 160; William, 70
Owens: Mardin, 186
OWENS: Nancy, 105
Owney, 115
P_HEN: Thomas Boswell, 51
PA__CAR: Alexander, 123

PACHAM: William, 148
Pacience, 113
Padie, 177
Page, 21, 26, 55
PAGE: Carter, 73; Eliza, 159; Jane B., 54; John, 54, 55; John C., 16; Lavinia, 100; Mann, 54; Mildred, 28; Nelly, 15; William B., 54
Paisley, 78
Pallas, 131, 158
PALMER: Mary, 12
Pamela, 17
Pampry, 155
Pantha, 123
PARADISE: John, 84, 94
PARANDINE: Elizabeth, 180
PARKE, 59
Parker, 26, 57, 141; Tom, 158
PARKER: James, 127
PARR: Anthony, 33; Elizabeth, 33
Parret: Tom, 73
PARRISH: Charles, 9; Garland, 63; James, 9; Joel, 9; John, 9; John H., 102; Joseph, 9; Mary, 9; William, 36
Parrot, 26
Parrott, 155
PARTHAN: Ann, 43; Betsy, 43; Ephrain, 43; Joanna, 43; Nicholas, 43; Thomas, 43
Parthena, 135
PARVER: Edward, 84
PARVER Jr: Edward, 84
Pat, 8, 28, 78, 79, 80, 82, 87, 89, 92, 93, 94, 95, 97, 148, 150, 154, 196
Pate, 94

PATES: Aaron, 172, 187; Jonas, 172, 187
Pati, 56
Patience, 10, 41, 44, 47, 61, 69, 105, 141, 154
PATILLO: James, 43; Martha, 43; Mary, 43; Solomon, 43
PATILLO minor: James, 43
Patram, 144
Patrick, 26, 64, 92, 113
Patrick Welsh, 113
Patsy, 35, 43, 71, 100
Patt, 26, 31, 36, 41, 46, 73, 85, 87, 88, 90, 91, 92, 140
PATTEN: William, 180
Patterson, 3
PATTERSON: Polly, 105
PATTESON: Agnes, 19; Ann, 1; Augustine, 20; Betsy, 20; Charles, 1; Charles Powhatan, 19; David, 19, 20; Hugh, 20; I.L., 20; James M., 19, 20; Jane, 20; John, 20; Lucy, 20; Richard L., 20; Thomas, 1; Virginia, 19; W.N., 19; William, 20
Patty, 11, 14, 16, 24, 26, 35, 56, 61, 66, 69, 77, 79, 100, 102, 117, 136, 140, 143, 145, 151, 154, 159, 164, 166
Paul, 96, 97, 141, 151, 191
Paulina, 17, 46, 61, 65
PAVEY: Adam, 179
PAYNE: M.M., 68
Payton, 25
PAYTON: Even, 181; John, 174
Peace, 31, 134
Peach, 41

PEACHY: John Blair, 5, 201; Mary M., 5, 201
PEARSON: Charles, 76, 135; Hannah, 76
PEEBLES: William, 32
PEETE: Dr. George W., 126
Peg, 19, 38, 53, 59, 65, 69, 79, 80, 82, 83, 84, 87, 94, 96, 113, 126, 141, 166, 180
Pegg, 31, 41, 88, 90, 92, 94, 97, 104, 134, 151, 188, 199
PEGGOTT: Frances, 84; Francis, 94; John, 94
Peggy, 14, 26, 42, 43, 46, 51, 54, 60, 64, 70, 76, 86, 93, 145, 152, 164, 165
Pembroke, 75
Pendelton, 158
PENDELTON: Philip B., 104
Pender, 73
Pendleton, 65
PENDLETON: Benjamin, 14; Edmund, 28; Hugh N., 28; John, 28; Mary, 14; Nace, 14; Sally, 14; William G., 74, 161
PENDLETON Jr.: Edmund, 28
Penellepet, 99
Penelope, 153
Penn, 125
Penny, 127
PERKEY: Jacob, 166; John, 166
Perkins, 94
PERKINS: Baker, 84; Benjamin M., 20; Daniel P., 20; Elijah, 14; Eliza A., 20; Hardin, 20; John M., 20; Mary, 84, 94; Mary L., 20; William P., 20

PERRY: Capt Peter, 33; Peter, 32; Richard, 32
Pers, 75
Person of Color: Mary O.D. Tinsley, 69; Polly O.D. Tinsley, 69
Peter, 9, 11, 12, 13, 15, 17, 19, 20, 21, 25, 26, 27, 33, 36, 39, 40, 41, 42, 43, 44, 45, 47, 54, 60, 65, 66, 68, 69, 78, 79, 80, 82, 85, 86, 87, 89, 90, 91, 92, 95, 96, 103, 104, 107, 109, 113, 115, 116, 119, 127, 130, 133, 134, 139, 140, 141, 142, 143, 144, 147, 148, 151, 152, 154, 155, 157, 172, 182, 185, 188, 189, 191, 197, 199
PETYON: John, 182
Peyton, 39, 51, 52, 94
PEYTON: John, 181, 183
Phebe, 10, 14, 28, 59, 60, 78, 79, 87, 88, 109, 145, 148, 151, 166
Phebee, 102
Pheby, 78, 79, 85, 89, 95, 113, 145, 154, 164, 166, 193
Pheobe, 116, 154
Phil, 7, 26, 29, 42, 61, 72, 75, 78, 79, 80, 81, 82, 84, 85, 86, 88, 89, 90, 92, 96, 141, 178, 191
Philip, 10, 12, 13, 19, 75, 85, 123
Philis, 17, 39
Phill, 26, 38, 41, 42, 45, 75, 106, 109, 145, 146, 169
Phillip, 12, 61, 69, 93
PHILLIPS: Etheline, 100; Lancelot, 68; William, 68

247

Phillis, 9, 14, 18, 19, 21, 24, 26, 27, 29, 40, 41, 42, 43, 46, 52, 65, 71, 72, 73, 75, 79, 80, 81, 82, 84, 85, 86, 87, 88, 89, 90, 91, 92, 93, 94, 95, 96, 99, 113, 114, 116, 130, 141, 145, 150, 152, 153, 154, 155, 161, 166, 172, 181, 188, 192, 196
Phobe, 151
Phoebe, 21, 25, 55, 64, 73, 85, 102, 116, 123, 154, 188, 192
Phoeby, 16, 24, 149
Phyllis, 88
Pickles, 104
Pierce, 129
PIERCE: John, 94
PIERCE Jr.: John, 94
PIGGOTT: Fielding D., 76; Francis, 76; Francis B., 76; Nathaniel, 76
PILCHER: George, 178; Mr., 111
PITT: Eleanor, 84, 94
PITZER: George, 7; James, 7; Robert, 7
Plato, 154
Plats, 148
Pleasant, 21, 26, 61, 66, 72, 77, 144, 161
PLEASANTS: Elizabeth, 73; Jane, 73; Jonathan, 73; Joseph, 73; Margaret, 73; Mary, 73; Robert, 73; Samuel, 73; Thomas, 73
PLEASANTS Sr.: John, 72
Plenty, 121
Plummer, 119
Pocker, 129
Pocon, 59

PODD: Dr. William B., 104; Marcus P., 104
Pointer, 90
Pol, 25
Polidore, 80
Polk, 158
Poll, 28, 38, 82, 155, 164
POLLARD: Benjamin, 60; Elizabeth P., 104; Peter Thornton, 104; Polly, 116; Thomas, 68; William, 60
Polly, 12, 16, 19, 24, 26, 35, 41, 42, 51, 54, 55, 56, 66, 67, 79, 81, 90, 92, 102, 106, 117, 119, 144, 152, 161, 162, 163, 165, 166
Pompey, 19, 35, 84, 88, 89, 126, 154, 196
Pomprey, 80, 81, 86, 92, 93, 96
Pompry, 80
Pompsy, 69
Pompy, 9, 145, 150
PONER: John, 84
Ponhatan, 78
Pool, 148
Pooley: Henry, 182
POORE: Polly Walker, 3; Robert Bolling, 3
Porc__, 88
Porter, 152
PORTER, 118; Ann, 130; Israel, 118; John, 130; Mary, 118
Portia, 28
PORVELL: William, 83
POSEY: Ann Kidley, 134; John Price, 134, 135; Martha, 134; Mrs., 135
Possom, 134
Pouringer, 94

POWELL: Elizabeth P., 153; Jennet, 166; Seamer, 194; William, 93
POWER: Edward, 94
POWER Jr.: Edward, 94
POYTHRESS: Jane, 154; Robert, 153; Susannah, 154; Tabetha, 154
PRATT: Burkett, 181
PRENTIS: Mary, 192; Susanna, 192
Prentise, 127
PRESSON: Nicholas, 191; Sarah, 191
Preston, 3, 8
PRESTON: Thomas, 8
PREWITT: Benjamin, 94
Price: Frances, 186
PRICE: Camilla, 66; Elizabeth T., 66; Lucien B., 66; Martha, 13; Mary Randolph, 66; Thaddeus, 66; Thomas, 66
PRIDE: Peter, 40
PRILLER: Mary, 77
Primus, 81, 83, 91, 93
Prince, 61, 81, 86, 92, 96, 154
Priscilla, 95, 97, 195
Priss, 69, 97, 134, 188
PROBY: Elizabeth, 148; Servante, 148
PROSSER: Letitia, 63
Pru, 46
Prudence, 14, 42, 141
Prycey, 157
Pugg, 36
PULLIAM: Sally, 59; Thompson Wilson, 66; William, 66
Pumetia, 90

Quarter Sam, 60
Quash: Charles, 169
Quashey, 193
Queen, 73, 161
Ra_h, 197
Rachael, 185
Rachel, 3, 7, 16, 17, 18, 20, 21, 24, 25, 26, 27, 31, 40, 41, 42, 43, 44, 47, 53, 56, 60, 62, 65, 67, 73, 78, 79, 80, 82, 84, 85, 86, 87, 88, 91, 92, 93, 94, 95, 96, 99, 102, 113, 114, 116, 117, 123, 129, 130, 131, 140, 141, 144, 148, 158, 164, 165, 166, 182, 191
Radnor, 84
RAINES: Dorothy, 28; Giles, 28
RAINEY: Margarey, 42
RALLS: Edward, 173, 179; John, 174, 175, 179, 187; Lydia Beck, 188; Margaret, 188
RALLS Sr.: John, 180
Rally, 21
Ralph, 26, 28, 37, 57, 60, 114, 119
Ramsey, 81
RAN_ISON: Harold, 84
Randal, 7, 68
Randall, 174, 175
RANDALL: Edward, 178
Randol, 25, 39, 63, 140
Randolph, 18, 26, 29, 66, 72, 79, 102, 106, 114, 130, 160; Free Negro Certificate, 130
RANDOLPH: Betty, 73; Edmund, 85, 94; Jacob, 130; John, 73, 161; Lucy, 73; Peyton, 73; Richard, 76, 148;

Richard Kidder, 73; Richard Ryland, 154; William, 73
RANLEY: Luc__ia E., 84
RANSONE: Sally, 57
Raphne, 158
RATCLIFFE: James, 84, 94
RATELIS: Richard, 194
Rawley, 88
RAWLINGS: Judith H., 13
RAWLISON: Hewlett, 94
RAWLS: Justin, 126; Sarah, 126
RAWLS Jr.: Uriah, 130
Read, 192
READ: Susan B., 64
REAMES: Simon, 43
Rebecca, 12, 41, 44, 47, 54, 102
Redwood, 84
REDWOOD: William, 94
REEKS: Nicholas, 155; Patsey C., 123; Susannah, 155; Thomas, 123; Thomas C., 123
REEMS: Simon, 43; William, 43
REEVES: John, 166; William, 166
REID: Samuel McDowell, 21
RETCHIE: Archibald, 105; Patsy Hipkins, 105
Reuben, 13, 26, 79, 89, 93, 103, 104, 115, 123, 166
REYNOLDS: Frances, 28; John, 28
Rhoda, 7, 11, 18, 123, 144
Rhode, 26
Rhody, 145
Rice, 94
RICE: Levi, 118; William, 37

Richard, 20, 26, 39, 41, 78, 81, 86, 92, 115, 119, 136, 141, 142, 143, 151, 162
Richard Higgins, 126
Richard Jr., 115
RICHARDS: Lucy, 28; Thomas, 28
RICHARDSON: Allen, 85; Anna, 31; Betty Matilda, 59; Dudley, 85, 95; Edward, 84, 95; John, 31; Mary, 85, 95; Stan__, 85, 95; Turner, 31; William, 84, 85, 95
RICHARDSON Jr.: Dudley, 85, 95
Rico, 155
RIDDICK: Benjamin, 127; Josiah, 130; Richard, 128
RIDDICK Jr.: Josiah, 130
Riger, 136
Riley: Barnaby, 175
Rina, 19
Rippon, 84, 94, 95
RITCHIE: Ann Eliza, 151; Isabella, 151; Thomas, 151
RIVERCOMB: Rebecca, 38
RIVES: Robert, 74, 161
RIXEBY: Margaret, 3
ROANE: Alexander, 28; Samuel, 104; Sarah, 28; Thomas, 28, 104
Robbin, 26, 71
Robert, 14, 18, 25, 42, 47, 54, 63, 68, 77, 78, 88, 102, 115, 123, 133, 134, 141, 147, 153, 161, 171, 173, 179, 195
ROBERT__: Patty, 143
ROBERTS: Elizabeth C., 123
ROBERTSON: David, 3; Eliza S., 3; Elizabeth, 162; James

E., 3; John, 144, 162; Mary P., 3; Melvina J., 144
Robin, 10, 26, 33, 42, 53, 56, 64, 69, 72, 79, 83, 85, 86, 89, 90, 93, 94, 95, 102, 104, 108, 113, 117, 130, 148, 149, 165, 188, 191, 194
ROBINSON: Alicy, 101; Benjamin, 180; James, 158; Lucy, 117; Peter, 144; William, 187
Robison: James, 158
Rochambeau, 26
Rochester, 12, 44, 47
Rodger, 188
Roger, 9, 33, 41, 46, 82, 84, 85, 86, 91, 92, 93, 94, 96, 113, 143, 148, 196
ROGERS: Achillis, 29; Betsey Whitt, 36; Catharine B., 29; Dorcas, 36; George, 29; Isaac, 29; Jamima J., 142; John, 36, 89; Kirkland, 36; Lucy, 29; Martha, 36; Mary, 24; Mildred, 29; Molley, 25; Polly, 29; Reuben, 29; William, 36
Rolling, 141
Roper, 79, 89, 134
ROPER: Martha, 150
ROSCOW: James, 191
Rose, 14, 17, 21, 22, 26, 28, 29, 37, 42, 45, 51, 52, 53, 56, 68, 69, 75, 82, 85, 92, 95, 97, 126, 129, 131, 139, 148, 158, 160, 161, 171, 175, 179, 180
ROSE: Alexander, 179; Alexander F., 187; John, 184, 187; John N., 121; Patrick, 187; Sarah M., 121
Roseaty, 14
Rosey, 21, 75
Rosina, 54
ROSS Sr.: William, 182
ROSSER: Randolph, 94
ROUNTREE: Frances, 85
ROUT: Peter, 179, 185
ROW: Thomas, 107
ROWE: Hansford, 55
Rowland, 19, 144
ROWZEE: Richard, 29
ROY: James, 57; Martha, 57
Royal, 18, 143
ROYSTON: Mary B., 56
Rozelly, 14
Ruben, 81
RUDD: William C., 140
Ruffin, 102
RUFFIN: Sterling, 104
Rufus, 128
Russell, 117
RUSSELL: Armistead, 134, 136
RUST: Samuel, 199; Thomas, 199
Ruth, 51, 52
Ryland, 13
RYLAND: Ann S., 118; Dora, 118; John N., 105; Josephine, 118; Maria P., 118; Pricilla E., 118; Robert S., 118; Rosey, 103; Sally B., 118; Susan F., 118; Willentina, 118; William S., 118
S__ney, 193
S_rry, 43
Sabia, 80
Sabina, 93, 97
Sabra, 89

Sal, 25, 62, 76, 78, 81, 82, 83, 84, 86, 87, 94, 96, 126, 166, 172
Salena, 106
Sall, 9, 25, 26, 27, 36, 38, 40, 41, 42, 44, 68, 78, 81, 82, 84, 86, 87, 88, 90, 91, 92, 93, 94, 96, 97, 113, 147, 148, 152, 153, 165
Sallie, 128
Sally, 8, 9, 15, 16, 19, 21, 26, 38, 42, 43, 44, 45, 52, 54, 60, 61, 64, 66, 67, 70, 71, 75, 77, 78, 79, 81, 88, 99, 101, 104, 114, 115, 116, 121, 127, 133, 141, 143, 144, 145, 147, 152, 160, 197, 200
Sally Haxhall, 15
Sam, 1, 3, 10, 12, 13, 14, 15, 16, 20, 21, 24, 25, 26, 31, 34, 36, 41, 42, 45, 51, 52, 55, 56, 57, 60, 61, 62, 65, 68, 71, 73, 76, 77, 78, 79, 80, 81, 84, 85, 86, 87, 88, 90, 91, 92, 94, 96, 97, 102, 103, 104, 106, 107, 109, 113, 114, 115, 119, 123, 126, 127, 128, 130, 131, 133, 134, 136, 137, 140, 141, 143, 145, 148, 149, 153, 155, 158, 185, 188
Sam Sr., 128
SAMBERTH: Archer Williams, 67
Sambo, 86, 96, 113, 117, 141
Sampson, 18, 19, 31, 43, 45, 71, 86, 96, 116
Samuel, 20, 130, 166, 197
SANDAGE: Jane, 118; John, 118
Sanday, 93
Sanders, 21
Sandy, 21, 26, 85
Sanford, 106
SANFORD: Robert, 85, 95
Sanny, 80
Sapho, 184
Sara, 61, 69, 81
Sara Jane, 119
Sarah, 1, 10, 11, 19, 20, 21, 24, 25, 26, 27, 29, 31, 35, 36, 46, 51, 52, 55, 56, 60, 61, 62, 65, 73, 78, 81, 82, 83, 85, 86, 87, 89, 90, 91, 92, 93, 95, 96, 97, 104, 105, 109, 113, 115, 119, 121, 129, 133, 134, 135, 139, 143, 153, 154, 155, 158, 159, 165, 166, 172, 173, 174, 188, 191, 192, 196, 199
Sarah Moll, 9
Sarey, 78, 85, 86, 93, 95
Sary, 19, 20, 59, 91, 92, 96, 97, 106
SAUNDERS: Archer, 92; Daniel M., 20; Dorotha, 28; Elizabeth, 20; John, 85, 95; William, 106
SAVAGE: Jesse R., 130
Sawne, 29
Sawney, 25, 53, 64, 82, 92, 101, 154; Doctor, 20
Sawny, 16, 103
Sawyer, 55
Sawyers, 117
SCHOOLS: Elijah, 105; George, 105; Jeremiah, 105; John, 105; Major, 105; Nancy, 105; Polly, 105; Rebecca, 105; Thomas, 105; Waller, 105
Scipio, 1, 46, 86, 96, 181

252

Scirpio, 1
Scott, 36, 154; Betsy, 20; Wilson, 20
SCOTT: Ann, 43; Caroline M., 161; Christian, 106; Dianelia, 41; Dr. Samuel, 188; Hannah, 41; James, 43; John, 41; Joseph, 161; Seymour, 74, 161; Thomas, 41; William, 43
SCOTT Jr.: James, 160
SCRUGGS: E.A., 13
SCULLY: John G., 85, 95
Scylla, 65
Scypio, 88
Seal, 118
Sealy, 65, 127
Seanah, 154
Seany, 93
SEARS: Thomas, 105
SEATON: Augustine, 118; Betty, 118; George, 118; George Watson, 118; Jenny, 118
SEAWELL: Francis, 55; John, 55; John P., 55; Overton, 55; Sterling Thornton, 55; Thornton, 55
SEAY: Anna, 119; Gidean, 118; James, 118; Jesse, 119; John, 119
SEBURN: James, 186
SEGOUGUE: Lewis, 109
Sek, 84
Sela, 166
SELDON: Samuel, 193; Sarah, 115
Seleg, 85
Seley, 84
Sella, 83

Sellah, 82
Seller, 27, 93
Senah, 92
Sepio, 89
Seraphina, 179
Servant: Anderson, 104; Anderson, John, 178; Ash, John, 176; Basset, Joseph, 186; Bolling, Francis, 182; Bowen; Hugh, 181; Box, Geoffrey, 179; Brown, John, 187; Bryan; John, 179; Butler, William, 178; Campbell, James, 186; Campbell, Joanna, 173; Cocklin, Margaret, 173; Coleman, John, 179; Coo, William, 187; Cornwall, Margaret, 182; Cove, William, 182; Crann, Peter, 182; Crose, James, 176; Darbey, William, 178; Darby; William, 177; Daves, Randall, 174; Davis, Randall, 175; Dillon, Ann, 186; Early, Honour, 174; Elliott, Jane, 186; Elliott, William, 178; Frazier; Isbell, 184; Frazier, Mary, 185; Furguson, Duncan, 164; Gray, Ann, 173; Harvey, Daniel, 186; Holt, John, 177, 178; Jack, 104; Jane Osborne, 175; Jefferson, Joseph, 186; Kelly; William, 179; Lowry, Ann, 186; Lynaugh; Rose, 179; Mason, Mary, 173; McCollister, Agnes, 187; McEntire, Matthew, 173; Mills, Jamima, 182; Moore,

Isabell, 184; Neale, Joseph, 182; Neighing; Francise, 180; Orphus, 173; Owens, Mardin, 186; Page, Thomas, 185; Pairinain, Thomas, 178; Park, Joseph, 176; Pebbles, John, 174; Pepples; James, 181; Philip, Thomas, 177; Pooley, Henry, 182; Price, Frances, 186; Regan, James, 175; Riley, B arnaby, 175; Shehon; Daniel, 181; Smith, Isabell, 185; Smith, John, 104, 185; Smith, Margaret, 183; Storm, Michael, 178; Thompson, Jane, 182; Turner, John, 176; Walker, Alosis, 173; Waller, Elizabeth, 186; Watson, William, 185; Wheeler; Padie, 177; Whitaker, Rachael, 185; Whitehouse, Thomas, 177; Williams, John, 186; Williams, Thomas, 173; Williamson, Mary, 184; Young, Margaret, 177

Seth, 62, 90, 169
SHACKLEFORD: Laura A.H., 142; Sarah F., 142; Zachary, 166
Shadrack, 16, 25, 40, 43, 59
Shadrick, 65
SHAFFER: John, 167; Nicholas, 167
Sham, 155
SHANDS: Thomas, 32
Shardack, 19
Sharlot, 62
Sharper, 73, 117

Shawn, 104
Shed, 16
SHEDDON: Thomas, 152
SHELBURNE: James, 95
Shem, 26
Shephard, 17
SHEPHERD: Mildred, 105; Robert, 105; Samuel, 105
Sheppard, 17, 21
SHEPPARD: Mary C.G., 60; William, 105
SHEPPERSON: Peggy, 42
SHERMER: Ann, 136; Anne, 76; John, 76, 136
SHERWOOD: William, 32
SHIELD: Samuel, 193
SHIELDMAN: James, 85
SHIELDS: James, 85, 95; John, 85; John P., 95; Page, 85, 95; Rebecca, 76
SHIELDS Sr.: James, 76
Shill, 104
Shion, 113
Shirley, 115
SHORE: Eliza, 67
SHORT: John, 180
SHORTS: John, 173
SHOTTY: William, 85
Sib, 84
Siby, 87
Sidney, 141
Silas, 83, 93
Silis, 113
Sillah, 86
Siller, 62, 82, 83, 86, 87, 91, 92, 94, 96, 97
Siloe, 40
Silva, 22, 61, 139
SILVAN: Catharine, 106
Silvanus, 86, 96

Silvey, 21, 22, 85, 90, 93, 94, 95, 97, 148
Silvia, 65, 80, 81, 83, 84, 86, 140
Silvy, 89, 90, 96
Sily, 66
SIMMONS: Benjamin, 10; Henry, 10; Mason, 10; Thomas, 9, 10
SIMMS: Betty, 38; James, 38; Martin, 38; Sally Jones, 38
Simon, 1, 17, 27, 54, 56, 80, 85, 88, 91, 95, 101, 113, 114, 115, 116, 140, 141, 145, 148, 152, 164
Simpson: Jusanna, 174
SIMPSON: Diana, 184
SIMS: Anne, 31; Peggy, 67; William, 67
Sinah, 158
Sinder, 145
Sindi, 141
Sipeo, 27
Sippio, 44, 45
Sis, 33, 87
SIZER: Augustus, 119; Hannah, 119; John, 119
SKILLERN: Elizabeth, 8; George, 8; William Preston, 8
SKINKER: John, 111, 187; Samuel, 111; Thomas, 111
SLATER: Rebecca, 85, 95; William, 95
Slaughter, 86
SMART: William, 56
Smith, 183; Isabell, 185; John, 104; Margaret, 183
SMITH, 193; Ann, 23, 60; Arthur, 130, 131; Caroline, 109; Dorothea Ann, 105; Dr. William, 105; Edwin, 126, 130; Eleanor A., 102; Gregory, 60; Henry, 176; John, 67, 185; Joseph, 176, 184; Margaret Maria, 126; Martha, 126; Martha Jane Louisa, 130; Mary, 44, 47; Mary Effa, 126; Park, 59; Robert B., 105; Thomas, 34, 182
Smith Bob, 108
SMITHER: Eliza, 106; James, 106; William T., 56
SNEAD: Robert, 67; Sophia, 67
SOANE: Capt Henry, 36; Rebecca Hubbard, 36
Sofia, 79
Soloman, 47
Solomon, 10, 11, 18, 43, 44, 54, 65, 81, 92, 95, 102, 141, 143, 144, 158, 165, 199
Sooky, 19
Sophia, 47, 65, 78, 86, 115, 141
Sophromia, 106
SOUTHALL: James, 85, 95
SPAIRS: John, 74
SPEED: John, 123
Spencer, 12, 15, 18, 21, 26, 29, 85, 95, 106, 115; William, 67
SPENCER: John, 106; Lewellin, 85, 95; Mary, 20; Polly Ruffin, 100; Sarah, 85, 95; William W., 106
Spenser, 118
SPILLER: Grace, 52
Spotswood, 24, 26
SPOTSWOOD: Robert, 60
SPRAGGINS: Mary, 86; William, 92

SPRATTEY: William, 95
SPRATTOY: Kezia, 85
SPRIGGINS: Mary, 95
Squire, 37, 84, 85, 89, 95
St. JOHN: Eliza, 103
Stafford, 85, 180
STAINBACK: Littleberry E., 43
STAMPER: James, 136
Stan, 144
STARK: James, 176
Stephen, 15, 18, 20, 21, 41, 46, 54, 66, 78, 85, 86, 88, 94, 95, 108, 114, 128, 133, 144, 152, 155, 164
STEPHEN, 185; Adam, 185; Alexander, 186
Stepney, 94, 133, 169, 193
Sterling, 41, 83, 139, 152
STEVEN: Adam, 186
STEVENSON: Polu, 152
STHRESHLEY: Thomas, 29
STIFF: Catharine, 67; John, 67
Stirling, 154
STITH: Holly, 9; Thomas, 9
STOKES: Martha, 44; Sterling, 44
STONE: Caleb, 1; Elijah, 1; Frances Taylor, 1; Hezekiah, 1; Marbel, 1; Thomas, 1; William, 1
STRATTON: Benoni, 178
STREET: Charles P., 67; Henry G., 67; Joseph, 67; Sarah B., 144
STUART: David, 188; John, 176, 184; William, 106
STUCKEY: Anne, 191
STURDIVANT: James, 154
STURDIVANT Sr.: John, 154

Su_ea, 144
SUBLETT: William, 20
Suck, 68, 93
Sucke, 96
Suckey, 12, 19, 26, 41, 65, 86, 93, 104, 140, 151, 155, 161
Sucky, 12, 16, 17, 26, 43, 73, 80, 139, 147
SUDDUTH: Mary, 185
Sudley, 39
Sue, 24, 36, 39, 47, 69, 78, 79, 83, 85, 87, 92, 94, 113, 114, 133, 148, 152, 154, 172, 175, 188, 199
Suke, 154
Sukey, 8, 10, 16, 17, 26, 35, 68, 72, 78, 79, 81, 82, 84, 85, 88, 91, 94, 114, 119, 128, 148, 157, 158, 166, 172, 187
Suky, 19, 90
SULLIVAN: Eugene, 85, 95
Surrey, 148
Surry, 148
Susan, 16, 17, 44, 60, 65, 66, 103, 115, 141, 144
Susanna, 24
Susannah, 14, 26, 145, 171
Sussex, 45, 162
Susy, 56
SUTTON: R.J., 106
SWEENY: Sarah Burdett, 158
SWEET: John L., 116
SYDNOR: Ann, 68; Elizabeth, 144
Syfox, 141
Syliva, 38
Sylla, 140
Syller, 158
Sylva, 21, 65
Sylvey, 94, 96

Sylvia, 60, 72, 79, 81, 84, 86, 95, 116, 136, 160, 179, 184
Sylvy, 85, 89, 91, 141
SYLVY: John, 187
Sypha__, 73
Syrus, 40, 88, 94, 96, 155
Tab, 86, 96
Taba, 47
Tabb, 36, 39, 61, 73
TABB: Robert, 56; William, 56
Tabby, 75, 161
Taber, 44
Tabetha, 36
Tabitha, 61, 140
Taff, 94
TALBOT: C.M., 136; Salley, 17
TALIAFERRO: Benjamin, 96; Charles, 86, 96; Col. Richard, 86, 97; Rebecca, 77; Richard, 77, 96; Sally, 97
TALLEY: Ekhanah, 68
TALLEY Sr.: Charles, 68
TALLY: Elkano, 68
Tamar, 16
Tamer, 62, 64
Tammy, 11
Tamor, 92
Tamos, 76
Tamsend, 188
TANDY: Patsy, 144
Taner, 134
Tanor, 67
TAPLEY: John, 46
TAPSCOTT: Henry Breeton, 199; Martin, 199
Tarah, 16
Tarr, 85
TARRY: Elvira E., 123
Tarta, 9

TAULMAN: Benjamin, 164; Lidda, 164
TAURMAN: Martha H., 8, 67; William, 8
Tawney, 60
Tayler: Spencer, 115
TAYLOE: Ann, 111; Benjamin Ogle, 111; John, 111, 184
TAYLOE Jr.: John, 111
Taylor, 65, 128, 143, 144; Joe, 130
TAYLOR: Ann B., 76; Archibald, 74; B., 95; Edmund, 76, 77, 86, 96; Elizabeth, 86, 96; Fanny, 99; Frances, 28, 102, 106; Francis, 106; Henley, 86, 96; Isham, 86, 96; Jeremiah, 86, 96; John, 106; Leticia H., 74; Mary, 150; Pinkethman, 86, 96; Pinkethman W., 77; Rebecca W., 77; Richard, 150; Richardson W., 77; Robert, 28, 86, 96; Sally M., 77; Samuel, 106; Sarah, 77; Susanna Catherine, 77; Wesley H., 77; William, 86, 106; William M., 77
TAYLOR Sr.: Edmund, 77
TAYOR: Richardson, 96
Tazewell, 79
TAZEWELL: Henry, 77; Sophia Ann, 77
Tazwell, 86, 89, 145
TAZWELL: Henry, 86, 96; Littleton, 96
TEASBROOK: Elizabeth, 191
TEASLEY: Sarah, 160
TEBBS: Betsy, 157
Ted, 10, 152

257

Tellah, 82
Teller, 92
Temfry, 41
Temp, 92, 93, 114
Temple, 159
TEMPLE: Catharine, 103; Ella, 66; Eurgenia, 66; James, 79, 115; John T., 66; Maria Louisa, 66; Mary, 115; Thomas P., 66; William, 150
Tena, 22, 115
Tenah, 22
Tenh, 194
TENNY: James, 86
Tenor, 83, 85, 88
TERRELL: Ann, 68
TERRIL: Mary, 19; William, 19
TERRILL: James, 29
Terry, 82
Thaddius, 105
Thandy: Tom, 201
Therman: Nan, 165
THILMAN Sr.: Jane, 27; John, 27
Thoedosia, 85, 95
Thomas, 34, 78, 82, 84, 86, 87, 88, 94, 97, 100, 141, 172, 173, 177, 178, 185; Mary, 172; Milly, 172
THOMAS: John, 173, 183; Phillip, 33; Thomas, 20
Thomas-Anthony, 19
Thompson, 42; Jane, 182
THOMPSON: Alfred, 5; Ann F., 44, 47; Elizabeth, 68; Elizabeth C., 44, 47; Emily, 44, 47; Helen Ann, 5; Henry, 47; John, 68; Joseph, 68; Robert, 44, 47; Robert L., 47;
Robert S., 44; Susan Jane, 142; William, 47
THORNBURY: John, 180; William, 177
Thornton, 26, 29, 157, 171
THORNTON: Francis, 55; Sterling, 55; William, 121; William M., 13
THROGMORTON: John, 158; Mary Ann, 158
THURSTON: Edward T., 121; Robert, 55; William S., 121
THWEATT: Henry, 44; James, 44; Jane, 44; John, 154; John James, 154; Thomas, 44
Tildy, 19
Tillah, 26, 104
Tillar, 103
Tiller, 89, 90
TILLMAN: Mary, 10
Tillor, 45
Tim, 92, 199
TIMBERLAKE: Benjamin Arthur, 69; Chapman, 69; David, 64; Francis, 136; Henry, 69; Henry Austin, 69; Reuben, 69; Sally, 64; Sophia, 69
Timer, 35
Times, 171
Timothy, 81, 93, 113
Timothy Bryant, 113
Timson, 80
Tinah, 92
Tinken, 93
TINNY: Sally, 154
Tinsley: Mary O.D., 69; Polly O.D., 69

TINSLEY: Charles, 69; Col. Thomas, 65; Peter, 69; Sarah, 160; Susanna, 65
Tippis, 113
Titus, 13, 43, 86, 153, 154, 182
Tobe, 18
Tobey, 71
Toby, 75, 79, 89, 102, 148, 194
TODD: Joseph, 140; Nancy, 99
TOLEY: Mrs., 68
Toliman, 65
Tolre, 41
Tom, 7, 10, 11, 12, 14, 21, 22, 26, 27, 28, 29, 31, 32, 34, 35, 36, 37, 39, 40, 41, 42, 43, 54, 57, 59, 60, 61, 62, 64, 65, 68, 69, 73, 77, 78, 79, 80, 81, 82, 83, 84, 86, 87, 88, 89, 90, 91, 92, 93, 94, 96, 99, 100, 102, 104, 105, 106, 113, 114, 119, 121, 128, 131, 133, 135, 141, 144, 145, 147, 148, 151, 152, 153, 154, 158, 163, 165, 166, 172, 176, 178, 179, 188, 195, 196
Tom Bigbe, 12
Tomboy, 11, 153, 193
Tommy, 115, 158
Tomos, 80
Tompkin, 155
Tomson, 54
Tone, 17
Tony, 31, 34, 39, 42, 81, 83, 84, 86, 91, 93, 94, 96, 127, 129, 140, 152, 155
TOPLAY: Elizabeth, 191
Topsam, 86
Tossey, 81
TOWLES: John, 38
Trak, 87

Travis, 41
TRAVIS: Champion, 86, 96; Sam, 96
Trecy, 130
Tremont, 19
TRENT: Elizabeth, 21
TRICE: G.W., 103; Godney, 29; James, 29, 119; Jane, 103; Judy, 29
TRIGG: William, 197
TRIMBLE: James, 8
TRO_VER: Elizabeth, 135
TROTTER: Thomas, 125
Truckey, 43
Truelove, 26
Truman, 145
Tub, 80
Tubby, 179
TUCK: Catharine, 114
TUCKER: Danny, 154; John, 148; Joseph, 45; Mary, 44, 47; Richard, 154; Thomas, 154
Tulip, 160
Tulor, 152
Tun, 45
Tunin, 141
TUREMAN: Ignatius, 38
Turner: John, 176
TURNER: Elizabeth, 28; John, 180; Sarah, 28
TYLER: John, 183; Wat H., 36, 69
TYLOR: William, 32
TYNE: Mary, 86
TYREE: Mary, 136
Unity, 26
Uriah, 26
Ursely, 26
Ursley, 59

USHER Sr.,: Hamilton, 85
Ussy, 154, 161
VAIDEN: Henry, 136; Isaac, 136; Jerimiah, 136; John, 136
VALENTINE: Capt. John, 78; Jacob, 101
VALENTINE: John, 96
VALENTINE Jr.: John, 86
Vanderwall: Daniel P., 162
VANDEWALL: Ann, 71; Sally, 71
VANGHAN: Nicholas, 32; William, 32
VAUGHAN: Ambrose, 106; Caroline S., 56; Cornelius, 106; Eliza M., 39; Elizabeth, 106; James, 106; James L., 56; John, 106; John H., 56; Ledford, 56; Lucy C., 56; Mary U., 56; Peter, 44, 47; William T., 56
Venus, 8, 9, 21, 36, 46, 52, 53, 60, 64, 68, 80, 81, 83, 87, 88, 90, 93, 96, 97, 105, 113, 126, 131, 136, 176, 184, 192, 193, 194
Veria, 126
Vernal, 102
VIDAL: William George, 102
Vido, 129
Vilate, 26
Vilett, 141
Vina, 14, 47, 103
Vince, 115
Vincent, 11
Viney, 97, 114, 148, 149, 157
Viny, 67
Violet, 8, 26, 43, 81, 82, 86, 91, 96, 104, 109, 113, 117, 121
Violett, 27, 127

Virgin, 158
Vivian, 145
Voll, 152
WADE: Ch__y, 87; David, 87, 97; Eilliam, 87; Judith, 87, 97; Matthew, 87, 97; Sally, 66; William, 97
Waggery, 172
WALDEN: Edward, 107; Maria, 106; William, 107
WALDEN Jr.: Richard, 107
WALDEN Sr.: Richard, 106
Walker, 3, 24, 28, 29, 66, 102, 105, 173; John, 183; Tom, 54
WALKER: _ueser, 45; Abby W., 151; Bolling M., 44; Bolling Munford, 45; Capt. Robert, 86; Clarissa, 45; David, 45, 87, 96; Elizabeth, 45; James N., 87, 97; John, 86, 87, 97; Kitty, 149; Mary Ann, 45; Richard, 45; Robert, 45, 46, 97; Theodore, 45; William, 87, 97
WALKER Sr.: John, 97
WALKINS: John, 162; Polly, 18; William, 18; Willyam, 21
WALL: Isaac, 45; Sally, 45
Wallace, 125
WALLACE: Dr. Michael, 184
Waller, 66; Elizabeth, 186
WALLER: Edward, 56
WALLIS: Robert H., 87
WALTER: Capt. John, 83
WALTHALL: John, 72, 160
WALTHINS: Palina, 14
WALTON: Agnes, 67; Edward, 19; Joel, 67; Nevell, 64; Newell, 70; Sarah, 67; Sarah

A., 195; Thomas, 21; William, 21, 67
WAMACK: Jane, 7
Wappier, 199
Wappin, 45
Wapping, 102
WARBURTON, 91; John, 96
Warden: John, 133
WARDROP: Ann, 131; John, 131
WARE: Lydia, 107; Robert A., 108; Robert Spence, 107; Sarah, 119; Spencer, 107, 108; Thomas, 119
Warner, 60, 63, 102, 116
WARREN: Benjamin, 10; Temberance, 10
Warrick, 113
Warwich, 42
Warwick, 73, 85, 95
Wasefield, 180
WASH: Croshe, 65; Edmund, 195; James C., 195; Lucy Ann, 195; Nancy, 195; Polly, 65; Richard, 195; William, 195
Washington, 24, 63, 68, 119, 128
WASHINGTON: John, 173; Kitty, 51, 52
Wasner, 55
WATKINS: Elizabeth Willis, 12; John, 45; Sally, 144; Sele, 12
Watt, 65, 85, 94, 113, 157; William, 80
Wattes, 115
WATTS: Alice, 45; Arthur, 45; Betty, 45; Edward, 46; John, 29, 46; Lucy, 38; Richard, 29; Sarah, 46; William, 45
WAYLAND: Adam, 38; Hannah, 38; John, 38
WEATHERS: John, 87, 96; Thomas, 179
WEBB: Abraham M., 21; George, 21; John, 21; Martin, 21; Mary S., 147; Merry, 21; Rachel, 21; Robert, 21; William, 21
WEEKS: Elizabeth, 151
WEELINS: Joseph, 1; William, 1
WELCH: Reuben, 69
Wellington, 3, 54
WELLS: Carty, 177, 180; Henrietta K., 142; Turner, 84
Wesley: John, 54
WHEADON: Mary, 195
Whinney, 57
Whitaker: Rachael, 185
WHITAKER: Richard, 97
White: Charles, 72; Jack, 151; John, 73, 161
WHITE: Archibald, 130; Elizabeth, 100; George, 187; John, 81; Matthew I., 131
White Jack, 31
WHITECOTTON: Sarah, 184
WHITEHEAD: William B., 128, 130; William H., 127
WHITHEAD, 194; William B., 127
WHITING: Agatha, 56; Francis, 56, 57; John, 56; John R., 61; Leticia, 56; Louisa, 61
WHITLOCK: Agnes, 69; David, 69; Frances, 69;

James, 69; Mary, 69; Matthew, 69; Temperance, 69
WHITLOCKE: Frances E., 71; Henry, 71
WHITNEY: Jeremiah, 21; Josiah, 21, 22; Susannah, 22
Wiatt, 21
WIATT: Elizabeth Mary, 157; Fanny L., 54; Francis C., 54; Frank F., 54; John M., 54; Virginia I., 54; William, 157
WICHAM: Mr., 5
Wieson, 133
Wiggin, 166
Wilbert, 116
Wilds: Nanny, 41
Wile, 187
WILEY: Eleanor, 52; William, 51, 52
WILKENSON: John, 25
WILKINS: Robert, 74
WILKINSON: Catharine, 5; Elizabeth, **97**; Elizabeth C., 97; John D., 87, 97; Joseph, 5; William, 97
WILKINSON Jr.: William, 87
WILKINSON Sr.: William, 87, 97
Will, 7, 10, 17, 18, 25, 26, 31, 32, 33, 34, 36, 38, 39, 40, 42, 43, 46, 55, 59, 61, 62, 66, 69, 71, 72, 74, 78, 79, 80, 81, 82, 83, 84, 85, 86, 87, 88, 89, 92, 93, 95, 96, 97, 107, 108, 109, 113, 114, 119, 125, 140, 145, 148, 155, 172, 173, 180, 182, 184, 188, 191, 195, 199
WILLCOX: Susanna, 149; Thomas H., 35

Willey, 41
William, 12, 14, 15, 24, 26, 41, 44, 46, 47, 54, 61, 63, 65, 67, 79, 80, 84, 85, 94, 99, 100, 102, 105, 111, 115, 116, 119, 130, 133, 141, 143, 153, 157, 171, 177, 178, 179, 182, 185, 187, 192
Williams: John, 186
WILLIAMS: Ann, 43; Ann A., 145; Anna L., 145; Bartlett, 137; Benjamin, 188; Camelia R., 144; Catharine, 145; Charles, 188; Daniel, 131; David D., 145; David G., 145; Dudley, 96; Eliza J., 144; Frank S., 145; George, 188; Jacob, 173, 180; James, 43; James L., 145; James T., 145; Jesse, 188; Joel B., 144; John, 83, 93; John B., 154, 155; John Pope, 188; Joseph G., 145; Lettice G., 145; Martha G., 145; Martha V., 145; Mary, 154; Mary A., 145; Mary J., 154; Mourning, 131; Nathaniel, 188; Richard H., 144; Samuel G., 145; Sarah G., 145; Susannah, 150; Thomas, 145; Thomas R., 145; Thomas W., 145; William, 145; William O., 145
WILLIAMS Sr.: Richard, 154
WILLIAMSON: Benjamin, 28; Elizabeth, 87; George, 28; James, 123; John, 28, 69; Richard, 74; Robert, 28; Thomas, 74
Willianna, 74, 161

Willis, 21, 44, 126, 127, 130
WILLIS: David, 131; Elizabeth, 35; James, 87; Robert, 131
Willis Sr., 127
Wills, 155
WILLS: Ann, 196; Dorothy, 196; Elizabeth, 195, 196; John, 194, 195, 196; John S., 131; Mary, 195, 196
WILLS the elder: Thomas, 196
WILLSHIRE: Ellen V., 195; William B., 195
Wilshier, 71
Wilson, 14, 15, 55, 76, 103, 137, 155
WILSON: Arthur, 128; Charles, 145; Francis, 109; John, 143, 145; Lucretia, 128; Rachel, 145; Sarah, 128; William, 22; William B., 145; Zachariah, 29
WILSON Jr.: William, 128
Windsor, 81, 91
Winefred, 194
WINGFIELD: Martha P., 65
WINN: Eliza, 60; Jane, 145, 146; Peter, 146
Winney, 37, 39, 40, 42, 46, 51, 79, 80, 84, 88, 91, 94, 104, 106, 114, 115, 145, 148, 152, 158, 165, 172, 188
Winny, 141, 171, 176, 183
Winston, 21
WINSTON: Edward, 69; Jemina, 61; John, 70; John G., 69; John Geddis, 69; Susannah, 60
WITHERS: Elizabeth, 45; James, 188; John, 42; Thomas, 46

WODDROP: Alexander, 131; Ann, 131
WOLL_NDGE: George, 20
Wood, 40
WOOD: Elizabeth, 38; John, 107; John Scott, 38; Joseph, 38; Thomas, 38
WOODLIEF: George, 34; John, 34; Thomas, 34
WOODMAN: William H., 40
WOODS: Eliza, 188; William, 22
Woodson, 16, 66
WOODWARD: Fanny B., 29, 109; Martha, 133; Thomas, 29
Woody, 85
WOODY: Catharine, 117
WOOLFOLK: Augustine, 64, 70; Joseph, 64, 70
WOOTEN: Thomas, 196; William, 196; Willis, 196
WOOTIN: John F., 100; Mary, 100
Worcester, 78, 81, 91
WORDY: Martha P., 115
WORSHAM: Elizabeth, 46; Lewelling, 46; Lucy, 46; Margaret, 46; Martha, 46; Phillip, 46
Worster, 88
WRENN: Charles, 131
WRIGHT: David, 46; Elizabeth, 46; James S., 146; Louisa W., 46; Mary T., 46; Nancy, 136; Thomas, 78, 88
WULL: John, 25
Wyath, 143
Wyatt, 3, 18, 197

WYATT: Alice, 149; Ann, 149; Anthony, 155; Edward, 155; Hubbard, 155; James, 57; John, 109, 155; Katherine, 155; Margaret, 149; Mary, 155; Nicholas, 155; Peter, 57; Thomas Turner, 109
WYNNE: Elizabeth, 196; Humphrey H., 196; Mary, 196
WYTHE: Elizabeth, 196; Nathaniel, 196
Y.__rte, 83
YANCEY: Joel, 64; Katey Garland, 64; Sarah, 64
Yarrow, 171
YATES: Benjamin, 46; Robert, 186; William, 41, 144
YEATES: John, 131

YELTON: James, 177, 178
YINSLEY: Sarah, 60
York, 43, 78, 81, 82, 87, 91, 92, 113, 117, 149, 151
YOUNG: William, 192
Younker, 148
Yousy, 113
Yunker, 148
Zack, 67
Zaga, 31
ZARKLE: Ludwich, 167
Zelpha, 130
Zephamiah, 162
Zilla, 8
Zinea, 191
Zion, 65
ZIRCHEL/ZIRKLE: Lewis, 167
ZIRCLE: Ludwick, 167

www.ingramcontent.com/pod-product-compliance
Lightning Source LLC
Chambersburg PA
CBHW062006220426
43662CB00010B/1248